STECK-VAUGHN

transitions
preparing for college mathematics

Dr. Paul Kennedy

Steck Vaughn.

HOUGHTON MIFFLIN HARCOURT

www.SteckVaughn.com/AdultEd
800-289-4490

Special thanks to CSU graduate student, William Bromley, for his contributions to the solutions.

Photo Acknowledgements: Page cover © MedioImages/Corbis; 5 © Lew Robertson/Corbis; 41 © Tom Grill/ Corbis; 103, 151, 211 © Corbis.

Printed in the United States of America.

ISBN 13: 978-1-419-07475-2
ISBN 10: 1-419-07475-X

3 4 5 6 7 8 9 10 0956 15 14 13 12 11

4500279524   A B C D E F G

Contents

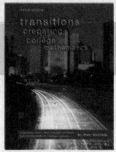

Using this Book

The *Transitions: Preparing for College* series moves adult learners successfully into a college classroom without having to spend valuable time or money on remedial, not-for-credit courses. Specifically written with adult learners in mind, this two-book series provides learners with the skills necessary for mastering college entrance exams and college coursework.

The *Transitions: Preparing for College Mathematics* book is designed to provide learners with opportunities to place into college-level mathematics courses. Unit 1 is a review of basic arithmetic and the elementary algebra skills necessary to be successful in this course. Units 2–5 are sequenced to provide learners with opportunities to master the concepts and skills related to equations, inequalities, and functions. Key features include exploration of new ideas; tips about common errors, calculators, and mental math; and many practice opportunities.

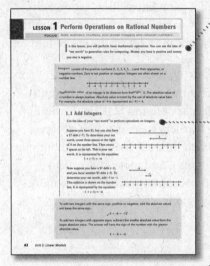

Informal Introduction

Each lesson begins with an introduction of the target concept using language and contexts that adult learners will understand and connect with, including real-world applications and examples.

Formalization

The formalization is divided into sections throughout each lesson. The actual "teaching" part of the lesson, these sections present the lesson's target academic skill in small chunks that allow learners to master the concepts gradually. Blue boxes are used to highlight important mathematical properties or definitions.

Explore It

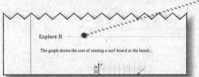

Some lessons include an *Explore It* section as part of the formalization. This section outlines a scenario and asks learners to answer a series of questions about it. Learners use this Socratic process to discover and define a concept or property independently.

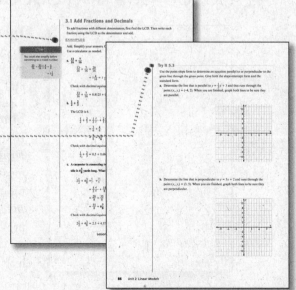

Example

After each formalization section, learners are shown how to apply the concept in carefully scaffolded, guided examples. Answers are provided so that learners can assess their own understanding of the material.

Try It

This section challenges learners to apply their new knowledge to independent practice problems. Workspace is provided so that students may work out solutions in the book. The complete solution for each problem is given at the back of the book.

Calculator Tip

Each lesson ends with a *Calculator Tip*. While the lessons are not calculator-driven, many college-placement exams allow the use of graphing calculators. These tips help learners build confidence in their calculator skills and understand basic graphing calculator functions.

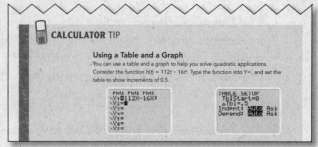

Self-Assessment

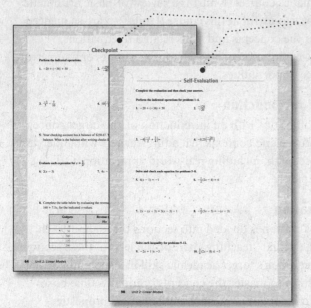

Checkpoint and Self-Evaluation

Each unit includes a mid-unit Checkpoint, a 15-question evaluation that allows learners to assess their progress through the first three lessons, and a cumulative 30-question Self-Evaluation, which allows learners to monitor and ensure their mastery of the entire unit.

Are You Ready to Go On?

This feature appears at the end of the end of every Checkpoint and Self-Evaluation, prompting learners to assess their progress thus far to determine if they should continue with the lessons—and move to the next unit—or go back and practice a little more before moving on.

- Check your answers in the *Solutions* section at the back of the book. Reading the solution for each problem will help you understand why the correct answers are right and will allow you to see each step of the solutions.
- On the chart below, circle the problem numbers that you did not solve correctly. If you answered more than one problem per lesson incorrectly, you should review that lesson before moving to the next unit.

Performance Analysis Chart

LESSON	PROBLEM NUMBER
1	1, 2, 3, 4, 24
2	5, 6, 7, 8, 25
3	9, 10, 11, 12, 26

Resources and Support

Tips

In every lesson, side-margin callouts give learners general tips, mental math strategies, hints, notes, common errors, guidance, and extra support.

Student Resources

In the back of the book, learners are provided with a *Formulas* page that allows learners to quickly reference the most important formulas in the book, stepped out *Solutions* for every Try It and Assessment problem, a *Glossary*, and an *Index*. Learners can also access *Student Tips for Success*, which provides survival tips for making the most of campus resources as well as time management tips and college best practices to make their collegiate experience a successful one.

Complete problems 1 and 2.

1. Determine the greatest common factor of 30, 24, and 36.

2. Which is greater: $\frac{3}{4}$ or $\frac{13}{16}$?

Convert each percent to a decimal and a fraction.

3. 75%

4. 35%

Convert each fraction to a decimal and a percent.

5. $\frac{4}{5}$

6. $\frac{2}{3}$

Perform the indicated operation for problems 7–12.

7. $2\frac{5}{6} + \frac{5}{6}$

8. $\frac{3}{4} - \frac{2}{3}$

Continue on next page.

9. $3\dfrac{1}{4} - 2\dfrac{3}{8}$

10. $\dfrac{5}{9} \cdot \dfrac{6}{25}$

11. $1\dfrac{2}{5} \div \dfrac{7}{10}$

12. What is 25% of 120?

Combine like terms.

13. $6x + 5 - x - 1$

14. $\dfrac{3}{4}x - \dfrac{1}{2}x$

Solve for the value of x in problems 15–18.

15. $x - \dfrac{2}{3} = \dfrac{1}{6}$

16. $\dfrac{3}{4}x = 12$

17. $2x - 1 = 15$

18. $\dfrac{2}{3}x - 1 = 5$

Pretest Solutions and Performance Analysis Chart

The Unit 1 Pretest allows you to assess your basic algebra skills. Use the chart below to check your solutions.

Solutions for Test Items	
1. GCF = 6	**10.** $\frac{2}{15}$
2. $\frac{13}{16}$	**11.** 2
3. $75\% = 0.75 = \frac{3}{4}$	**12.** 30
4. $35\% = 0.35 = \frac{7}{20}$	**13.** $5x + 4$
5. $\frac{4}{5} = 0.8 = 80\%$	**14.** $\frac{1}{4}x$
6. $\frac{2}{3} = 0.\overline{6} = 66\frac{2}{3}\%$	**15.** $x = \frac{5}{6}$
7. $3\frac{2}{3}$	**16.** $x = 16$
8. $\frac{1}{12}$	**17.** $x = 8$
9. $\frac{7}{8}$	**18.** $x = 9$

If you answered all problems correctly, you may skip Unit 1 and begin Unit 2. If you answered a test item incorrectly, place a check mark (✔) next to that item on the *Performance Analysis Chart* below. You will need to complete the Unit 1 lesson that corresponds to that test item. Completing all of Unit 1 will help you build the basic skills needed to be successful in college mathematics.

Performance Analysis Chart

TEST ITEMS	NEED TO REVIEW (✔)	LESSON
1, 2		1
3, 4, 5, 6		2
7, 8, 9		3
10, 11, 12		4
13, 14		5
15, 16, 17, 18		6

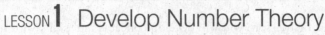

This unit, *Gateway to Algebra*, is designed to help you build the foundational skills needed to be successful in the other units. The abilities to work with fractions, decimals, and percents and to solve simple equations are some of most important skills needed for success in algebra.

LESSON **1** Develop Number Theory

In this first lesson, you will develop concepts and skills with numbers that will enable you to complete operations with fractions, decimals, and percents. The set of counting numbers, or **natural numbers**, N, is usually shown in brackets.

$$N = \{1, 2, 3, 4, 5, 6, 7,...\}$$

A **factor** of a counting number is any number that divides the counting number evenly, or without a remainder. For example, the factors of 6 are 1, 2, 3, and 6 because they divide into 6 evenly.

$$\frac{6}{6} = 1 \qquad \frac{6}{3} = 2 \qquad \frac{6}{2} = 3 \qquad \frac{6}{1} = 6$$

A composite number is any number greater than 1 that has more than two factors. A number is a **prime number** if it has exactly two factors: itself and 1. Listed below are the first four composite numbers and prime numbers.

Composite Number	Factors		Prime Number	Factors
4	1, 2, 4		2	1, 2
6	1, 2, 3, 6		3	1, 3
8	1, 2, 4, 8		5	1, 5
9	1, 3, 9		7	1, 7

The set of prime numbers is called P.

$$P = \{2, 3, 5, 7, 11,...\}$$

1.1 Write Numbers in Prime Factored Form

A counting number written as a factor of only prime numbers is in **prime factored form**. For example, the prime factorization of 36 is:

$$36 = 2 \cdot 2 \cdot 3 \cdot 3$$

EXAMPLES

Write each number as a product of prime numbers.

a. 8

$8 = 4 \cdot 2$
$\quad = 2 \cdot 2 \cdot 2$

b. 12

$12 = 4 \cdot 3$
$\quad = 2 \cdot 2 \cdot 3$

c. 48

$48 = 8 \cdot 6$
$\quad = 2 \cdot 2 \cdot 2 \cdot 2 \cdot 3$

d. 75

$75 = 25 \cdot 3$
$\quad = 5 \cdot 5 \cdot 3$

[HINT]

$\frac{6}{1}$ is the same as $6 \div 1$.

NOTE

The number 1 is neither composite nor prime.

[TIP]

A simple way to determine the prime factorization of a number is to determine two factors of the number. Then find the factors of those factors and continue until you have only prime factors.

$36 = 6 \cdot 6$
$\quad = 2 \cdot 2 \cdot 3 \cdot 3$

■

Try It 1.1

Write each number as a product of prime numbers.

a. 16

b. 20

c. 32

d. 100

1.2 Find the Greatest Common Factor (GCF)

The **greatest common factor (GCF)** of two or more numbers is the greatest counting number that divides evenly into the given numbers. For example, the GCF of 36 and 24 is 12. To find the greatest common factor, you can write each number in prime factored form. Then identify and multiply the common prime factors.

$$36 = 2 \cdot 2 \cdot 3 \cdot 3$$
$$24 = 2 \cdot 2 \cdot 2 \cdot 3$$

The common prime factors of 24 and 36 are 2, 2, and 3. Note that these are circled above. Multiply those factors, and the product is the GCF of 24 and 36:

$$2 \cdot 2 \cdot 3 = 12$$

EXAMPLES

Determine the GCF.

a. 8 and 12
$8 = 2 \cdot 2 \cdot 2$
$12 = 2 \cdot 2 \cdot 3$
The GCF is $2 \cdot 2 = $ **4**.

b. 25 and 20
$25 = 5 \cdot 5$
$20 = 2 \cdot 2 \cdot 5$
The GCF is **5**.

c. 72 and 48
$72 = 2 \cdot 2 \cdot 2 \cdot 3 \cdot 3$
$48 = 2 \cdot 2 \cdot 2 \cdot 2 \cdot 3$
The GCF is $2 \cdot 2 \cdot 2 \cdot 3 = $ **24**.

d. 18, 12, and 20
$18 = 2 \cdot 3 \cdot 3$
$12 = 2 \cdot 2 \cdot 3$
$30 = 2 \cdot 3 \cdot 5$
The GCF is $2 \cdot 3 = $ **6**.

> **NOTE**
>
> *Notice the numbers in example **b** only have one common factor. In cases like this, the only factor is the greatest common factor.*

Determine the GCF.

a. 14 and 16   **b.** 30 and 40

c. 100 and 75   **d.** 8, 24, and 32

1.3 Find the Least Common Multiple (LCM)

The multiple of a number is the product of the number with another counting number. For example, 36 is a multiple of 9 because $9 \cdot 4 = 36$. The **least common multiple (LCM)** of two numbers is the smallest number into which each number can divide evenly. The LCM of 36 and 24 is 72 since it is the smallest number that both 36 and 24 can divide evenly. To find the LCM, first determine the GCF. Then multiply the GCF by all the remaining factors.

$$36 = 2 \cdot 2 \cdot 3 \cdot 3$$
$$24 = 2 \cdot 2 \cdot 2 \cdot 3$$

The GCF is $2 \cdot 2 \cdot 3 = 12$. There are two remaining factors, 2 and 3. Multiply the GCF and all the remaining factors to find the LCM of 36 and 24:

$$12 \cdot 2 \cdot 3 = 72$$

EXAMPLES

Determine the LCM.

a. 8 and 12
    $8 = 2 \cdot 2 \cdot 2 = 4 \cdot 2$
    $12 = 2 \cdot 2 \cdot 3 = 4 \cdot 3$
    The LCM is $4 \cdot 2 \cdot 3 = \mathbf{24}$.

b. 25 and 20
    $25 = 5 \cdot 5$
    $20 = 2 \cdot 2 \cdot 5$
    The LCM is $5 \cdot 5 \cdot 2 \cdot 2 = \mathbf{100}$.

c. 16 and 48
    $16 = 2 \cdot 2 \cdot 2 \cdot 2 = 16$
    $48 = 2 \cdot 2 \cdot 2 \cdot 2 \cdot 3 = 16 \cdot 3$
    The LCM is $16 \cdot 3 = \mathbf{48}$.

d. 18 and 12
    $18 = 2 \cdot 3 \cdot 3 = 6 \cdot 3$
    $12 = 2 \cdot 2 \cdot 3 = 6 \cdot 2$
    The LCM is $6 \cdot 3 \cdot 2 = \mathbf{36.}$

Try It 1.3

Determine the LCM.

a. 4 and 6

b. 30 and 15

c. 8 and 12

d. 24 and 32

CALCULATOR TIP

Finding the Prime Factorization of a Number

You can use a graphing calculator to determine the prime factorization of numbers. Consider the number 132. Key in 132 and press ENTER. Divide that "answer" (ANS) by 2 until the answer is not an even number.

```
132
                132
Ans/2
                 66
                 33
```

You have determined that 132 = 2 · 2 · 33 because you divided by 2 twice. Now take a look at 33, and ask yourself if 33 is a prime number. You know that 33 is divisible by 3 and 11, so it is not a prime number. Divide 33 by 3 to continue the prime factorization.

```
132
                132
Ans/2
                 66
                 33
Ans/3
                 11
■
```

Ask yourself if 11 is a prime number. Since the only factors of 11 are 1 and 11, you know that 11 is a prime number. This means the prime factorization of 132 is:

$$132 = 2 \cdot 2 \cdot 3 \cdot 11$$

LESSON 2 Convert Fractions, Decimals, and Percents

FOCUS Use equivalent fractions to convert among fractions, decimals, and percents

DEFINITION
The *quotient* is the answer in a division problem.

$$3 \div 4 = \frac{3}{4}$$

In this lesson, you will learn how to represent fractions as decimals and percents. You use fractions, decimals, and percents in many situations involving building, cooking, and money. A fraction such as $\frac{3}{4}$ is a quotient of two counting numbers; 3 is the numerator and 4 is the denominator. The denominator is the number of equal parts into which the whole is divided. The numerator indicates how many of those parts you have. A number line is an easy way to visualize fractions.

$$\begin{array}{ccccc} \vdash & \mid & \mid & \mid & \dashv \\ 0 & \frac{1}{4} & \frac{2}{4} & \frac{3}{4} & 1 \end{array}$$

You can see that $\frac{2}{4}$ is in the same position that $\frac{1}{2}$ would be. Fractions such as $\frac{1}{2}$ and $\frac{2}{4}$ are called **equivalent fractions** because they have the same value. To form equivalent fractions, multiply or divide both the numerator and the denominator by the same number, or a fraction equal to 1. Below are two examples of equivalent fractions.

NOTE

Notice that 1 has many equivalent fractions.

$$1 = \frac{2}{2} = \frac{3}{3} = \frac{4}{4} = \dots$$

Multiplication		Division
$\frac{1}{2} = \frac{1 \cdot 2}{2 \cdot 2} = \frac{2}{4}$ and		$\frac{2}{4} = \frac{2 \div 2}{4 \div 2} = \frac{1}{2}$
$\frac{3}{4} = \frac{3 \cdot 5}{4 \cdot 5} = \frac{15}{20}$ and		$\frac{15}{20} = \frac{15 \div 5}{20 \div 5} = \frac{3}{4}$

2.1 Compare Fractions

You can use equivalent fractions to compare any two fractions. On the number line above, you see that three-fourths is greater than one-half. This is written as:

$$\frac{3}{4} > \frac{1}{2}$$

You can also say the one-half is less than three-fourths, or $\frac{1}{2} < \frac{3}{4}$. Each of these statements is called an **inequality**, a statement that compares two or more quantities.

To compare two fractions, first find the **least common denominator (LCD)**, and then convert each fraction to that denominator. The LCD is the least common multiple of the denominators.

For example, to compare $\frac{1}{2}$ and $\frac{3}{4}$, find the LCM of the denominators, which is 4. This is the least common denominator (LCD). Then write $\frac{1}{2}$ with a denominator of 4.

$$\frac{1}{2} = \frac{1 \cdot 2}{2 \cdot 2} = \frac{2}{4}$$

Since $\frac{2}{4} < \frac{3}{4}$, you know $\frac{1}{2} < \frac{3}{4}$.

EXAMPLES

Compare each pair of fractions by writing an inequality.

a. $\frac{3}{4}$ and $\frac{5}{6}$ Find the LCD.

The LCD is 12.

$$\frac{3}{4} = \frac{3 \cdot 3}{4 \cdot 3} = \frac{9}{12}$$

$$\frac{5}{6} = \frac{5 \cdot 2}{6 \cdot 2} = \frac{10}{12}$$

Convert each fraction to an equivalent fraction with a denominator of 12.

Since $\frac{9}{12} < \frac{10}{12}$, you know that $\frac{3}{4} < \frac{5}{6}$.   Compare. Write as an inequality.

b. **Compare the two wrench sizes: $\frac{11}{16}$ and $\frac{5}{8}$. First find the LCD.**

The LCD is 16.

$$\frac{5}{8} = \frac{5 \cdot 2}{8 \cdot 2} = \frac{10}{16}$$

Convert $\frac{5}{8}$ to an equivalent fraction with a denominator of 16.

Since $\frac{10}{16} < \frac{11}{16}$, you know that $\frac{5}{8} < \frac{11}{16}$.   Compare. Write as an inequality.

c. **Evett had $\frac{5}{12}$ of her book left to read while Roger had $\frac{3}{8}$ left to read.**

The LCD is 24.

$$\frac{5}{12} = \frac{5 \cdot 2}{12 \cdot 2} = \frac{10}{24}$$

$$\frac{3}{8} = \frac{3 \cdot 3}{8 \cdot 3} = \frac{9}{24}$$

Convert each fraction to an equivalent fraction with a denominator of 24.

Since $\frac{10}{24} > \frac{9}{24}$, you know that $\frac{5}{12} > \frac{3}{8}$.   Compare. Write as an inequality.

Compare each pair of fractions by writing an inequality.

a. $\frac{1}{4}$ and $\frac{1}{6}$

b. $\frac{7}{10}$ and $\frac{1}{2}$

c. Mylah has completed $\frac{5}{12}$ of her Spanish homework and $\frac{7}{18}$ of her English homework.

2.2 Convert Percents to Decimals and Fractions

Percents are used widely in the real world to compute taxes, to find discounts, and for many other applications. A percent can be written as a fraction with a denominator of 100. For example, $25\% = \frac{25}{100}$. Decimals can be written as fractions with denominators 10, 100, 1,000, and so on. As a decimal, $25\% = \frac{25}{100} = 0.25$, which is read "twenty-five hundredths." The place value of a number is a fundamental concept in working with fractions and decimals. For example, in the number 0.25, 2 is in the tenths place and 5 is in the hundredths place.

DEFINITION
A fraction is in lowest terms when the GCF of the numerator and the denominator is 1.

You can also use equivalent fractions to write a percent as a fraction in simplest form:

$$25\% = \frac{25}{100}$$
$$= \frac{25 \div 25}{100 \div 25} = \frac{1}{4}$$

EXAMPLES

Convert each percent to a decimal and a fraction.

a. 75%

$$75\% = \frac{75}{100} = \mathbf{0.75} \qquad\qquad 75\% = \frac{75}{100} = \frac{75 \div 25}{100 \div 25} = \frac{3}{4}$$

b. Write an 8% sales tax as a decimal and a fraction.

$$8\% = \frac{8}{100} = \mathbf{0.08} \qquad\qquad\qquad 8\% = \frac{8 \div 4}{100 \div 4} = \mathbf{\frac{2}{25}}$$

c. 37.5%

$$37.5\% = \frac{37.5}{100} = \frac{375}{1,000} = \mathbf{0.375} \qquad\qquad 37.5\% = \frac{37.5}{100} = \frac{375 \div 125}{1,000 \div 125} = \frac{3}{8}$$

[TIP]

To eliminate the decimal in the fraction, multiply by 10 to create an equivalent fraction:

$$\frac{37.5 \cdot 10}{100 \cdot 10} = \frac{375}{1,000}$$

Try It 2.2

Convert each percent to a decimal and a fraction.

a. 50%

b. Write a 6% automobile tax as a decimal and a fraction.

c. 62.5%

2.3 Convert Fractions to Decimals and Percents

Converting fractions to decimals and percents is easy when you are able to form an equivalent fraction with a denominator of 100.

$$\frac{3}{4} = \frac{3 \cdot 25}{4 \cdot 25} = \frac{75}{100} = 0.75 = 75\%$$

Some fractions such as $\frac{1}{3}$ aren't as easily converted. Let's again consider $\frac{3}{4}$. Note that you can convert $\frac{3}{4}$ by dividing 4 into 3.

$$\begin{array}{r} 0.75 \\ 4\overline{)3.00} \\ -28 \\ \hline 20 \\ -20 \\ \hline 0 \end{array}$$

You can use this same process with any fraction. When you convert $\frac{1}{3}$, you also divide, but you get a repeating decimal.

$$
\begin{array}{r}
0.333... \\
3\overline{)1.000} \\
\underline{-9} \\
10 \\
\underline{-9} \\
10 \\
\underline{-9} \\
1
\end{array}
$$

To indicate that the 3 repeats, you place a bar over the first 3 and drop the two remaining 3s.

$$\frac{1}{3} = 0.333... = 0.\overline{3}$$

To write $\frac{1}{3}$ as a percent, first write as a decimal and then convert to a percent. Note that this percent includes a fraction.

$$\frac{1}{3} = 0.333... = 0.33\overline{3} = 33.\overline{3}\% = 33\frac{1}{3}\%$$

EXAMPLES

Convert each fraction to a decimal and a percent.

a. $\frac{3}{5}$

$$\frac{3}{5} = \frac{3 \cdot 20}{5 \cdot 20} = \frac{60}{100} = 0.60 = 60\%$$

$$\frac{3}{5} = 0.6 = 60\%$$

b. $\frac{1}{8}$

$$\frac{1}{8} = \frac{1 \cdot 125}{8 \cdot 125} = \frac{\cdot 125}{1,000} = 0.125 = 12.5\%$$

$$\frac{1}{8} = 0.125 = 12.5\%$$

c. $\frac{5}{6}$

$$
\begin{array}{r}
0.8\overline{3} \\
6\overline{)5.00}
\end{array}
\text{ and } 0.8\overline{3} = 83.\overline{3}\% = 83\frac{1}{3}\%
$$

$$\frac{5}{6} = 0.8\overline{3} = 83\frac{1}{3}\%$$

Try It 2.3

Convert each fraction to a decimal and a percent.

a. $\frac{2}{5}$

b. $\frac{7}{8}$

c. $\frac{2}{3}$

CALCULATOR TIP

Convert Repeating Decimals to Fractions

You can use a graphing calculator to convert fractions to repeating decimals and then covert the answer back to a fraction. Consider the fraction $\frac{5}{6}$. First divide 6 into 5.

```
5/6
          .8333333333
```

You can see that the answer has a repeating decimal. Go to the MATH menu, and choose Frac to convert the repeating decimal to a fraction.

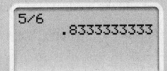

```
5/6
          .8333333333
Ans▸Frac
                 5/6
■
```

LESSON 3 Add and Subtract Fractions and Decimals

In this lesson, you will build on what you know about equivalent fractions to add and subtract fractions. To add fractions, each fraction must have the same denominator. Suppose you jog around a three-quarter mile track. If you do two laps, you can find the total by adding.

$$\frac{3}{4} + \frac{3}{4} = \frac{6}{4}$$

Note that $\frac{6}{4}$ is greater than 1 because it can be simplified and written as a mixed number. A mixed number such as $1\frac{1}{2}$ contains a whole number and a fraction.

$$\frac{6}{4} = \frac{4}{4} + \frac{2}{4} = 1 + \frac{2}{4} = 1\frac{1}{2}$$

You can also add decimal equivalents to find a sum.

$$\frac{3}{4} + \frac{3}{4} = 0.75 + 0.75 = 1.50 = 1.5$$

In general, you can rewrite fractions greater than 1 as mixed numbers by dividing and taking the remainder as the new numerator.

$$\frac{11}{4} = 4\overline{)11} \begin{array}{c} 2\frac{3}{4} \\ \underline{-8} \\ 3 \end{array}$$

To write a mixed number as a fraction, multiply the whole number by the denominator and add the product to the numerator. The denominator will stay the same. Consider $2\frac{3}{4}$: multiply 2 by 4 and add 3.

$$2\frac{3}{4} = \frac{4 \cdot 2 + 3}{4} = \frac{11}{4}$$

3.1 Add Fractions and Decimals

To add fractions with different denominators, first find the LCD. Then write each fraction using the LCD as the denominator and add.

EXAMPLES

Add. Simplify your answers. Check your answers by adding the decimal equivalents. Use a calculator as needed.

a. $\dfrac{13}{16} + \dfrac{7}{16}$

$$\frac{13}{16} + \frac{7}{16} = \frac{20}{16} \qquad\qquad \text{Add the numerators.}$$

$$= 1\frac{4}{16} = 1\frac{4 \div 4}{16 \div 4} = 1\frac{1}{4} \qquad \text{Write the fraction in simplest form.}$$

Check with decimal equivalents:

$$\frac{13}{16} + \frac{7}{16} = 0.8125 + 0.4375 = 1.25 = 1\frac{1}{4}$$

b. $\dfrac{1}{2} + \dfrac{2}{3}$ ⠀⠀⠀⠀⠀⠀⠀⠀⠀⠀⠀⠀⠀⠀⠀⠀⠀⠀⠀ Find the LCD.

The LCD is 6.

$$\frac{1}{2} + \frac{2}{3} = \frac{1 \cdot 3}{2 \cdot 3} + \frac{2 \cdot 2}{3 \cdot 2} \qquad \text{Convert both denominators to 6.}$$

$$= \frac{3}{6} + \frac{4}{6} \qquad\qquad\qquad \text{Add.}$$

$$= \frac{7}{6} = 1\frac{1}{6} \qquad\qquad\quad \text{Simplify.}$$

Check with decimal equivalents:

$$\frac{1}{2} + \frac{2}{3} = 0.5 + 0.666\ldots = 1.166\ldots = 1.1\overline{6} = 1\frac{1}{6}$$

c. A carpenter is connecting two sides of a patio. One side is $2\frac{1}{2}$ yards long, and the other side is $4\frac{3}{8}$ yards long. What is the combined length?

$$2\frac{1}{2} + 4\frac{3}{8} = \frac{5}{2} + \frac{35}{8} \qquad \text{Write the mixed numbers as fractions.}$$

$$= \frac{5 \cdot 4}{2 \cdot 4} + \frac{35}{8} \qquad \text{Convert } \frac{5}{2} \text{ to a fraction with a}$$
$$\qquad\qquad\qquad\qquad \text{denominator of 8, the LCD.}$$

$$= \frac{20}{8} + \frac{35}{8} \qquad\quad \text{Add.}$$

$$= \frac{55}{8} = 6\frac{7}{8} \qquad\quad \text{Simplify.}$$

Check with decimal equivalents:

$$2\frac{1}{2} + 4\frac{3}{8} = 2.5 + 4.375 = 6.875 = 6\frac{7}{8} \text{ yards}$$

■ Try It 3.1

Add. Simplify your answers. Check your answers by adding the decimal equivalents. Use a calculator as needed.

a. $\frac{7}{8} + \frac{5}{8}$

b. $\frac{3}{4} + \frac{1}{3}$

c. Katie volunteered for $2\frac{1}{3}$ hours and worked for $1\frac{5}{6}$ hours. How many hours is that?

3.2 Subtract Fractions and Decimals

Some subtraction problems can be completed mentally by "adding up." Suppose a carpenter cuts a $2\frac{3}{4}$ -foot piece of wood from a board that is $4\frac{1}{2}$ feet long. To find the length of the board after the cut, the carpenter can "add up." First he adds $\frac{1}{4}$ to $2\frac{3}{4}$ to get 3 feet.

$$2\frac{3}{4} + \frac{1}{4} = 3$$

Then he adds $1\frac{1}{2}$ to 3 to get $4\frac{1}{2}$.

$$3 + 1\frac{1}{2} = 4\frac{1}{2}$$

This means he has $\frac{1}{4} + 1\frac{1}{2} = 1\frac{3}{4}$ feet of the board left.

You can also convert the fractions to decimals and subtract.

$$4\frac{1}{2} - 2\frac{3}{4} = 4.5 - 2.75$$
$$= 1.75$$

To subtract fractions, each fraction must have the same denominator. To subtract fractions with different denominators, first find the LCD and write each fraction in the same denominator. Then you can subtract. The subtraction for the situation above is:

$$4\frac{1}{2} - 2\frac{3}{4} = 4\frac{2}{4} - 2\frac{3}{4} = \frac{18}{4} - \frac{11}{4} = \frac{7}{4} = 1\frac{3}{4}$$

Subtract. Simplify your answers. Check your answers by subtracting the decimal equivalents. Use a calculator as needed.

a. $\dfrac{13}{16} - \dfrac{7}{16}$

$$\dfrac{13}{16} - \dfrac{7}{16} = \dfrac{6}{16}$$

$$= \dfrac{6 \div 2}{16 \div 2}$$

$$= \mathbf{\dfrac{3}{8}}$$

b. $\dfrac{2}{3} - \dfrac{1}{2}$

$$\dfrac{2}{3} - \dfrac{1}{2} = \dfrac{2 \cdot 2}{3 \cdot 2} - \dfrac{1 \cdot 3}{2 \cdot 3}$$

$$= \dfrac{4}{6} - \dfrac{3}{6}$$

$$= \mathbf{\dfrac{1}{6}}$$

Check with decimal equivalents:

$$\dfrac{13}{16} - \dfrac{7}{16} = 0.8125 - 0.4375$$

$$= 0.375 = \dfrac{3}{8}$$

Check with decimal equivalents:

$$\dfrac{2}{3} - \dfrac{1}{2} = 0.666\ldots - 0.5$$

$$= 0.166\ldots = 0.1\overline{6} = \dfrac{1}{6}$$

c. **Sue cuts a $1\dfrac{3}{8}$ -foot piece from a $3\dfrac{1}{2}$ -foot long board. How much is left?**

The LCD is 8. Begin by writing the mixed numbers as fractions.

$$3\dfrac{1}{2} - 1\dfrac{3}{8} = \dfrac{7}{2} - \dfrac{11}{8}$$

$$= \dfrac{7 \cdot 4}{2 \cdot 4} - \dfrac{11}{8}$$

$$= \dfrac{28}{8} - \dfrac{11}{8}$$

$$= \dfrac{17}{8}$$

$$= \mathbf{2\dfrac{1}{8} \text{ feet}}$$

Check with decimal equivalents:

$$3\dfrac{1}{2} - 1\dfrac{3}{8} = 3.5 - 1.375$$

$$= 2.125 = 2\dfrac{1}{8}$$

[Mental Math]

Add $\dfrac{5}{8}$ to $1\dfrac{3}{8}$ to get 2. Then add $1\dfrac{1}{2}$ to 2 to get $3\dfrac{1}{2}$.

$$\dfrac{5}{8} + 1\dfrac{1}{2} = \dfrac{5}{8} + \dfrac{12}{8}$$

$$= \dfrac{17}{8}$$

■ **Try It 3.2** ⋯⋯⋯⋯⋯⋯⋯⋯⋯⋯⋯⋯⋯⋯⋯⋯⋯⋯⋯⋯⋯⋯⋯⋯⋯⋯⋯⋯⋯⋯⋯⋯⋯⋯

Subtract. Simplify your answers. Check your answers by subtracting the decimal equivalents. Use a calculator as needed.

a. $\dfrac{7}{8} - \dfrac{5}{8}$

b. $\dfrac{3}{4} - \dfrac{1}{3}$

c. Ben studied for his math test for $2\dfrac{1}{3}$ hours. He studied for his science test for $1\dfrac{5}{6}$ hours. How many more hours did he study math than science?

CALCULATOR TIP

Using the Fraction Function to Subtract Fractions

You can use a graphing calculator to add or subtract numbers and to covert the answer to a fraction. Consider the subtraction problem $3\dfrac{1}{2} - 1\dfrac{3}{8}$. Rewrite the mixed numbers as $\left(3+\dfrac{1}{2}\right) - \left(1+\dfrac{3}{8}\right)$, and enter into your calculator.

```
(3+1/2)-(1+3/8)
            2.125
■
```

Note the decimal answer. Under the MATH menu, choose Frac.

```
(3+1/2)-(1+3/8)
            2.125
Ans▶Frac
             17/8
■
```

You see that the solution is $3\dfrac{1}{2} - 1\dfrac{3}{8} = \dfrac{17}{8} = \mathbf{2\dfrac{1}{8}}$.

Complete problems 1–5.

1. Write 60 in prime factored form.

2. Determine the GCF of 24, 36, and 48.

3. Determine the LCM of 15 and 20.

4. Write an inequality to compare $\frac{9}{16}$ and $\frac{7}{12}$.

5. Write an inequality to compare $\frac{3}{5}$ and $\frac{7}{10}$.

Convert each percent to a decimal and a fraction.

6. 80%   7. 5%

Convert each fraction to a decimal and a percent.

8. $\frac{4}{5}$ 9. $\frac{5}{8}$

10. $\frac{5}{9}$

Continue on next page.

Add or subtract. Simplify your answers. Check your answers by adding or subtracting the decimal equivalents. Use a calculator as needed.

11. $\frac{3}{4} + \frac{3}{4}$

12. $\frac{5}{9} + \frac{1}{2}$

13. $1\frac{3}{4} + 2\frac{5}{16}$

14. $\frac{3}{5} - \frac{1}{2}$

15. $2\frac{1}{2} - 1\frac{3}{4}$

Check your answers in the *Solutions* section at the back of the book. If you missed more than one answer from problems 1 to 5, review lesson 1. If you missed more than one answer from problems 6 to 10, review lesson 2. If you missed more than one answer from problems 11 to 15, review lesson 3.

To multiply fractions, you will multiply the numerators and denominators, and then simplify.

$$\frac{3}{4} \cdot \frac{5}{6} = \frac{15}{24} = \frac{15 \div 3}{24 \div 3} = \frac{5}{8}$$

You can also simplify by dividing diagonal numerators and denominators by common factors before you multiply. In the example below, 3 and 6 are both divisible by 3.

$$\frac{3}{4} \cdot \frac{5}{6} = \frac{\overset{1}{\cancel{3}}}{4} \cdot \frac{5}{\underset{2}{\cancel{6}}} = \frac{5}{8}$$

4.1 Solve Percent Problems

You can solve simple percent problems by multiplying by fraction and decimal equivalents. Some of the common percents and their fraction-decimal equivalents are listed in the table below.

Fraction	$\frac{1}{10}$	$\frac{1}{5}$	$\frac{1}{4}$	$\frac{3}{10}$	$\frac{1}{3}$	$\frac{2}{5}$	$\frac{1}{2}$	$\frac{3}{5}$	$\frac{2}{3}$	$\frac{7}{10}$	$\frac{3}{4}$	$\frac{4}{5}$	$\frac{9}{10}$
Decimal	0.1	0.2	0.25	0.3	$0.\overline{3}$	0.4	0.5	0.6	$0.\overline{6}$	0.7	0.75	0.8	0.9
Percent (%)	10	20	25	30	$33\frac{1}{3}$	40	50	60	$66\frac{2}{3}$	70	75	80	90

Suppose you want to leave a 20% tip on a dinner that cost $34.78. You can estimate the tip by rounding the cost to the nearest whole number and then multiplying by $\frac{1}{5}$:

$$20\% \text{ of } 35 = \frac{1}{\underset{1}{\cancel{5}}} \cdot \frac{\overset{7}{\cancel{35}}}{1} = \$7$$

You could also multiply by the decimal:

$$20\% \text{ of } 35 = 0.2(35) = \$7$$

[HINT]

Since 35 and 5 are diagonal to each other and both divisible by 5, you can reduce by dividing out the common factor (5) before multiplying.

NOTE

*Look at example **b**. When the answer is a whole number, the fraction and decimal will look the same.*

[Mental Math]

Look at example **c**. Use mental math to subtract 10% from 65.

$$65 - 0.1(65) = 65 - 6.5$$

EXAMPLES

Solve each problem as a fraction and as a decimal.

a. 75% of 15

$$75\% \text{ of } 15 = \frac{3}{4} \cdot \frac{15}{1} = \frac{45}{4} = 11\frac{1}{4}$$

$$75\% \text{ of } 15 = 0.75(15) = \textbf{11.25}$$

b. $66\frac{2}{3}\%$ of 15

$$66\frac{2}{3}\% \text{ of } 15 = \frac{2}{\underset{1}{\cancel{3}}} \cdot \frac{\overset{5}{\cancel{15}}}{1} = \textbf{10}$$

$$66\frac{2}{3}\% \text{ of } 15 = 0.666(15) = \textbf{10}$$

c. 90% of 65

$$90\% \text{ of } 65 = \frac{9}{\underset{2}{\cancel{10}}} \cdot \frac{\overset{13}{\cancel{65}}}{1} = \frac{117}{2} = \textbf{58}\frac{1}{2}$$

$$90\% \text{ of } 65 = 0.9(65) = \textbf{58.5}$$

Try It 4.1   ···

Solve each problem as a fraction and a decimal.

a. 25% of 18

b. 60% of 25

c. 10% of 120

4.2 Multiply Fractions

[RECALL]

The area of a rectangle is the length times the width and is written as units squared.

You can use an area model to visualize the multiplication of fractions. Suppose the area of a farm is three-fourths of a mile by a one-half a mile. Draw an area model to represent this situation. Start by drawing a square to represent 1-square mile. Divide it vertically into halves and horizontally into fourths. Then shade a portion to show $\frac{3}{4} \times \frac{1}{2}$. The part where the shading overlaps shows the product.

The area model shows that
$\frac{3}{4} \cdot \frac{1}{2} = \frac{3}{8}$ of a square mile.

To find the area of the same farm in acres, you multiply $\frac{3}{8}$ by the number of acres in 1-square mile, 640 acres.

$$\frac{3}{8} \cdot 640 = \frac{3}{8} \cdot \frac{\overset{80}{\cancel{640}}}{\underset{1}{1}} = 240 \text{ acres}$$

The farm is $\frac{3}{8}$ of a square mile or 240 acres.

EXAMPLES

Solve each problem.

[HINT]

You could also multiply first and then divide.

$$\frac{3}{4} \cdot \frac{2}{3} = \frac{6 \div 6}{12 \div 6} = \frac{1}{2}$$

a. $\frac{3}{4} \cdot \frac{2}{3}$

$$\frac{3}{4} \cdot \frac{2}{3} = \frac{\overset{1}{\cancel{3}}}{\underset{2}{\cancel{4}}} \cdot \frac{\overset{1}{\cancel{2}}}{\underset{1}{\cancel{3}}} = \frac{1}{2}$$

b. $2\frac{2}{3} \cdot \frac{3}{4}$

$$2\frac{2}{3} \cdot \frac{3}{4} = \frac{8}{3} \cdot \frac{3}{4} = \frac{\overset{2}{\cancel{8}}}{\underset{1}{\cancel{3}}} \cdot \frac{\overset{1}{\cancel{3}}}{\underset{1}{\cancel{4}}} = 2$$

c. A farm is $\frac{3}{4}$ miles by $1\frac{1}{2}$ miles. What is the area in acres?

$$\frac{3}{4} \cdot 1\frac{1}{2} = \frac{3}{4} \cdot \frac{3}{2} = \frac{9}{8} = 1\frac{1}{8}$$ First compute the square miles.

[HINT]

There are 640 acres in 1-square mile.

$$\frac{9}{8} \cdot 640 = \frac{9}{\cancel{8}} \cdot \frac{\overset{80}{\cancel{640}}}{\cancel{1}} = 720$$ Compute the number of acres.

The farm is $1\frac{1}{8}$ square miles, which is **720 acres.**

Try It 4.2

Solve each problem.

a. $\frac{3}{4} \cdot \frac{1}{3}$

b. $\frac{2}{3} \cdot 1\frac{3}{4}$

c. A farm is $1\frac{3}{4}$ miles by 2 miles. What is the area of the farm in acres?

4.3 Divide Fractions

Division problems ask the question, "How many of one thing are in another?" This means the division $2 \div \frac{2}{3}$ is asking for the number of two-thirds in 2. You can see from the model below that there are 3 two-thirds in 2, which means $2 \div \frac{2}{3} = 3$.

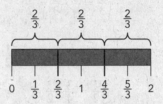

This is the same as $2 \cdot \frac{3}{2} = 3$. **Reciprocals** are numbers whose product is 1. You know that $\frac{2}{3}$ and $\frac{3}{2}$ are reciprocals because $\frac{2}{3} \cdot \frac{3}{2} = 1$. To divide by a fraction, you multiply by the reciprocal.

$$2 \div \frac{2}{3} = \frac{2}{1} \cdot \frac{3}{2} = 3$$

EXAMPLES

Divide.

a. $\frac{3}{4} \div \frac{9}{10}$

$$\frac{3}{4} \div \frac{9}{10} = \frac{3}{4} \cdot \frac{10}{9} = \frac{\overset{1}{3}}{\underset{2}{4}} \cdot \frac{\overset{5}{10}}{\underset{3}{9}} = \frac{5}{6}$$

b. $4\frac{1}{2} \div \frac{3}{4}$

$$4\frac{1}{2} \div \frac{3}{4} = \frac{9}{2} \cdot \frac{4}{3} = \frac{\overset{3}{9}}{\underset{1}{2}} \cdot \frac{\overset{2}{4}}{\underset{1}{3}} = 6$$

c. How many quarters are there in two dollars and fifty cents?

This can be written as $2\frac{1}{2} \div \frac{1}{4} = ?$

$$2\frac{1}{2} \div \frac{1}{4} = \frac{5}{2} \cdot \frac{4}{1} = \frac{5}{\underset{1}{2}} \cdot \frac{\overset{2}{4}}{1} = 10$$

There are **10 quarters** in two dollars and fifty cents.

■ **Try It 4.3**

Divide.

a. $1\frac{3}{4} \div \frac{2}{5}$

b. $2\frac{2}{3} \div \frac{4}{9}$

c. How many $\frac{1}{3}$-foot long pieces can be cut from an 8-foot long board?

CALCULATOR TIP

Dividing Fractions

You can use a graphing calculator to multiply or divide and then convert the answer to a fraction. Consider the division problem $4\frac{1}{2} \div \frac{3}{4}$. Rewrite the problem as $\left(4 + \frac{1}{2}\right) \div (3 \div 4)$. Without the parentheses, you would be dividing by three and then by four. Then enter into your calculator.

```
(4+1/2)/(3/4)
                  6
■
```

You see that $4\frac{1}{2} \div \frac{3}{4} = 6$.

LESSON 5 Evaluate and Simplify Algebraic Expressions

You have worked with **numeric expressions** such as $\frac{3}{4} \cdot \frac{1}{2}$. Numeric expressions contain only numbers and operation symbols. Suppose you make $12 per hour. You can represent your earnings with the **algebraic expression** $12x$, which means 12 times x, the number of hours you work. The **variable**, x in this expression, is a letter or symbol that can be replaced by a number. The number 12 in this expression is called the **coefficient** of x.

If you plan to work 30 hours this week, you can evaluate the expression $12x$ by replacing x with 30.

$$12x = 12(30) = 360$$

If you work 30 hours, you will make $360.

[RECALL]

Remember that a percent can be converted to a decimal by dividing by 100.

5.1 Write and Evaluate Algebraic Expressions

There are many real-world situations that can be represented with algebraic expressions. For example, the typical tip for a meal in a restaurant is about 20%. The tip for a meal that costs d dollars could be represented with the expression $0.2d$.

EXAMPLES

Translate each situation into an algebraic expression, and then evaluate for the variable.

a. **You leave a 20% tip for a meal that costs d dollars. If your meal cost $24, what would the tip be?**

$$0.2d = 0.2(\$24) \qquad \text{Write an expression and substitute for } d.$$
$$= \$4.80 \qquad \text{Simplify.}$$

The tip would be **$4.80.**

b. **You use a $15 off coupon when you buy x dollars of merchandise. If the merchandise cost $225 before you use the coupon, what is the cost after you use the coupon?**

$$x - 15 = \$225 - 15 \qquad \text{Write an expression and substitute for } x.$$
$$= \$210 \qquad \text{Simplify.}$$

You would spend **$210** with the coupon.

c. **Find the number of hours equal to m minutes. Evaluate when $m = 150$.**

$$\frac{m}{60} = \frac{150}{60} \qquad \text{Write an expression and substitute for } m.$$
$$= 2.5 \qquad \text{Simplify.}$$

150 minutes is equal to **2.5 hours.**

■ Try It 5.1

Translate each situation into an algebraic expression, and then evaluate.

a. You leave a 25% tip for a meal that costs d dollars. If your meal cost $15, what would the tip be?

b. You pay $8 for shipping on x dollars of merchandise. Evaluate when $x = \$39.95$ of merchandise.

c. Find the number of weeks equal to d number of days. Evaluate for 364 days.

5.2 Combine Like Terms

Earlier you wrote the expression $12x$ as the earnings made for work at $12 per hour. Suppose you receive a 50¢ per hour raise. This additional amount you will receive can be represented with the expression, $0.5x$. Your earnings can now be represented by:

$$12x + 0.5x = 12.5x$$

This is called combining like terms. You can evaluate each side of the equation for 30 hours to find your new pay with the raise:

$$
\begin{aligned}
12x + 0.5x &= 12(30) + 0.5(30) & 12.5x &= 12.5(30) \\
&= \$360 + \$15 & &= \$375 \\
&= \$375
\end{aligned}
$$

Combine like terms. Check by evaluating the original expression and the answer for $x = 10$. If the solutions are the same, you know the value of the variable is correct.

a. $2x + 5 + 4x - 3$

$$2x + 5 + 4x - 3 = 2x + 4x + 5 - 3 \qquad \text{Regroup so like terms are adjacent.}$$
$$= 6x + 2 \qquad \text{Combine like terms.}$$

Check when $x = 10$.

$$2x + 5 + 4x - 3 = 2(10) + 5 + 4(10) - 3 \qquad 6x + 2 = 6(10) + 2$$
$$= 20 + 5 + 40 - 3 \qquad\qquad = 60 + 2$$
$$= 62 \qquad\qquad\qquad = 62$$

b. $\frac{2}{3}x + \frac{3}{4}x$

$$\frac{2}{3}x + \frac{3}{4}x = \left(\frac{2}{3} + \frac{3}{4}\right)x \qquad \text{Combine like terms.}$$
$$= \left(\frac{8}{12} + \frac{9}{12}\right)x \qquad \text{Write equivalent fractions using the LCD.}$$
$$= \frac{17}{12}x \qquad \text{Add.}$$

Check when $x = 10$.

$$\frac{2}{3}x + \frac{3}{4}x = \frac{2}{3}(10) + \frac{3}{4}(10) \qquad\qquad \frac{17}{12}x = \frac{17}{12}(10)$$
$$= \frac{20}{3} + \frac{30}{4} \qquad\qquad\qquad = \frac{170}{12}$$
$$= \frac{80}{12} + \frac{90}{12}$$
$$= \frac{170}{12}$$

c. $7x - 3 - x$

$$7x - 3 - x = 7x - x - 3 \qquad \text{Regroup so like terms are adjacent.}$$
$$= 6x - 3 \qquad \text{Combine like terms.}$$

Check when $x = 10$.

$$7x - 3 - x = 7(10) - 3 - 10 \qquad\qquad 6x - 3 = 6(10) - 3$$
$$= 70 - 3 - 10 \qquad\qquad\qquad = 60 - 3$$
$$= 67 - 10 \qquad\qquad\qquad = 57$$
$$= 57$$

Try It 5.2

Combine like terms. Check by evaluating the original expression and the answer for $x = 10$. If the solutions are the same, you know the value of the variable is correct.

a. $x + 10 + 7x - 1$

b. $\frac{5}{2}x - \frac{3}{4}x$

c. $3x - 3 - 2x$

CALCULATOR TIP

Using the Store (STO) Key

You can use a graphing calculator to evaluate an expression for several values of x by using the store key (STO). Consider the expressions $12x + 0.5x$ and $12.5x$. To determine if the expressions are equal, evaluate both expressions for $x = 30$.

First, type in 30 STO, and then press the X key and ENTER. Then type in each expression and press ENTER. This will give you the value of each expression when $x = 30$.

```
30→X
                        30
12X+.5X
                       375
12.5X
                       375
■
```

Since the expressions have the same value when $x = 30$, they are equal.

LESSON 6 Solve Equations

In this lesson, you will learn the basic skills needed to solve equations. An **equation** is a mathematical sentence that shows that two expressions are equivalent. Equations can be used to model many real-world events. Suppose you buy a long-distance cell-phone plan that costs $7 a month plus 5¢ per minute. If your monthly bill is $19, how many minutes did you pay for? This situation can be modeled as an equation, where x is the number of minutes you paid for:

$$0.05x + 7 = 19$$

In the next few sections, you will develop methods for solving that kind of equation.

6.1 Solve Equations Using Addition and Subtraction

Suppose you go to the department store with a $40 coupon. If you paid $225 with the coupon, how much would you have spent without the coupon? This situation can be modeled with the equation $x - 40 = 225$. To solve for x, you can "undo" the subtraction by adding 40 to both sides.

$$x - 40 = 225$$
$$x - 40 + 40 = 225 + 40$$
$$x = 265$$

Add 40 to both sides.

Note: $40 - 40 = 0$.

You would have spent $265 without the coupon.

EXAMPLES

Add or subtract to find the value of x.

a. $x + 14 = 20$

$$x + 14 = 20$$
$$x + 14 - 14 = 20 - 14$$
$$x = 6$$

Subtract 14 from both sides.

Note: $14 - 14 = 0$.

b. A video is discounted $1.25 to $10. What was the original price?
   Use the equation $x - 1.25 = 10$.

$$x - 1.25 = 10$$ Add 1.25 to both sides.
$$x + 1.25 - 1.25 = 10 + 1.25$$ Note: $1.25 - 1.25 = 0$.
$$x = 11.25$$

The original price was **$11.25**.

c. $x + \dfrac{3}{4} = 2\dfrac{1}{2}$

$$x + \frac{3}{4} = 2\frac{1}{2}$$

$$x + \frac{3}{4} - \frac{3}{4} = \frac{5}{2} - \frac{3}{4}$$ Subtract $\dfrac{3}{4}$ from both sides.

$$x = \frac{10}{4} - \frac{3}{4}$$ Find the LCD and subtract.

$$x = \frac{7}{4} = 1\frac{3}{4}$$

■ Try It 6.1

Add or subtract to find the value of x.

a. $x + 4 = 16$

b. After studying 6.75 hours, Morgan still has 1.25 hours left to study. How many hours will she study? Use the equation $x - 6.75 = 1.25$.

c. $x - \dfrac{1}{2} = \dfrac{2}{3}$

6.2 Solve Equations Using Multiplication and Division

Suppose 60% of students in a freshman class at a college are female. If there are 2,100 women in the class, how would you determine the total number of students in the class? Use your fraction-percent equivalents: $60\% = \frac{3}{5}$. You can write and solve the equation:

$$\frac{3}{5}x = 2{,}100$$

To find the total number of students x, multiply both sides by the reciprocal of $\frac{3}{5}$.

$$\frac{5}{3} \cdot \frac{3}{5}x = \frac{5}{3} \cdot 2{,}100$$

$$x = \frac{5}{\cancel{3}} \cdot \cancel{2{,}100}^{\,700}_{\,1}$$

$$x = 3{,}500$$

There are 3,500 students in the freshman class.

EXAMPLES

Multiply or divide to find the value of x.

a. $2x = 5$

$$2x = 5$$

$$\frac{2x}{2} = \frac{5}{2} \qquad \text{Divide both sides by 2.}$$

$$x = \frac{5}{2} = \mathbf{2.5} \qquad \text{Simplify.}$$

b. $\frac{2}{3}x = 10$

$$\frac{2}{3}x = 10$$

$$\frac{3}{2} \cdot \frac{2}{3}x = \frac{3}{2} \cdot 10 \qquad \text{Multiply both sides by } \frac{3}{2}.$$

$$x = \frac{3}{2} \cdot \cancel{10}^{\,5}_{\,1} \qquad \text{Cross divide by 2.}$$

$$x = \frac{3}{1} \cdot 5 = \mathbf{15} \qquad \text{Simplify.}$$

[RECALL]

Remember that the reciprocal of $\frac{3}{5}$ is $\frac{5}{3}$ because $\frac{3}{5} \cdot \frac{5}{3} = 1$.

NOTE

Notice that $\frac{2x}{2} = 1x = x$.

[RECALL]

Remember that the product of reciprocals is 1:

---

c. Patrick makes $20 per hour at his job. If his weekly earnings are $750, how many hours does he work?

Write an equation where x is the number of hours worked.

$$20x = 750$$

$$\frac{20x}{20} = \frac{750}{20} \qquad \text{Divide both sides by 20.}$$

$$x = 37.5 \qquad \text{Simplify.}$$

Patrick works $37\frac{1}{2}$ **hours** per week.

Try It 6.2

Multiply or divide to find the value of x.

a. $4x = 15$

b. $\frac{4}{5}x = 12$

c. Mallory gets paid overtime for any hours she works over 40 hours. Overtime pay is 1.5 times her regular hourly rate. If her overtime pay is $13.50 per hour, what is her regular hourly rate?

6.3 Solve Two-Step Equations

You will combine the skills you learned in the last two sections to solve two-step equations, such as $2x + 1 = 5$, by first adding or subtracting and then multiplying or dividing.

EXAMPLES

Solve for x.

a. $2x + 1 = 5$

$$2x + 1 - 1 = 5 - 1$$ Subtract 1 from both sides.

$$\frac{2x}{2} = \frac{5}{2}$$ Divide both sides by 2.

$$x = \textbf{2.5}$$ Simplify.

b. $\frac{3}{4}x - 4 = 2$

$$\frac{3}{4}x + 4 - 4 = 2 + 4$$ Add 4 to both sides.

$$\frac{4}{3} \cdot \frac{3}{4}x = \frac{4}{3} \cdot 6$$ Multiply both sides by $\frac{4}{3}$.

$$x = \frac{4}{\overset{}{\underset{1}{3}}} \cdot \overset{2}{6}$$ Cross divide by a common factor.

$$x = \textbf{8}$$ Simplify.

c. You buy a long-distance cell-phone plan that costs \$7 a month plus 5¢ per minute. If your bill for last month is \$19, how many minutes did you use last month?

Write an equation where x is the number of minutes used.

$$0.05x + 7 = 19$$
$$0.05x + 7 - 7 = 19 - 7$$ Subtract 7 from both sides.
$$0.05x = 12$$

$$\frac{0.05x}{0.05} = \frac{12}{0.05}$$ Divide both sides by 0.05.

$$x = \frac{12 \cdot 100}{0.05 \cdot 100}$$ Multiply by 100 to eliminate the decimal.

$$x = \frac{1,200}{5} = 240$$ Simplify.

You used **240 minutes** last month.

NOTE

You could also multiply both sides by 20 to find 1x.

$$20 \cdot 0.05x = 20 \cdot 12$$
$$x = 240$$

Try It 6.3

Solve for x.

a. $3x - 1 = 11$

b. $\frac{1}{2}x + 2 = 5$

c. A shipping company charges $10 per crate plus $1.50 per pound to ship. If the cost to ship a crate is $28.75, what is its weight?

CALCULATOR TIP

Checking Solutions

You can use a graphing calculator to check solutions to an equation by evaluating one side for the value of x. Consider the equation $0.05x + 7 = 19$ and its solution $x = 240$. Check the solution by evaluating the left side for $x = 240$.

```
.05(240)+7
                    19
■
```

You can see the total charge is $19, so you know the solution is correct.

Self-Evaluation

Complete problems 1–4.

1. Write 80 in prime factored form.

2. Determine the GCF of 30, 20, and 60.

3. Determine the LCM of 16 and 24.

4. Write an inequality to compare $\frac{6}{16}$ and $\frac{3}{8}$.

Convert each percent to a decimal and a fraction. Simplify your answers.

5. 70%

6. 15%

Convert each fraction to a decimal and a percent. Simplify your answers.

7. $\frac{3}{5}$

8. $\frac{3}{8}$

9. $\frac{1}{6}$

Add or subtract for problems 10–15. Simplify your answers. Check your answer by adding or subtracting the decimal equivalents. Use a calculator as needed.

10. $\frac{8}{9} + \frac{7}{9}$

11. $\frac{3}{4} + \frac{2}{3}$

12. $3\frac{1}{4} + 2\frac{3}{8}$

13. $\frac{5}{9} - \frac{2}{9}$

14. $\frac{7}{9} - \frac{1}{2}$

15. $4\frac{1}{5} - 1\frac{7}{10}$

Solve problems 16–20.

16. 40% of 120

17. $\frac{5}{6} \cdot \frac{3}{10}$

18. $1\frac{2}{3} \cdot 1\frac{4}{5}$

19. $3\frac{3}{5} \div \frac{3}{10}$

20. How many $\frac{3}{4}$-foot pieces can be cut from a 9-foot board?

Translate each situation into an algebraic expression, and evaluate for the variable.

21. You leave a 15% tip for a meal that costs d dollars. How much was the tip? Evaluate for $d = 15$.

22. You use a \$25 off coupon to pay x dollars of merchandise. How much did you spend? Evaluate for $x = \$135$.

Combine like terms.

23. $6x + 5 + x - 1$

24. $\frac{1}{2}x - \frac{1}{4}x$

Continue on next page.

Solve each equation for x.

25. $x - \dfrac{1}{2} = \dfrac{5}{6}$

26. $\dfrac{1}{3}x = 12$

27. $3x + 4 = 25$

28. $\dfrac{3}{4}x - 1 = 5$

Write and solve an equation for problems 29 and 30.

29. George makes $12 per hour. If his weekly wages are $402, how many hours does he work per week?

30. Sheri joins a CD club. She pays $10 per month plus $12.50 per CD. If her monthly bill is $97.50, how many CDs did she buy?

- Check your answers in the *Solutions* section at the back of the book. Reading the solution for each problem will help you understand why the correct answers are right and will allow you to see each step of the solutions.
- On the chart below, circle the problem numbers that you did not solve correctly. If you answered more than one problem per lesson incorrectly, you should review that lesson before moving to the next unit.

Performance Analysis Chart

LESSON	PROBLEM NUMBER
1	1, 2, 3, 4
2	5, 6, 7, 8, 9
3	10, 11, 12, 13, 14, 15
4	16, 17, 18, 19, 20
5	21, 22, 23, 24
6	25, 26, 27, 28, 29, 30

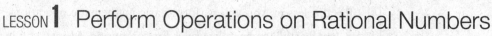

UNIT 2   Linear Models

In this unit, you will work with linear equations. There are many real-world applications that involve linear equations. For example, simple business applications dealing with cost, revenue, and profit can be represented with equations such as:

$$C(x) = 1,000 + 25x$$

$$R(x) = 45x$$

$$P(x) = 45x - (1,000 + 25x)$$
$$= 20x - 1,000$$

LESSON 1 Perform Operations on Rational Numbers

In this lesson, you will perform basic mathematic operations. You can use the idea of "net worth" to generalize rules for computing. Money you have is positive and money you owe is negative.

Integers consist of the positive numbers {1, 2, 3, 4, 5, ...} and their opposites, or negative numbers. Zero is not positive or negative. Integers are often shown on a number line.

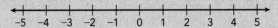

The **absolute value** of an integer is its distance from the **origin**, 0. The absolute value of a number is always positive. Absolute value is noted by the use of absolute-value bars. For example, the absolute value of −4 is represented as $|-4| = 4$.

1.1 Add Integers

Use the idea of your "net worth" to perform operations on integers.

Suppose you have $3, but you also have a $7 debt (−7). To determine your net worth, count three spaces to the right of 0 on the number line. Then count 7 spaces to the left. This is your net worth. It is represented by the equation:

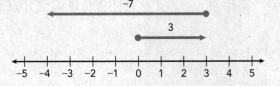

$$3 + (-7) = -4$$

Now suppose you have a $1 debt (−1), and you incur another $3 debt (−3). To determine your net worth, add −3 to −1. This addition is shown on the number line. It is represented by the equation:

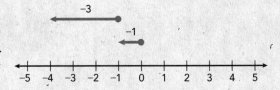

$$-1 + (-3) = -4$$

To add two integers with the same sign, positive or negative, add the absolute values and keep the same sign.

$$-4 + -8 = -12$$

To add two integers with opposite signs, subtract the smaller absolute value from the larger absolute value. The answer will have the sign of the number with the greater absolute value.

$$4 + -8 = -4$$

Add.

a. $25 + (-37) = 25 - 37 = -12$ **b.** $-50 + (-15) = -65$

c. $4 + (-16) + (-20) = 4 + (-36) = -32$

Try It 1.1

Add.

a. $76 + (-24) =$ **b.** $-47 + (-13) =$

c. $-12 + 5 + (-27) =$

1.2 Subtract Integers

You can also use the net worth idea to understand how to subtract integers.

Suppose you have a $100 debt (–100), and you pay off $60 debt (–60), which means you subtract –$60 of debt. Subtracting –60 is the same as adding 60 to your net worth. This can be represented by the equation:

$$-100 - (-60) = -100 + 60 = -40$$

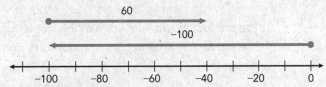

To subtract a negative integer from another negative integer, add its opposite.

DEFINITION
When you add the **opposite** of a negative integer, you are adding the positive. Remember that opposites have a sum of 0.

EXAMPLES

Subtract.

a. $-12 - (-37) = -12 + 37 = 25$ **b.** $-50 - (-15) = -50 + 15 = -35$

c. After a cold front, the temperature drops 40°F from 25°F. What is the temperature after the drop?

$$25 - 40 =$$
$$25 + (-40) = -15$$

After the drop, the temperature is **−15°F.**

Subtract.

a. $5 - (-40) =$

b. $-14 - (25) =$

c. A submarine at a depth of 100 feet (−100) dives another 250 feet. What is the depth?

1.3 Multiply and Divide Integers

Thinking about net worth will help you develop a method for multiplying integers.

Suppose you made three $100 purchases. You can represent this with the equation $3(-100) = -300$. Your net worth decreases by $300 (−300).

Now suppose you negate, or pay off, three $100 debts. You can model this with the equation $-3(-100) = 300$. Your net worth increases by $300.

> The *product* of two integers with the *same sign*, positive or negative, is *positive*.
> The *product* of two integers with *opposite signs*, one positive and one negative, is *negative*.

The same rules apply for division.

> The *quotient* of two integers with the *same sign* is *positive*.
> The *quotient* of two integers with *opposite signs* is *negative*.

EXAMPLES

Multiply or divide.

a. $-12(-15) = 180$

b. $-50(-15) = 750$

c. $\dfrac{-27}{-9} = 3$

Try It 1.3

Multiply or divide.

a. $-13(3) =$

b. $-12(-10) =$

c. $\dfrac{-300}{4} =$

1.4 Perform Operations on Rational Numbers

The numbers $\dfrac{-4}{3} = -1.\overline{3}$ and $\dfrac{10}{4} = 2.25$ are both examples of rational numbers.
The integers are all rational numbers. For example, you can write -5 as $\dfrac{-5}{1}$.

Rational numbers are of the form $\dfrac{a}{b}$, where a and b are integers and b is not 0.

The Distributive Property is a useful tool for computing products mentally.

The Distributive Property states that for any numbers a, b, and c:
$$a(b + c) = ab + ac$$

[Mental Math]

Some numbers may be difficult to use in mental math. Break these numbers into easier-to-use numbers. This will make mental calculations simpler. For example, think of 96 as $(100 - 4)$.

For example, to multiply $-25(96)$, write 96 as $100 - 4$.
$$-25(96) = -25(100 - 4)$$
$$= -25(100) - (-25)(4)$$
$$= -2,500 - (-100)$$
$$= -2,500 + 100$$
$$= \mathbf{-2,400}$$

You could also write -25 as $\dfrac{-100}{4}$ and then solve.

$$-25(96) = \dfrac{-100}{4} \cdot 96 = -100 \cdot 24 = \mathbf{-2,400}$$

Note that the rules for performing operations with rational numbers are the same as the rules for performing operations on integers—the order of operations still applies.

a. Solve $-4\left(\dfrac{-3}{4} + \dfrac{5}{8}\right)$ by finding a common denominator.

$$-4\left(\dfrac{-3}{4} + \dfrac{5}{8}\right) = -4\left(\dfrac{-6}{8} + \dfrac{5}{8}\right) \qquad \text{Find a common denominator.}$$

$$= -4\left(\dfrac{-1}{8}\right) \qquad \text{Multiply.}$$

$$= \dfrac{4}{8} = \mathbf{\dfrac{1}{2}} \qquad \text{Simplify.}$$

b. Solve $-4\left(\dfrac{-3}{4} + \dfrac{5}{8}\right)$ using the Distributive Property.

$$-4\left(\dfrac{-3}{4} + \dfrac{5}{8}\right) = -4\left(\dfrac{-3}{4}\right) + (-4)\left(\dfrac{5}{8}\right) \qquad \text{Use the Distributive Property.}$$

$$= 3 + \left(\dfrac{-5}{2}\right)$$

$$= \dfrac{6}{2} + \left(\dfrac{-5}{2}\right) \qquad \text{Add.}$$

$$= \mathbf{\dfrac{1}{2}} \qquad \text{Simplify.}$$

c. Multiply $-0.25\left(\dfrac{-8}{5}\right)$. Write your answer as a decimal.

$$-0.25\left(\dfrac{-8}{5}\right) = -\dfrac{1}{4}\left(\dfrac{-8}{5}\right) \qquad \text{Convert the decimal to fraction.}$$

$$= \dfrac{2}{5} = \mathbf{0.4}$$

> **NOTE**
> *Notice that the answer can be written as a decimal or a fraction.*

Try It 1.4

a. Use a common denominator:

$$10\left(\dfrac{-3}{2} + \dfrac{4}{5}\right) =$$

b. Use the Distributive Property:

$$10\left(\dfrac{-3}{2} + \dfrac{4}{5}\right) =$$

c. Multiply: $-0.75\left(\dfrac{-20}{3}\right) =$

CALCULATOR TIP

Perform Computations

You can use a graphing calculator to perform computations. Consider the expression:

$$-\frac{2}{3}\left(\frac{10}{7} - \left(\frac{-21}{5}\right)\right)$$

Method 1:

```
-2/3*(10/7-(-21/
5))
        -3.752380952
```

Enter the expression into your calculator as shown. Be sure to use parentheses appropriately. Note the difference between the subtraction symbol and the negative symbol—the subtraction symbol is lower and longer.

```
-2/3*(10/7-(-21/
5))
        -3.752380952
Ans▶Frac
          -394/105
■
```

Some calculators will convert your decimal answer to a fraction as shown. See your calculator manual for specific instructions.

You can see that:

$$-\frac{2}{3}\left(\frac{10}{7} - \left(\frac{-21}{5}\right)\right) \approx -3.75 \approx \frac{-394}{105}$$

Method 2:

```
(-2/3)(10/7)-(-2
/3)(-21/5)
        -3.752380952
Ans▶Frac
          -394/105
```

You could also use the Distributive Property to perform the computation on your calculator. You can see how the fraction $-\frac{2}{3}$ is multiplied in two places.

You can see that:

$$\left(-\frac{2}{3}\right)\left(\frac{10}{7}\right) - \left(-\frac{2}{3}\right)\left(\frac{-21}{5}\right) \approx -3.75 \approx \frac{-394}{105}$$

Note that the answer is the same using both methods.

LESSON 2 Solve Linear Equations

DEFINITION
A **linear equation** is any equation that forms a line when graphed.

In this lesson, you will solve **linear equations** with one variable: x. You can use basic business applications to develop the methods for solving equations.

Suppose you have your own business making gadgets. Your fixed costs are $1,000 per month, and your variable costs are $25 per gadget. Use the expression $1,000 + 25x$ to indicate the cost. You charge $45 per gadget, so your revenue expression is $45x$.

In the linear expression, $1,000 + 25x$, the **term** 1,000 is **constant**.

For the term, 25x, 25 is called the **coefficient** and x is called the **variable**.

To evaluate an expression for x, substitute a value for x into the expression.

To evaluate $1,000 + 25x$ for $x = 10$, substitute 10 for x as shown.

$$1,000 + 25(10) = 1,000 + 250 = 1,250$$

2.1 Build a Table

Build a table to compare your cost and your revenue by evaluating each expression for the indicated x-value.

Gadgets: x	Revenue ($): $45x$	Cost ($): $1,000 + 25x$
0	$45(0) = 0$	$1,000 + 25(0) = 1,000$
10	$45(10) = 450$	$1,000 + 25(10) = 1,250$
20	$45(20) = 900$	$1,000 + 25(20) = 1,500$
30	$45(30) = 1,350$	$1,000 + 25(30) = 1,750$
40	$45(40) = 1,800$	$1,000 + 25(40) = 2,000$
50	$45(50) = 2,250$	$1,000 + 25(50) = 2,250$
60	$45(60) = 2,700$	$1,000 + 25(60) = 2,500$

The break-even point occurs when the number of units sold, $x = 50$, has the same revenue and cost, $2,250. This means that after you sell 50 gadgets, you begin to make a profit. You can see that when you sell 60 gadgets, you make a $200 profit because your revenue is greater than your cost.

EXAMPLES

a. **Evaluate the revenue expression, 2.5x, and the cost expression, 175 + 1.5x, for the indicated x-values. What is the break-even point?**

Gadgets: x	Revenue ($): 2.5x	Cost ($): 175 + 1.5x
0	2.5(0) = 0	175 + 1.5(0) = 175
50	2.5(50) = 125	175 + 1.5(50) = 250
100	2.5(100) = 250	175 + 1.5(100) = 325
150	2.5(150) = 375	175 + 1.5(150) = 400
200	2.5(200) = 500	175 + 1.5(200) = 475

Note that you don't see the break-even point in the table, but you can see that somewhere between 150 and 200 gadgets sold, the revenue becomes greater than the cost. This means the break-even point is between 150 and 200. You can use 175 as a starting point to guess and check: 2.5(175) = 437.5 and 175 + 1.5(175) = 437.5. This means the break-even point occurs at **x = 175**, when both the revenue and cost are $437.50.

[Mental Math]

You might also have noticed the difference between the coefficient of the revenue and cost is $1, and you could have concluded that you must sell 175 gadgets to break even.
2.5x = 175 + 1.5x
1x = 175

[HINT]

Book Club B is only the better deal when it costs less than Book Club A.

b. **You can buy books from Book Club A for a $100 membership fee plus $25 per book (100 + 25x) or from Book Club B for a $225 fee plus $20 per book (225 + 20x). Use a table to compare the book clubs. When is Book Club B the better deal?**

Books: x	Book Club A: 100 + 25x	Book Club B: 225 + 20x
5	100 + 25(5) = 225	225 + 20(5) = 325
10	100 + 25(10) = 350	225 + 20(10) = 425
15	100 + 25(15) = 475	225 + 20(15) = 525
20	100 + 25(20) = 600	225 + 20(20) = 625
25	100 + 25(25) = 725	225 + 20(25) = 725
30	100 + 25(30) = 850	225 + 20(30) = 825

You would have to buy **more than 25 books** for Book Club B to be the better deal.

Try It 2.1

a. Evaluate the revenue expression, 30x, and the cost expression, 1,500 + 20x, for the indicated x-values.

Gadgets: x	Revenue ($): 30x	Cost ($): 1,500 + 20x
0		
50		
100		
150		
200		

Lesson 2: *Solve Linear Equations* **49**

b. You can rent videos from Rental Store A for a $10 monthly fee plus $2.50 per video or from Rental Store B for $12.50 a month plus $2.00 per video. Complete this table to compare the rental stores.

Videos: x	Rental Store A: $10 + 2.5x$	Rental Store B: $12.5 + 2x$
5		
10		
15		
20		
25		
30		

2.2 Write and Solve Equations

To find break-even points, you can write and solve equations. Consider the business example from section 2.1. The revenue expression is $45x$, and the cost expression is $1,000 + 25x$. Set the two expressions as equal, and then solve. The solution is the break-even point.

$$45x = 1,000 + 25x$$
$$45x - 25x = 1,000 + 25x - 25x \quad \text{Subtract 25x from both sides.}$$
$$20x = 1,000$$
$$\frac{20x}{20} = \frac{1,000}{20} \quad \text{Divide both sides by 20.}$$
$$x = 50 \quad \text{The break-even point is 50.}$$

Check your solution to be sure the break-even point is correct.

$$45(50) = 2,250 \quad \text{Substitute 50 into each expression.}$$
$$1,000 + 25(50) = 2,250$$

EXAMPLES

a. Write and solve an equation to find the break-even point for the revenue expression, $2.5x$, and the cost expression, $175 + 1.5x$.

$$2.5x = 175 + 1.5x \quad \text{Set the expressions to be equal.}$$
$$2.5x - 1.5x = 175 + 1.5x - 1.5x \quad \text{Subtract 1.5x from both sides.}$$
$$x = 175$$

Check:

$$2.5(175) = 437.5 \quad \text{Substitute 175 into each expression.}$$
$$175 + 1.5(175) = 437.5$$

The break-even point occurs at $x = 175$ when the revenue and cost are both $437.50.

b. You can join Gym A for a $100 membership fee plus $25 per month ($100 + 25x$) or join Gym B for a $225 fee plus $20 per month ($225 + 20x$). After how many months is the cost the same? Write and solve an equation.

$$100 + 25x = 225 + 20x \qquad \text{Set the expressions to be equal.}$$
$$100 - 100 + 25x = 225 - 100 + 20x \qquad \text{Subtract 100 from both sides.}$$
$$25x - 20x = 125 + 20x - 20x \qquad \text{Subtract 20x from both sides.}$$
$$\frac{5x}{5} = \frac{125}{5} \qquad \text{Divide both sides by 5.}$$
$$x = 25$$

Check:

$$100 + 25(25) = 725 \qquad \text{Substitute 25 into each expression.}$$
$$225 + 20(25) = 725$$

Both gyms cost the same when you buy **25 months.**

Try It 2.2

a. Write and solve an equation to find the break-even point for the revenue expression, $30x$, and the cost expression, $1{,}500 + 20x$.

b. You can rent a carpet steamer from Rental Place A for a $10 fee plus $2.50 per hour or from Rental Place B for a $12.50 fee plus $2.00 per hour. After how many hours is the cost the same? Write and solve an equation.

2.3 Solve Equations

In the previous section, you used some of the properties that are used to solve a variety of linear equations. These properties indicate that you can add, subtract, multiply, or divide equals.

Properties of Equality

Addition: If $a = b$ and $c = d$, then $a + c = b + d$.

Subtraction: If $a = b$ and $c = d$, then $a - c = b - d$.

Multiplication: If $a = b$ and $c = d$, then $ac = bd$.

Division: If $a = b$ and $c = d$ when $c \neq 0$ and $d \neq 0$, then $\frac{a}{c} = \frac{b}{d}$.

You can also use reciprocals.

The **reciprocal** of $\frac{a}{c}$ is $\frac{c}{a}$. Note that $\frac{a}{c} \cdot \frac{c}{a} = \frac{ac}{ac} = 1$.

EXAMPLES

a. **Solve the equation for x.**

$$\frac{3}{4}x - 1 = 5$$

$$\frac{3}{4}x - 1 + 1 = 5 + 1 \qquad \text{Add 1 to both sides.}$$

$$\frac{3}{4}x = 6$$

$$\frac{4}{3} \cdot \frac{3}{4}x = \frac{4}{3} \cdot 6 \qquad \text{Multiply by the reciprocal: } \frac{4}{3}.$$

$$x = 8$$

Check your answer by substituting 8 as the value of x into the original equation:

$$\frac{3}{4}x - 1 \stackrel{?}{=} 5$$

$$\frac{3}{4}(8) - 1 \stackrel{?}{=} 5$$

$$6 - 1 \stackrel{?}{=} 5$$

$$5 = 5$$

Your solution of $x = 8$ is correct because the equality is true: 5 is equal to 5.

b. Solve the equation for x.

$$-2(x - 3) = x + 7$$

$-2x + 6 = x + 7$	Distribute -2.
$-2x + 6 - 6 = x + 7 - 6$	Subtract 6.
$-2x - x = x - x + 1$	Subtract x.
$\dfrac{-3x}{-3} = \dfrac{1}{-3}$	Divide by -3.

$$x = -\frac{1}{3}$$

Check your answer by substituting $-\frac{1}{3}$ into the original equation.

$$-2\left(-\frac{1}{3} - 3\right) \overset{?}{=} -\frac{1}{3} + 7$$

$$-2\left(-\frac{1}{3} - \frac{9}{3}\right) \overset{?}{=} -\frac{1}{3} + \frac{21}{3}$$

$$-2\left(-\frac{10}{3}\right) \overset{?}{=} \frac{20}{3}$$

$$\frac{20}{3} = \frac{20}{3}$$

c. Solve the equation for x.

$$\frac{4}{5}(2x - 5) = 3x - (4x + 1)$$

$\dfrac{8}{5}x - 4 = 3x - 4x - 1$	Distribute on the left and on the right.
$\dfrac{8}{5}x - 4 = -x - 1$	Combine like terms.
$\dfrac{8}{5}x - 4 + 4 = -x - 1 + 4$	Add 4 to both sides.
$\dfrac{8}{5}x + x = -x + x + 3$	Add x to both sides.
$\dfrac{5}{13} \cdot \dfrac{13}{5}x = \dfrac{5}{13} \cdot 3$	Multiply by the reciprocal.

$$x = \frac{15}{13}$$

Check your answer by substituting $\frac{15}{13}$ into the original equation.

$$\frac{4}{5}(2x - 5) \overset{?}{=} 3x - (4x + 1)$$

$$\frac{4}{5}\left(2\left(\frac{15}{13}\right) - 5\right) \overset{?}{=} 3\left(\frac{15}{13}\right) - \left(4\left(\frac{15}{13}\right) + 1\right)$$

$$\frac{4}{5}\left(\frac{30}{13} - \frac{65}{13}\right) \overset{?}{=} \frac{45}{13} - \left(\frac{60}{13} + \frac{13}{13}\right)$$

$$\frac{4}{5}\left(-\frac{35}{13}\right) \overset{?}{=} \frac{45}{13} - \left(\frac{73}{13}\right)$$

$$-\frac{28}{13} = -\frac{28}{13}$$

a. Solve for the value of x: $-\frac{1}{2}x + 7 = 9$

b. Solve for the value of x: $4(2x - 5) = 5 - (2x - 1)$

c. Solve for the value of x: $\frac{2}{3}(2x - 3) = -(x + 4)$

CALCULATOR TIP

Check Solutions

You can use your graphing calculator to check solutions. Suppose that for the equation was $\frac{4}{5}(2x - 5) = 3x - (4x + 1)$, you determined the solution was $x = \frac{15}{13}$. There are two methods you can use to check your solution.

Method 1:

```
(4/5)(2*15/13-5)
          -2.153846154
3(15/13)-(4(15/1
3)+1)
          -2.153846154
■
```

Key in each part of the original equation separately, and be sure to substitute for the value of x. If the answers are the same, then you know your solution is correct.

You can see that the answers are the same, so you know that $x = \frac{15}{13}$ is the correct solution.

Method 2:

```
15/13→X
          1.153846154
```

You can also use the store feature of a graphing calculator to store your solution as x. See your calculator manual for specific instructions.

```
(4/5)(2X-5)
          -2.153846154
3X-(4X+1)
          -2.153846154
■
```

After you have saved the value of x, you may key in each expression from the original equation to see if they have the same value. Your calculator will automatically substitute $\frac{15}{13}$ for x. If the answers for both expressions are the same, then you know your solution is correct.

Again, you can see that the answers are the same, so your solution, $x = \frac{15}{13}$, is correct.

LESSON 3 Solve Linear Inequalities

In this lesson, you will solve **linear inequalities in one variable**, x. You can build on the revenue cost ideas from Lesson 2 and investigate inequalities by thinking about profit.

The inequality symbols are:

< less than

> greater than

≤ less than or equal to

≥ greater than or equal to

DEFINITION
A **linear inequality in** x is any inequality that can be expressed in one of the following forms:

$ax + c < 0$
$ax + c > 0$
$ax + c \leq 0$
$ax + c \geq 0$

Note that $a \neq 0$.

Suppose again that you own a business that makes gadgets. Your fixed costs are $1,000 per month, and your variable costs are $25 per gadget. You use the expression $1,000 + 25x$ to indicate the cost. Now suppose you charge $45 per gadget. Your revenue expression is $45x$.

Profit is revenue minus cost (or *revenue − cost = profit*). This means the expression for profit at your business is:

$$45x - (1,000 + 25x) = 20x - 1,000$$

Suppose you want to determine when your profit is at least $3,000, which means your profit is equal to or greater than $3,000. You can represent this situation with the inequality:

$$20x - 1,000 \geq 3,000$$

There are many solutions to this inequality. The **solution of an inequality in one variable** is a value or set of values that satisfies the inequality. Use $x = 300$ as a starting point. If you evaluate $20x - 1,000$ for $x = 300$, you see that:

$$20(300) - 1,000 = 6,000 - 1,000 = 5,000$$

This means that you make a $5,000 profit when you sell 300 gadgets. Since 5,000 is greater than 3,000, $x = 300$ is one solution to the inequality $20x - 1,000 \geq 3,000$.

3.1 Solve Simple Inequalities

To solve inequalities, you can use many of the same methods you used to solve equations. Consider your profit inequality: $20x - 1{,}000 \geq 3{,}000$.

$$20x - 1{,}000 \geq 3{,}000$$

$$20x - 1{,}000 + 1{,}000 \geq 3{,}000 + 1{,}000 \qquad \text{Add 1,000 to both sides.}$$

$$20x \geq 4{,}000$$

$$\frac{20x}{20} \geq \frac{4{,}000}{20} \qquad \text{Divide both sides by 20.}$$

$$x \geq 200$$

To check your answer, choose an x value greater than 200 and see if it satisfies the inequality. Let's try 201.

$$20(201) - 1{,}000 \overset{?}{\geq} 3{,}000$$

$$4{,}020 - 1{,}000 \overset{?}{\geq} 3{,}000$$

$$3{,}020 \geq 3{,}000$$

Since 201 satisfies the inequality, you know that if you sell at least 200 gadgets, you will make a profit of at least $3,000.

EXAMPLES

a. **For the revenue expression, 2.5x, and the cost expression, 175 + 1.5x, write and solve an inequality to determine how many units you must sell for the profit to exceed $500.**

Remember that *revenue − cost = profit*. You must set up an equation to represent profit.

$$2.5x - (175 + 1.5x) = x - 175$$

You see that profit is $x - 175$. To determine when the profit is greater than $500, you must set up the inequality: $x - 175 > 500$. Then solve for x.

$$x - 175 > 500$$

$$x - 175 + 175 > 500 + 175 \qquad \text{Add 175 to both sides.}$$

$$x > 675$$

This means you must sell **more than 675 units** for the profit to exceed $500.

b. You can buy books from Book Club A for a $100 membership fee plus $25 per book $(100 + 25x)$ or from Book Club B for $225 plus $20 per book $(225 + 20x)$. Write and solve an inequality to determine the greatest number of books you can purchase in order for Book Club A to be cheaper than (less than) Book Club B.

$$100 + 25x < 225 + 20x$$
$$100 - 100 + 25x < 225 - 100 + 20x \qquad \text{Subtract 100 from both sides.}$$
$$25x - 20x < 125 + 20x - 20x \qquad \text{Subtract 20x from both sides.}$$
$$\frac{5x}{5} < \frac{125}{5} \qquad\qquad\qquad\qquad \text{Divide both sides by 5.}$$
$$x < 25$$

Book Club A is cheaper when you buy **less than 25 books.**

Try It 3.1

a. For the revenue expression, $30x$, and the cost expression, $1,500 + 20x$, write and solve an inequality to determine how many units must be sold so that the profit exceeds $3,000.

b. You can rent videos from Rental Shop A for a $10 monthly fee plus $2.50 per video or from Rental Shop B for a $12.50 monthly fee plus $2.00 per video. Write and solve an inequality to determine how many videos you must rent for Rental Shop A to be more expensive (greater than) Rental Shop B.

3.2 Solve Compound Inequalities

Consider again the profit expression $20x - 1{,}000$. Suppose you are interested in what sales will result in a profit of at least \$1,000 but less than \$4,000. You can represent this situation with the compound inequality:

$$1{,}000 \le 20x - 1{,}000 < 4{,}000$$

The solution method is much the same as before.

$$1{,}000 \le 20x - 1{,}000 < 4{,}000$$
$$1{,}000 + 1{,}000 \le 20x - 1{,}000 + 1{,}000 < 4{,}000 + 1{,}000 \qquad \text{Add 1,000.}$$
$$2{,}000 \le 20x < 5{,}000$$
$$\frac{2{,}000}{20} \le \frac{20x}{20} < \frac{5{,}000}{20} \qquad \text{Divide by 20.}$$
$$100 \le x < 250$$

Selling at least 100 gadgets but less than 250 gadgets will result in a profit of at least \$1,000 but less than \$4,000.

In general, the **compound inequality** is:
$$a < x < b$$

This means that $x > a$ and $x < b$.

Note that the compound inequality can also be written as:
$$b > x > a$$

EXAMPLES

a. For the cost expression $175 + 1.5x$, write and solve an inequality to determine how many units must be sold for the cost to be greater than \$300 but not more than \$1,000.

First, write the inequality, which is $300 < 175 + 1.5x \leq 1,000$. Then solve.

$$300 < 175 + 1.5x \leq 1,000$$
$$300 - 175 < 175 + 1.5x - 175 \leq 1,000 - 175 \qquad \text{Subtract 175.}$$
$$125 < 1.5x \leq 825$$
$$\frac{125}{1.5} < \frac{1.5x}{1.5} \leq \frac{825}{1.5} \qquad \text{Divide by 1.5.}$$
$$83.3 < x \leq 550 \qquad \text{Round to the nearest whole number.}$$
$$83 < x \leq 550$$

CALCULATOR TIP

You can use your calculator to divide by decimals.

```
125/1.5
           83.33333333
825/1.5
                   550
■
```

This means that **more than 83 units but no more than 550 units** must be sold for the cost to be greater than \$300 but not more than \$1,000.

b. You can join Gym A for a \$100 membership fee plus \$25 per month $(100 + 25x)$. How many months can you buy if you want to spend at least \$300 but not more than \$500?

Write and solve an inequality: $300 \leq 100 + 25x \leq 500$.

$$300 \leq 100 + 25x \leq 500$$
$$300 - 100 \leq 100 - 100 + 25x \leq 500 - 100 \qquad \text{Subtract 100.}$$
$$200 \leq 25x \leq 400$$
$$\frac{200}{25} \leq \frac{25x}{25} \leq \frac{400}{25} \qquad \text{Divide by 25.}$$
$$8 \leq x \leq 16$$

You can buy **at least 8 months but not more than 16 months** if you want to spend at least \$300 but not more than \$500.

Try It 3.2

a. For the revenue expression, $30x$, and the cost expression, $1,500 + 20x$, write and solve an inequality to determine when the profit is greater than \$4,000 but less than \$6,000.

b. You can rent a canoe for a $10 fee plus $2.50 per hour. How many hours can you rent the canoe if you want to spend at least $20 but not more than $50?

3.3 Solve Inequalities

You can generalize an important property of inequalities by investigating the following example. Consider the inequality $-4 < 6$.

Multiply both sides by -2.

$$-4 < 6$$
$$-2(-4) > -2(6)$$
$$8 > -12$$

Divide both sides by -2.

$$-4 < 6$$
$$\frac{-4}{-2} > \frac{6}{-2}$$
$$2 > -3$$

Notice that when you multiply or divide both sides of an inequality by a negative number, the inequality is reversed.

Properties of Inequality

If you *add or subtract the same number* to both sides of an inequality, the inequality *remains the same.*

If you *multiply or divide* an inequality by a *positive number*, the inequality *remains the same.*

If you *multiply or divide* an inequality by a *negative number*, the inequality is *reversed.*

EXAMPLES

a. Solve the inequality:

$$-2x - 1 \geq 5$$

$$-2x - 1 + 1 \geq 5 + 1 \qquad \text{First add 1 to both sides.}$$
$$-2x \geq 6$$
$$\frac{-2x}{-2} \leq \frac{6}{-2} \qquad \text{Divide by } -2, \text{ and reverse the inequality.}$$
$$x \leq -3$$

Check your answer by substituting a value less than or equal to -3:

$$-2(-4) - 1 \overset{?}{\geq} 5$$
$$8 - 1 \overset{?}{\geq} 5$$
$$7 \geq 5$$

Since the answer checks, you know that $x \leq -3$.

b. **Solve the inequality:**

$$4 < -2(x-3) < 7$$

$4 < -2x + 6 < 7$	Distribute −2.
$4 - 6 < -2x + 6 - 6 < 7 - 6$	Subtract −6.
$-2 < -2x < 1$	
$\dfrac{-2}{-2} > \dfrac{-2x}{-2} > \dfrac{1}{-2}$	Divide by −2, and reverse the inequality.
$1 > x > -\dfrac{1}{2}$	
$-\dfrac{1}{2} < x < 1$	Write in standard inequality form.

Check by substituting a value between $-\dfrac{1}{2}$ and 1.

$$4 \overset{?}{<} -2(0-3) \overset{?}{<} 7$$
$$4 < 6 < 7$$

Since the answer checks, you know that $-\dfrac{1}{2} < x < 1$.

c. **Solve the inequality:**

$$2x + 5 \geq 3x - (4x + 1)$$

$2x + 5 \geq 3x - 4x - 1$	Distribute on the right.
$2x + 5 - 5 \geq -x - 1 - 5$	Subtract 5.
$2x + x \geq -x + x - 6$	Combine like terms. Add x.
$\dfrac{3x}{3} \geq \dfrac{-6}{3}$	Divide by 3.
$x \geq -2$	

Check by substituting a value greater than or equal to −2:

$$2(-1) + 5 \overset{?}{\geq} 3(-1) - (4(-1) + 1)$$
$$-2 + 5 \overset{?}{\geq} -3 - (-3)$$
$$3 \geq 0$$

Since the answer checks, you know that $x \geq -2$.

Try It 3.3

Solve each inequality.

a. $-\dfrac{1}{2}x + 5 > 9$

b. $2x - 5 \geq 5 - (2x - 1)$

c. $-1 \leq -2x - 3 < 4$

CALCULATOR TIP

Check Solutions

You can use your graphing calculator to check the solutions to inequalities. Suppose you are given the inequality $4 < -2(x - 3) < 7$, and you determine that the solution is $-\dfrac{1}{2} < x < 1$.

You may check your solution by substituting any value for x that is between $-\dfrac{1}{2}$ and 1. Let's use the values and x = 0.25 and x = 0.5. Enter the original expression, $-2(x - 3)$, and remember to substitute the different values of x. If the answers are between 4 and 7 as shown in the inequality, then you know your solution is correct.

```
-2(-.25-3)
              6.5
-2(.5-3)
                5
```

Since both answers are between 4 and 7, you know that your solution, $-\dfrac{1}{2} < x < 1$, satisfies the inequality $4 < -2(x - 3) < 7$.

Perform the indicated operations.

1. $-20 + (-36) + 50$

2. $\dfrac{-250}{-40}$

3. $\dfrac{-3}{5} - \dfrac{7}{10}$

4. $10\left(\dfrac{-3}{2} + \dfrac{4}{5}\right)$

5. Your checking account has a balance of $258.67. You are charged a $25 fee for a negative balance. What is the balance after writing checks for $152.25, $48.67, and $112, including the fee?

Evaluate each expression for $x = \dfrac{1}{2}$.

6. $2(x - 5)$

7. $4x - (x + 2)$

8. Complete the table below by evaluating the revenue expression, $10x$, and the cost expression, $160 + 7.5x$, for the indicated x-values.

Gadgets: x	Revenue ($): $10x$	Cost ($): $160 + 7.5x$
0		
50		
100		
150		
200		

9. You can rent a bicycle from Bike Shop A for a $5 fee plus $2.50 per hour or from Bike Shop B for an $8 fee plus $2.00 per hour. After how many hours is the cost the same? Write and solve an equation. Then find the break-even point.

10. Solve and check the equation: $x - 5(x + 1) = 4(x - 1) + 2$

Find three solutions to each inequality by substituting values for x.

11. $2(x - 5) < 7$

12. $-4x - (x + 2) > 3$

13. For the revenue expression, $10x$, and the cost expression, $100 + 7.5x$, write and solve an inequality to determine when the revenue is greater than the cost. Then write and solve an inequality to determine when the profit described is between $500 and $1,000.

Solve each inequality.

14. $-\frac{1}{3}(2x + 6) \leq -4$

15. $4 < -\frac{1}{2}x + 4 < 10$

Check your answers in the *Solutions* section at the back of the book. If you missed more than one answer from problems 1 to 5, review lesson 1. If you missed more than one answer from problems 6 to 10, review lesson 2. If you missed more than one answer from problems 11 to 15, review lesson 3.

LESSON 4 Write and Graph Linear Functions

In this lesson, you will learn how to use **function notation** to represent some of the problems that you have already solved. A **function** is a rule that assigns only one output (y) to each input (x).

Imagine again that you are making gadgets. Your fixed costs are $1,000 per month, and your variable costs are $25 per gadget. Use the function $y = C(x) = 1,000 + 25x$ to represent this situation.

The input variable is x, the number of gadgets. The output variable, $y = C(x)$, indicates the cost of x gadgets.

NOTE

If you charge $45 per gadget, then your revenue function would be:

$$y = R(x) = 45x$$

To *evaluate* a function for x, *substitute* the input x into the function to determine the output y.

To evaluate the function $y = C(x) = 1,000 + 25x$ for $x = 10$, substitute 10 for x.

$$y = C(10)$$
$$= 1,000 + 25(10)$$
$$= 1,000 + 250$$
$$= 1,250$$

Ordered pairs are of the form (input, output) or (x, y) and are used to build graphs.

The ordered pair $(10, 1,250)$ is one solution to the function $y = C(x) = 1,000 + 25x$.

4.1 Graph Ordered Pairs and Determine the Point of Intersection

DEFINITION

A **coordinate** is the number used to identify the location of a point. On a coordinate plane, two coordinates are used, the x-coordinate and the y-coordinate.

You can build graphs of your cost and revenue functions using the ordered pairs in the table on the next page. **Ordered pairs** are the x- and y-coordinates that give the location of a point. The **x-coordinate** is the first number in an ordered pair and indicates the horizontal distance of a point from the origin on the coordinate plane. The **y-coordinate** is the second number in an ordered pair and indicates the vertical distance of a point from the origin on the coordinate plane. To graph point $(20, 1,500)$, count 20 units right from the **origin** along the x-axis, and then count 1,500 units up the y-axis.

Input: x	Output: $y = C(x) = 1,000 + 25x$	Ordered pair: (x, y)	Graph
0	$C(0)\ = 1,000 + 25(0)\ = 1,000$	$(0, 1,000)$	
20	$C(20) = 1,000 + 25(20) = 1,500$	$(20, 1,500)$	
40	$C(40) = 1,000 + 25(40) = 2,000$	$(40, 2,000)$	
60	$C(60) = 1,000 + 25(60) = 2,500$	$(60, 2,500)$	
80	$C(80) = 1,000 + 25(80) = 3,000$	$(80, 3,000)$	
	Note that the points lie on a straight line.		

Cost Function

DEFINITION

A linear function is defined by an equation that can be written in the form:

$$y = mx + b$$
or
$$f(x) = mx + b$$

The graph of a **linear function** is a line. For the linear function, $y = C(x) = 1,000 + 25x$, the **y-intercept** is 1,000, and 25 is the **rate of change**, or the **slope** of the line. This means that for every gadget you make your costs increase by \$25.

You can graph the revenue function, $y = R(x) = 45x$, on the same graph.

Input: x	Output: $y = R(x) = 45x$	Ordered pair: (x, y)	Graph
0	$R(0)\ = 45(0)\ = 0$	$(0, 0)$	
20	$R(20) = 45(20) = 900$	$(20, 900)$	
40	$R(40) = 45(40) = 1,800$	$(40, 1,800)$	
60	$R(60) = 45(60) = 2,700$	$(60, 2,700)$	
80	$R(80) = 45(80) = 3,600$	$(80, 3,600)$	

Cost and Revenue Functions

Break-even Point

The break-even point (50, 2,250) occurs when the number of gadgets, $x = 50$, gives the same revenue and cost value, 2,250. The break-even point is also known as the point of intersection, and $x = 50$ is the solution to the equation below which shows the cost and revenue as equal:

$$45x = 1,000 + 25x$$

EXAMPLES

a. **Consider the revenue and cost functions $R(x) = 2.5x$ and $C(x) = x + 90$. Graph the lines, and then find the break-even point (point of intersection).**

Determine and plot the ordered pairs for the revenue and cost functions.

$$R(0) = 2.5(0) = 0 \qquad\qquad (0, 0)$$
$$R(20) = 2.5(20) = 50 \qquad\quad (20, 50)$$

$$C(0) = 0 + 90 = 90 \qquad\qquad (0, 90)$$
$$C(20) = 20 + 90 = 110 \qquad (20, 110)$$

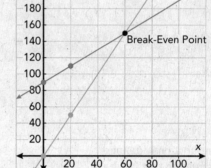

Graphically, the break-even point appears to be $(60, 150)$.

Check this by solving algebraically:
$$R(60) = 2.5(60) = 150$$
$$C(60) = 60 + 90 = 150$$

You can also solve the equation $R(x) = C(x)$ to check your solution.

First solve for the value of x:	Then substitute 60 as value of x into the revenue function and the cost function. If the y-values are the same, you know that the point of intersection is correct.
$R(x) = C(x)$ $2.5x = x + 90$ $\dfrac{1.5x}{1.5} = \dfrac{90}{1.5}$ $x = 60$	$R(60) = 2.5(60) = 150$ $C(60) = 60 + 90 = 150$

The solution checks, so the break-even point is $(60, 150)$.

b. **Graph the profit functions from example a. Then determine graphically and algebraically when the profit is $150.**

The profit function is:
$$P(x) = R(x) - C(x)$$
$$= 2.5x - (x + 90)$$
$$= 1.5x - 90$$

[Mental Math]

$-(x + 90) = -x - 90$

To interpret the problem graphically, use the **constant function** $y = 150$ to find when the profit reaches $150. Then solve the profit function for any 2 points. Use 0 to find the y-intercept and use 100.

$$P(0) = 1.5(0) - 90 = -90 \qquad\quad (0, -90)$$
$$P(100) = 1.5(100) - 90 = 60 \qquad (100, 60)$$

Graphically, the profit appears to be $150 at $x = 160$. To solve algebraically, substitute 160 into the profit function.

$$P(160) = 1.5(160) - 90$$
$$= 240 - 90$$
$$= 150$$

You can think of the constant function as $y = 150 = 150 + 0x$. No matter what the input value is, the output is always 150.

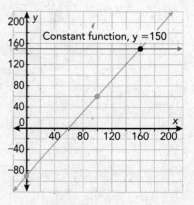

Constant function, $y = 150$

[Mental Math]

$$\frac{240}{1.5} = \frac{240}{\frac{3}{2}} = 240\left(\frac{2}{3}\right) = 160$$

You can also solve the equation $P(x) = 150$ to find the point of intersection.

$$1.5x - 90 = 150$$
$$\frac{1.5x}{1.5} = \frac{240}{1.5}$$
$$x = 160$$

c. **Suppose your business sets aside a $24,000 cash reserve at the beginning of the year to award the "employee of the month" with a $1,500 bonus at the end of each month. Graph the function $B(x) = 24,000 - 1,500x$, and then determine when the cash reserve will be $12,000.**

To interpret the problem graphically, use the constant function $y = 12,000$ to determine when the cash reserve is $12,000.

$$B(0) = 24,000 - 1,500(0) = 24,000 \qquad (0, 24,000)$$
$$B(6) = 24,000 - 1,500(6) = 15,000 \qquad (6, 15,000)$$

The cash reserve appears to be 12,000 at $x = 8$.

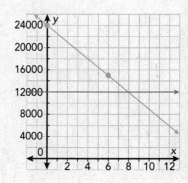

$$B(8) = 24,000 - 1,500(8)$$
$$= 12,000$$

You can also solve the equation:
$$24,000 - 1,500x = 12,000$$

$$\frac{-1,500x}{-1,500} = \frac{-12,000}{-1,500}$$
$$x = 8$$

a. Consider the revenue and cost functions $R(x) = 15x$ and $C(x) = 7.5x + 120$. Graph each function, and then interpret the point of intersection.

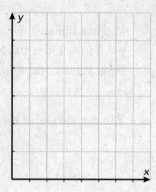

b. Graph the profit functions from problem **a.** Then determine graphically and algebraically when the profit is $300.

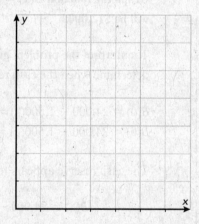

c. A 42,000-gallon irrigation tank empties at a rate of 50 gallons per minute. Write and graph a function for the number of gallons, $G(x)$, left in the tank. Determine when the tank reaches 20,000 gallons.

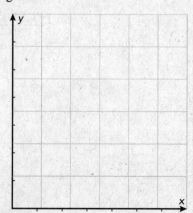

4.2 Determine Linear Functions from Graphs

You can determine linear functions by investigating graphs. There are two steps to complete:

1. Find the *y*-intercept.
2. Determine the rate of change.

Explore It

The graph shows the cost of renting a surf board at the beach.

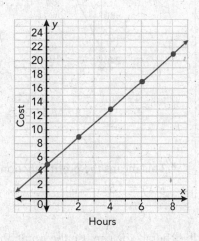

1. What is the initial cost?

2. What is the hourly rate?

3. Explain how you can use the graph to write a linear function to represent the problem.

Recall that for the linear function $y = C(x) = 1{,}000 + 25x$, the y-intercept is 1,000 and the rate of change, or slope of the line, is 25. The equation **$y = mx + b$** is called the **slope-intercept form** of the line, where **b** is the y-intercept and **m** is the slope.

Consider the graph of the profit function below.

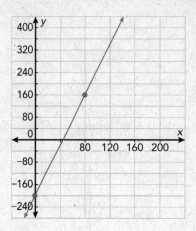

The y-intercept is -200. This means that $b = -200$ in the equation $y = mx + b$.

You can also see a point at $(80, 160)$, which means that when 80 units are sold, the profit is $160. To find the slope, m, substitute $x = 80$ and $y = 160$ into the equation $y = mx - 200$.

$$160 = m(80) - 200$$
$$\frac{80m}{80} = \frac{360}{80}$$
$$m = 4.5$$

This means the profit function is $y = P(x) = 4.5x - 200$, or more simply, $P(x) = 4.5x - 200$.

In general, you can use the notation **$f(x)$**, "f of x" to identify functions. This means a linear function can be written as **$f(x) = mx + b$**.

EXAMPLES

a. Determine a linear function of the form $f(x) = mx + b$ for the line shown on the graph.

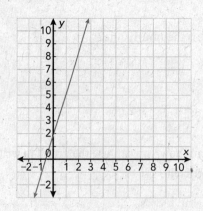

Note that the y-intercept is 2, which means $y = mx + 2$.

You can see the line passes through point $(1, 5)$. To find the slope, m, substitute $x = 1$ and $y = 5$ into the equation $y = mx + 2$.

$$5 = m(1) + 2$$
$$m = 3$$

The linear function is **$y = 3x + 2$, or $f(x) = 3x + 2$.**

b. Determine a linear function of the form $f(x) = mx + b$ for the line shown on the graph.

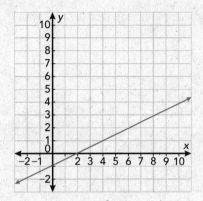

Note that the y-intercept is -1. This means that $y = mx - 1$.

The line passes through $(4, 1)$. To find the slope, m, substitute $x = 4$ and $y = 1$ into the equation $y = mx - 1$.

$$1 = m(4) - 1$$
$$\frac{4m}{4} = \frac{2}{4}$$
$$m = 0.5$$

The linear function is
$$y = 0.5x - 1, \text{ or } f(x) = 0.5x - 1.$$

Note that the x-intercept is $x = 2$ and that point $(2, 0)$ satisfies the linear function:

$$0 = 0.5(2) - 1$$
$$0 = 1 - 1$$
$$0 = 0$$

c. Determine a linear function of the form $f(x) = mx + b$ for the line shown on the graph.

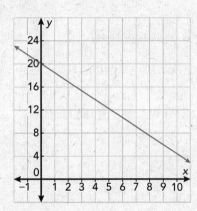

Note that the y-intercept is 20. This means that $y = mx + 20$.

The line passes through $(8, 8)$. To find the slope, m, substitute $x = 8$ and $y = 8$ into the equation $y = mx + 20$.

$$8 = m(8) + 20$$
$$\frac{8m}{8} = \frac{-12}{8}$$
$$m = -1.5$$

The linear function is
$$y = -1.5x + 20, \text{ or } f(x) = -1.5x + 20.$$

■ **Try It 4.2** ···

a. Determine a linear function of the form $f(x) = mx + b$ for the line shown.

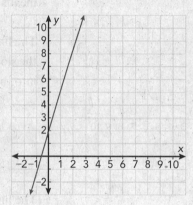

b. Determine a linear function of the form $f(x) = mx + b$ for the line shown.

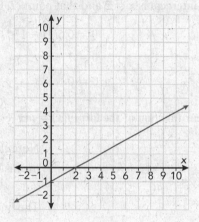

c. Determine a linear function of the form $f(x) = mx + b$ for the line shown.

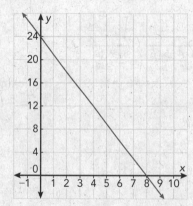

CALCULATOR TIP

Create Tables and Graphs

You can use a graphing calculator to build tables and graphs. Suppose you want to find the point of intersection for these cost and revenue functions:

$$y = C(x) = 1,000 + 25x \qquad \text{and} \qquad y = R(x) = 45x$$

First enter each function into the Y = menu.

Then set the table to show values every 10 units.

When you display the table, scroll down to find the break-even point. You can see that it is **(50, 2,250)**.

Note that the maximum x-value is 60 and the maximum y-value is about 3,000. You can guess that 10 should be the scale of the x-axis and that 500 should be the scale of the y-axis.

Then use the information from the table to set the window for the graph, which includes the maximum x and y values and the scale for each axis of the graph. Both scales should start at 0, the minimum value.

Remember that 50 was displayed in the table as the x-value for the break-even point. Use the trace mode, and enter 50 as the x-value. This will allow you to see the break-even point, or point of intersection. Note that the point of intersection is displayed at the bottom of the screen as x and y values.

The point of intersection is **(50, 2,250)**.

LESSON 5 Determine the Equation of a Line

In this lesson, you will build on your knowledge of functions, and formalize methods for writing the equations of lines in the form $y = mx + b$.

If you have a table of related values, you can write the equation of a line by looking at the differences.

Consider the data in the table at right. Since the cost is increasing \$3 per hour and the initial cost is \$4, the linear equation is:

Hours	Cost
0	4
1	7
2	10
3	13
4	16

$$y = 4 + 3x$$
or
$$y = 3x + 4$$

5.1 Determine Linear Functions from Ordered Pairs

DEFINITION
The slope is the "rise" over the "run". You will learn more about slope in section 5.2.

Since two points determine one line, you can determine linear functions if you know two points. First, find the rate of change or slope, and then find the y-intercept.

Explore It

Consider the cost data in the table.

1. What is the increase in cost, y?

Units, x	Cost, y
20	\$ 60
60	\$160

2. What is the increase in units, x?

3. Compute the cost per unit.

4. How can you find the cost for 0 units?

5. Use your answers from **3** and **4** above to write an equation of the form $y = mx + b$.

[TIP]

The subtraction must be completed above and below the division bar before the division can be completed.

Formalize your method from the Explore It. Note that for an increase of $60 - 20 = 40$ units, the cost increases $160 - 60 = 100$. Divide to find the variable cost per unit.

$$\frac{\text{change in } y}{\text{change in } x} = \frac{160 - 60}{60 - 20}$$

$$= \frac{100}{40}$$

$$= 2.5$$

This means the cost function is:

$$y = 2.5x + b$$

To find the y-intercept, or b, substitute either point into the equation, and then use the other point to check.

Suppose you start with the point $(20, 60)$. To find the value of b, substitute $x = 20$ and $y = 60$ into the equation $y = 2.5x + b$.

$$60 = 2.5(20) + b$$
$$60 = 50 + b$$
$$10 = b$$

This means the function is:

$$y = C(x) + b$$
$$= 2.5x + 10$$

You can check the function by substituting the other point $(60, 160)$ to see if it is a solution:

$$y = 2.5x + 10$$
$$160 = 2.5(60) + 10$$
$$160 = 150 + 10$$
$$160 = 160$$

Since the other point checks, you know that the function is correct.

a. **At Rental Place A, it costs $25 to rent a bicycle for 5 hours and costs $34 for 8 hours. Determine an equation for the linear cost function.**

Consider the data in the table at right, and then compute the hourly charge.

Hours, x	Cost, y
5	$25
8	$34

[TIP]

Use Δy to represent the change in y, and use Δx for the change in x.

$$\frac{\text{change in } y}{\text{change in } x} = \frac{\Delta y}{\Delta x} = \frac{34 - 25}{8 - 5}$$

$$= \frac{9}{3}$$

$$= 3$$

This means the cost function is $y = 3x + b$.

Next, determine the initial cost, or y-intercept, b. Use either point to solve for m. To find b for point (8, 34), substitute $x = 8$ and $y = 34$ into the equation $y = 3x + b$.

$$34 = 3(8) + b$$
$$34 = 24 + b$$
$$10 = b$$

This means the cost function is $y = 3x + 10$.

b. **You earn a profit of $300 for selling 60 units, but you lose $200 ($-200$) if you only sell 10 units. Determine an equation for the linear profit function.**

Consider the profit data in the table at right, and then compute the number of units.

Units, x	Profit, y
10	-200
60	300

$$\frac{\text{change in } y}{\text{change in } x} = \frac{\Delta y}{\Delta x} = \frac{300 - (-200)}{60 - 10}$$

$$= \frac{500}{50}$$

$$= 10$$

This means the profit function is $y = 10x + b$.

Next, determine the profit for zero units, or y-intercept, b. Use either point to solve for m. To find b for point (60, 300), substitute $x = 60$ and $y = 300$ into the equation $y = 10x + b$.

[RECALL]

Remember that adding a negative number is the same as subtracting.

$$300 = 10(60) + b$$
$$300 = 600 + b$$
$$b = -300$$

This means the profit function is $y = 10x - 300$.

a. At Rental Place B, it costs $100 for 5 hours and $145 for 8 hours. Determine an equation for the linear cost function.

b. You earn a profit of $600 for selling 200 units, but you lose $200 (−200) if you only sell 100 units. Determine an equation for the linear profit function.

5.2 Determine the Equation of the Line

DEFINITION
Rise is the increase or decrease along the *y*-axis, and *run* is the increase along the *x*-axis.

You can find the equation of a line that passes through any two points on a **coordinate plane**. First find the rate of change, or slope, and then find the *y*-intercept. The slope is simply the "rise" over the "run" represented as *m*.

$$m = \frac{\text{rise}}{\text{run}}$$

Consider the points on the graph, $(-3, -9)$ and $(4, 5)$. To find the equation of the line through the two points, first determine the slope.

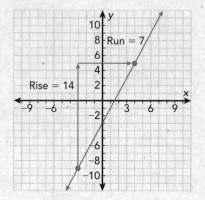

$$m = \frac{\Delta y}{\Delta x} = \frac{5 - (-9)}{4 - (-3)}$$

$$= \frac{14}{7}$$

$$= 2$$

[TIP]

When the coordinate plane is shown, you may also use it to find the *y*-intercept. You can see on this graph that the *y*-intercept is –3.

Now find the *y*-intercept, *b*. Use either point to solve for *m*. To find *b* for point $(-3, -9)$, substitute $x = -3$ and $y = -9$ into the equation $y = 2x + b$.

$$-9 = 2(-3) + b$$
$$-9 = -6 + b$$
$$b = -3$$

This means the equation of the line that passes through points $(-3, -9)$ and $(4, 5)$ is $y = 2x - 3$.

In general, for the two points (x_1, y_1), and (x_2, y_2) the slope formula is:

$$m = \frac{\Delta y}{\Delta x} = \frac{y_2 - y_1}{x_2 - x_1}$$

Recall the slope-intercept form, $y = mx + b$.

The **standard form of the linear equation** is:

$$ax + by = c$$

In the problem above, you can change the slope-intercept form to the standard form using the following steps:

$$y = 2x - 3$$
$$y - y + 3 = 2x - y - 3 + 3$$
$$3 = 2x - y$$
$$2x - y = 3$$

There are two special kinds of lines, horizontal lines and vertical lines. Horizontal lines are of the form $y = 0 \cdot x + b$, or simply $y = b$. They are called "constant" functions.

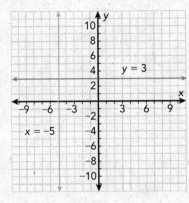

Vertical lines are of the form $x = a$ and are said to have "no slope."

The graph at the right shows the constant function $y = 3$ and the vertical line $x = -5$.

EXAMPLES

a. Sketch the graph when $(x_1, y_1) = (-2, 4)$ and $(x_2, y_2) = (3, -6)$, and determine the equation of the line. Give the slope-intercept form and the standard form.

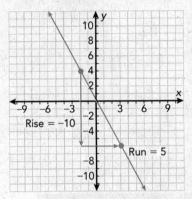

First, plot the points, and note that the rise is negative. Then compute the slope.

$$m = \frac{\Delta y}{\Delta x} = \frac{y_2 - y_1}{x_2 - x_1} = \frac{-6 - 4}{3 - (-2)} = \frac{-10}{5} = -2$$

Now find the y-intercept, b, using either point. To solve for point $(-2, 4)$, you write:

$$4 = -2(-2) + b$$
$$4 = 4 + b$$
$$0 = b$$

This means the slope-intercept form is $y = -2x$.

Now write in standard form. Remember that $b = 0$.

$$y = -2x$$
$$\mathbf{2x + y = 0}$$

Check by substituting point $(3, -6)$ into the standard form:

$$2x + y = 0$$
$$2(3) + (-6) \stackrel{?}{=} 0$$
$$0 = 0$$

Since point $(3, -6)$ checks, you know that the function is correct.

b. Sketch the graph when $(x_1, y_1) = (1, -4)$ and $(x_2, y_2) = (9, 2)$, and determine the equation of the line. Give the slope-intercept form and the standard form.

First, plot the points, and then determine the slope:

$$m = \frac{\Delta y}{\Delta x} = \frac{y_2 - y_1}{x_2 - x_1} = \frac{2 - (-4)}{9 - 1} = \frac{6}{8} = \frac{3}{4}$$

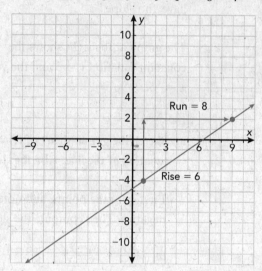

Now find the y-intercept, or b, using either point. To solve for point $(1, -4)$, you write:

$$-4 = \frac{3}{4}(1) + b$$

$$-4 = \frac{3}{4} + b$$

$$b = \frac{-16}{4} - \frac{3}{4}$$

$$b = \frac{-19}{4}$$

[TIP]

Convert -4 to a fraction with the same denominator as $\frac{3}{4}$.

This means the equation for the slope-intercept form is $y = \frac{3}{4}x - \frac{19}{4}$.

Now write in standard form by multiplying both sides by 4:

$$4y = 4\left(\frac{3}{4}x - \frac{19}{4}\right)$$
$$4y = 3x - 19$$
$$\mathbf{19 = 3x - 4y}$$

Check by substituting the other point $(9, 2)$ into the standard form.

$$3x - 4y = 19$$
$$3(9) - 4(2) \stackrel{?}{=} 19$$
$$27 - 8 \stackrel{?}{=} 19$$
$$19 = 19$$

Since the point $(9, 2)$ checks, you know that the function is correct.

a. Sketch the graph when $(x_1, y_1) = (-3, 2)$ and $(x_2, y_2) = (3, -4)$, and determine the equation of the line. Give the slope-intercept form and the standard form.

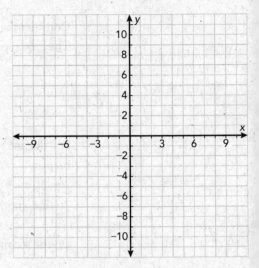

b. Sketch the graph when $(x_1, y_1) = (-1, 4)$ and $(x_2, y_2) = (3, -5)$, and determine the equation of the line. Give the slope-intercept form and the standard form.

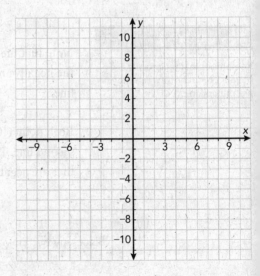

5.3 Graph Parallel and Perpendicular Lines

You have already seen that you can use the slope-intercept form to graph a line by identifying the y-intercept and one other point.

Consider the two lines given on the graph at right. They are represented by the equations:

$$y = 2x - 3$$

and

$$y = 2x + 5$$

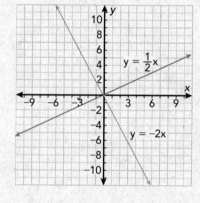

For the line $y = 2x - 3$, $(0, -3)$ is on the line because $y = 2(0) - 3 = -3$. If $x = 1$, then $y = 2(1) - 3 = -1$, and point $(1, -1)$ lies on the line. To find another point on the line, you may also use $\frac{\text{rise}}{\text{run}} = \frac{2}{1}$.

On the second line, you can see that both $(0, 5)$ $(1, 7)$ are on the line.

You can see from the graph that lines with the same slope are parallel. **Parallel lines** are lines that never intersect.

Now consider the two lines given on the graph at right. They are represented by the equations:

$$y = -2x$$

and

$$y = \frac{1}{2} x$$

[TIP]

Remember that reciprocals have a product of 1 when they are multiplied.

Note that the slope of the first equation, -2, is the negative reciprocal of the slope of the second line, $\frac{1}{2}$.

Both points $(0, 0)$ and $(1, -2)$ are on the first line. Both points $(0, 0)$ and $(2, 1)$ are on the second line. These lines are **perpendicular**, or form right angles. Lines that have slopes that are negative reciprocals are perpendicular when graphed.

Since any two points result in the same slope, you can derive the **point-slope form**.

$$m = \frac{y - y_1}{x - x_1}$$

$$y - y_1 = m(x - x_1)$$

$$y = m(x - x_1) + y_1$$

Use the point-slope form to determine an equation parallel to or perpendicular to the given line through the given point. Give both the slope-intercept form and the standard form.

a. **Determine the line that is parallel to $y = -2x - 1$ and that runs through the point $(x_1, y_1) = (4, 2)$.**

The slope of a parallel line is $m = -2$. Substitute the slope and the given point into the point-slope form:

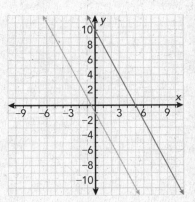

$$y = m(x - x_1) + y_1$$
$$y = -2(x - 4) + 2$$
$$y = -2x + 8 + 2$$
$$\mathbf{y = -2x + 10}$$

The standard form is $\mathbf{2x + y = 10}$.

You can see on the graph that the line $y = -2x + 10$ is parallel to line $y = -2x - 1$ and contains the point $(x_1, y_1) = (4, 2)$.

b. **Determine the line that is perpendicular to $y = -\frac{2}{3}x + 2$ and that runs through the point $(x_1, y_1) = (4, 5)$.**

The slope of a perpendicular line is $m = \frac{3}{2}$, which is the negative reciprocal of $-\frac{2}{3}$.

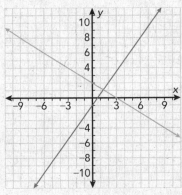

Substitute the slope and the given point into the point-slope form:

$$y = m(x - x_1) + y_1$$
$$y = \frac{3}{2}(x - 4) + 5$$
$$y = \frac{3}{2}x - 6 + 5$$
$$\mathbf{y = \frac{3}{2}x - 1}$$

The standard form is:

$$y = \frac{3}{2}x - 1$$
$$2y = 2\left(\frac{3}{2}x - 1\right)$$
$$2y = 3x - 2$$
$$\mathbf{3x - 2y = 2}$$

You can see on the graph that line $y = \frac{3}{2}x - 1$ is perpendicular to line $y = -\frac{2}{3}x + 2$ and contains the point $(x_1, y_1) = (4, 5)$.

Use the point-slope form to determine an equation parallel to or perpendicular to the given line through the given point. Give both the slope-intercept form and the standard form.

a. Determine the line that is parallel to $y = \frac{1}{2}x + 3$ and that runs through the point $(x_1, y_1) = (-4, 2)$. When you are finished, graph both lines to be sure they are parallel.

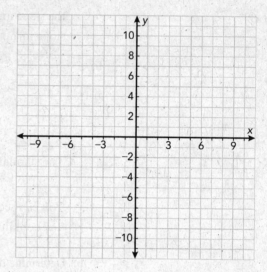

b. Determine the line that is perpendicular to $y = 3x + 2$ and runs through the point $(x_1, y_1) = (3, 5)$. When you are finished, graph both lines to be sure they are perpendicular.

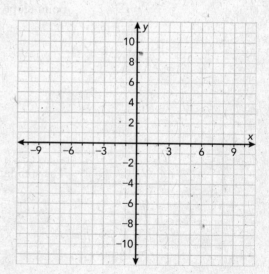

CALCULATOR TIP

Linear Modeling

You can use a graphing calculator to make predictions with real-world data. To do this, you will use a regression equation. *Regression equations* are used to model an approximate trend in a data set and to make predictions. A linear regression equation is of the form $y = ax + b$ where a is the slope and b is the y-intercept

For the population data below predict what the population will be in the year 2020.

Year	2002	2003	2004	2005	2006	2007	2008
Population	1,200	1,176	1,125	1,099	1,060	1,041	1,015

First, enter the population values for each year in the List menu. See your calculator manual for specific instructions. Note that you will consider 2002 to be year 0 because it is the beginning and because you are predicting what the population will be in the 18th year.

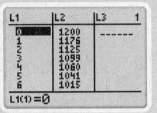

Then set an appropriate window for the data based on the information in the table. Even though the least x-value in the table is 0, use −2 to make it easier to read the y-axis on the graph. Since you are looking for the 18th year, set the maximum x-value to be a slightly greater number, such as 20. Under the 2nd Y= menu, choose the **scatter plot** as the type of graph.

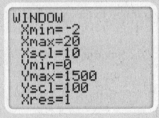

Display the scatter plot, and compute the regression equation, which will move into the Y= menu.

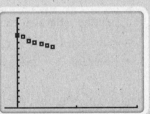

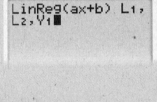

In trace mode, enter 18 as the x-value to represent the 18th year, 2020. The graph will show the predicted population as the y-value.

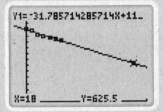

The predicted population in 2020 is **about 625.**

LESSON 6 Solve Systems of Linear Equations

In this lesson, you will build on the work you have been doing with functions, and formalize methods for solving systems of equations. A system of linear equations involves two or more linear equations in at least two variables. The break-even problems you have already completed were examples of solving systems of equations. You will see more business applications in the last section.

In general, a **system of linear equations** in two variables are pairs of equations like:

$$x + 2y = 5 \quad \text{and} \quad 3x - y = 1$$

The solution is the point that satisfies both equations. For this example, it is $(1, 2)$.

$$1 + 2(2) = 5 \quad \text{and} \quad 3(1) - 2 = 1$$

6.1 Solve Systems by Graphing

Because the equations can be graphed as lines, there are three possible situations as shown below. You must solve each equation for y before you can determine if there is a solution to the system of linear equations.

One Solution

Equation 1: $x + y = 4$ → $y = -x + 4$
Equation 2: $x - y = 6$ → $y = x - 6$

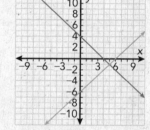

The solution is $(5, -1)$. This is the point of intersection. This is a **consistent system**, and the lines are independent of each other. This type of system is called an **independent system**.

No Solution—Parallel Lines

Equation 1: $2x + y = 4$ → $y = -2x + 4$
Equation 2: $-2x - y = 6$ → $y = -2x - 6$

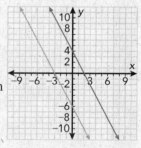

There is no solution; the lines are parallel. This type of system is called an **inconsistent system**.

Infinite Number of Solutions

$2x + y = 4$ or $y = -2x + 4$
$4x + 2y = 8$ $y = -2x + 4$

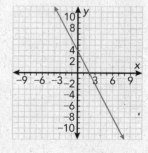

The graphs are the same. The solution set is infinite and consists of points on the line. This type of system is called a **dependent system**.

Solve each system of equations graphically. First, solve each equation for *y*. Then graph each line, and locate the point of intersection.

a.

> Equation 1: $x + 2y = 5$
> Equation 2: $x - y = -1$

Solve for *y* in each equation.

> Equation 1: $y = -\dfrac{1}{2}x + \dfrac{5}{2}$
>
> Equation 2: $y = x + 1$

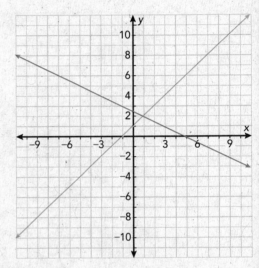

Then graph each line. You can see the solution, or point of intersection, is (1, 2).

Check by substituting the solution into each equation.

Equation 1:
$$x + 2y = 5$$
$$1 + 2(2) \overset{?}{=} 5$$
$$5 = 5$$

Equation 2:
$$x - y = -1$$
$$1 - 2 \overset{?}{=} -1$$
$$-1 = -1$$

b.

> Equation 1: $x + y = -4$
> Equation 2: $-x - y = -1$

Solve for *y* in each equation.

> Equation 1: $y = -x - 4$
> Equation 2: $y = -x + 1$

Then graph each line. You can see there is no solution because the lines are parallel. They will never intersect.

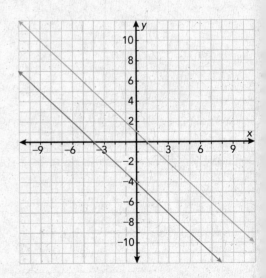

■ Try It 6.1 ⋯⋯⋯⋯⋯⋯⋯⋯⋯⋯⋯⋯⋯⋯⋯⋯⋯⋯⋯⋯⋯⋯⋯⋯⋯⋯⋯⋯

Solve each system of equations graphically. First, solve each equation for y. Then graph each line, and locate the point of intersection.

a.

$$2x - y = -7$$
$$x + 2y = -1$$

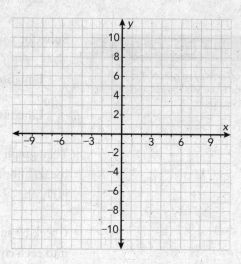

b.

$$2x - 4y = -8$$
$$-x + 2y = -4$$

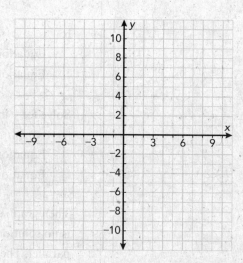

6.2 Solve Systems of Linear Equations Using the Substitution Method

There are many times when you can't easily determine the point of intersection, or solution to the system, by looking at the graph. This is when you use a method called substitution. To solve by substitution, isolate either variable from one equation and substitute into the other.

EXAMPLES

a. Solve this system using the substitution method.

$$4x + 3y = 3$$
$$2x - y = -6$$

The easiest variable to isolate is y in the second equation.

$$2x - y = -6$$
$$y = 2x + 6 \qquad \text{Solve for } y \text{ in the second equation.}$$

Use substitution.

$$4x + 3(2x+6) = 3 \qquad \text{Substitute } 2x + 6 \text{ for } y \text{ in the first}$$
$$4x + 6x + 18 = 3 \qquad \text{equation, and then solve for } x.$$

$$\frac{10x}{10} = \frac{-15}{10}$$

$$x = -\frac{15}{10} = -\frac{3}{2}$$

[**Mental Math**]

Use the Distributive Property here.

Use substitution again.

$$2\left(-\frac{3}{2}\right) - y = -6$$

$$-3 - y = -6 \qquad \text{Substitute } x = -\frac{3}{2} \text{ into the first equation,}$$
$$y = 3 \qquad \text{and then solve for } y.$$

The solution is $\left(-\frac{3}{2}, 3\right)$.

Check your answer.

$$4x + 3y = 3$$

$$4\left(-\frac{3}{2}\right) + 3(3) \stackrel{?}{=} 3 \qquad \text{Check by substituting the solution into}$$
$$\text{the second equation.}$$

$$-6 + 9 = 3$$

b. Solve this system using the substitution method.

$$3x - 2y = 1$$
$$2x - 3y = -11$$

First, isolate x in the second equation.

$$2x - 3y = -11$$
$$2x = 3y - 11$$

Solve for x in the second equation.

$$x = \frac{3}{2}y - \frac{11}{2}$$

Use substitution.

$$3x - 2y = 1$$

Substitute $\frac{3}{2}y - \frac{11}{2}$ for x in the first equation, and then solve for 7.

$$3\left(\frac{3}{2}y - \frac{11}{2}\right) - 2y = 1$$

$$\frac{9}{2}y - \frac{33}{2} - \frac{4}{2}y = \frac{2}{2}$$

$$\frac{5}{2}y = \frac{35}{2}$$

$$\frac{2}{5}\left(\frac{5}{2}y\right) = \frac{2}{5}\left(\frac{35}{2}\right)$$

$$y = 7$$

[Mental Math]

Write 2y as $\frac{4}{2}y$, and write 1 as $\frac{2}{2}$.

Use substitution again.

$$3x - 2(7) = 1$$
$$3x = 15$$
$$x = 5$$

Substitute $y = 7$ into the second equation, and then solve for x.

The solution is $(5, 7)$.

Check your answer.

$$3x - 2y = 1$$
$$3(5) - 2(7) \overset{?}{=} 1$$
$$15 - 14 = 1$$

Check by substituting the solution into the first equation.

Try It 6.2

Solve each system of linear equations using the substitution method.

a.

$$-x + y = 3$$
$$2x - y = -4$$

b.

$$6x - 2y = 1$$
$$-2x + 3y = 2$$

6.3 Solve Systems Using the Elimination Method

You have solved systems of linear equations graphically and by substitution. The method of elimination involves adding the two equations to eliminate one of the variables, and then solving for the other. For example, in the system $\begin{array}{l} x + y = 3 \\ x - y = -1 \end{array}$ if you add the two equations, the y variable is easily eliminated and x can be determined easily.

$$\begin{array}{r} x + y = 3 \\ + \ x - y = -1 \\ \hline 2x = 2 \\ x = 1 \end{array}$$

EXAMPLES

a. **Solve this system using the elimination method.**

$$x + 2y = 5$$
$$x - y = -1$$

Notice that if you multiply the second equation by 2, you can eliminate y by adding.

$$2(x - y) = 2(-1)$$
$$2x - 2y = -2$$

Multiply both sides of the second equation by 2.

$$x + 2y = 5$$
$$\underline{+\ 2x - 2y = -2}$$
$$3x = 3$$
$$x = 1$$

Add the first equation and the new second equation to eliminate y, and then solve for x.

Pick either equation to solve for y.

$$1 - y = -1$$
$$-y = -2$$
$$y = 2$$

Check the solution by substituting into the other equation.

$$x + 2y = 5$$
$$1 + 2(2) = 5$$

Since $x = 1$ and $y = 2$, the solution is **(1, 2)**.

b. **Solve this system using the elimination method.**

$$3x - 2y = 1$$
$$2x - 3y = -11$$

$$2(3x - 2y) = 2(1)$$
$$-3(2x - 3y) = -3(-11)$$

Multiply both sides of the first equation by 2, and multiply both sides of the second equation by -3 to eliminate x.

$$6x - 4y = 2$$
$$\underline{+\ -6x + 9y = 33}$$
$$5y = 35$$
$$y = 7$$

Add the equations to eliminate x, and then solve for y.

Pick either equation to solve for x.

$$3x - 2(7) = 1$$
$$3x = 15$$
$$x = 5$$

Check the solution by substituting into the other equation.

$$2x - 3y = -11$$
$$2(5) - 3(7) \stackrel{?}{=} -11$$
$$10 - 21 = -11$$

Since $x = 5$ and $y = 7$, the solution is **(5, 7)**.

[TIP]

Sometimes you may have to multiply both sides of an equation by the same number to eliminate one of the variables.

---

c. A company makes two kinds of skis: beginner and advanced. The beginner ski takes 2 hours in assembly and 1 hour in finishing. The advanced ski takes 3 hours in assembly and 2 hours in finishing. The assembly department has 2,000 hours per week allocated, and the finishing department has 1,200 hours allocated. How many of each ski should be made in order to create as many skis as possible within the hours allocated?

First, assign a variable to each type of ski. Call the number of beginner skis, x, and the number of advanced skis, y.

Then create a table to show the number of hours it takes to make each ski.

Hours	Beginner	Advanced	Total
Assembly	$2x$	$3y$	2,000
Finishing	x	$2y$	1,200

Then write equations for assembly hours and for finishing hours.

$$2x + 3y = 2,000$$
$$x + 2y = 1,200$$

Write an assembly equation.

Write a finishing equation.

$$2x + 3y = 2,000$$
$$-2(x + 2y) = -2(1,200)$$

Multiply the finishing equation by -2.

$$\begin{array}{r} 2x + 3y = 2,000 \\ + -2x - 4y = -2,400 \\ \hline -y = -400 \\ y = 400 \end{array}$$

Add the equations to eliminate x, and solve for y.

Pick either equation to solve for x.
$$x + 2y = 1,200$$
$$x + 2(400) = 1,200$$
$$x = 400$$

Check the solution by substituting into the other equation.

$$2(400) + 3(400) = 2,000$$
$$800 + 1,200 = 2,000$$

The solution is **(400, 400)**, or 400 beginner skis and 400 advanced skis.

Try It 6.3

Solve each system using the elimination method.

a.

$$x + y = 5$$
$$x - y = -1$$

b.

$$2x - y = 2$$
$$x - 3y = -4$$

c. A company makes canoes and kayaks. To manufacture a canoe, it takes 4 hours in assembly and 2 hours in finishing. To manufacture a kayak, it takes 20 hours in assembly and 11 hours in finishing. The assembly department has 600 hours per week allocated, and the finishing department has 320 hours allocated. How many of each type should be manufactured to run at capacity?

CALCULATOR TIP

Solving Systems

You can use a graphing calculator to solve systems by first solving each equation for y. Then you can graph and calculate the point of intersection. Solve the system:

$$4x + 3y = 3$$

$$2x - y = 6$$

Solving each equation for y gives you the system:

$$y = -\frac{4}{3}x + 1$$

$$y = 2x + 6$$

Enter both equations into the Y = menu.

```
Plot1  Plot2  Plot3
\Y1■-(4/3)X+1
\Y2■2X+6
\Y3=■
\Y4=
\Y5=
\Y6=
\Y7=
```

Set the window of the graph by using ZOOM Standard which gives you the window shown. If you don't see the point of intersection, Zoom out to change the window settings.

```
WINDOW
 Xmin=-10
 Xmax=10
 Xscl=1
 Ymin=-10
 Ymax=10
 Yscl=■
 Xres=1
```

Under the CALCULATE screen, choose the option to calculate the point of intersection.

```
CALCULATE
1:value
2:zero
3:minimum
4:maximum
5:intersect
6:dy/dx
7:∫f(x)dx
```

Then graph the point of intersection. You can see that it is (–1.5, 3).

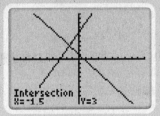

Self-Evaluation

Complete the evaluation and then check your answers.

Perform the indicated operations for problems 1–4.

1. $-20 + (-36) + 50$

2. $\dfrac{-120}{-20}$

3. $-4\left(\dfrac{-1}{2} + \dfrac{3}{4}\right) =$

4. $-0.25\left(\dfrac{-20}{7}\right)$

Solve and check each equation for problems 5–8.

5. $4(x - 1) = -1$

6. $-\dfrac{1}{2}(2x - 4) = 6$

7. $2x - (x - 3) = 3(x - 3) - 1$

8. $-\dfrac{2}{3}(3x - 5) = -(x - 3)$

Solve each inequality for problems 9–12.

9. $-2x + 1 \geq -3$

10. $\dfrac{3}{4}(2x - 8) \leq -3$

11. $-3 < -x - 1 < 4$

12. $3 < \frac{1}{2}x - 4 < 5$

Determine the linear function for problems 13–16.

13.

Profit

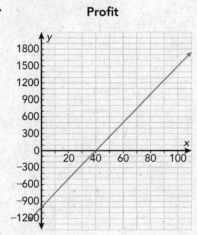

14.

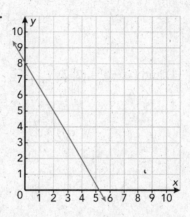

15.

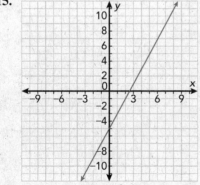

16.

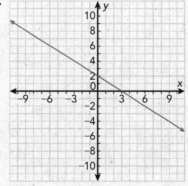

Continue on next page.

Determine an equation of a line using the two points given in problems 17–19. Write in slope-intercept form and then in standard form.

17. $(x_1, y_1) = (-3, 0)$ and $(x_2, y_2) = (1, 4)$ **18.** $(x_1, y_1) = (1, -5)$ and $(x_2, y_2) = (3, -2)$

19. $(x_1, y_1) = (-4, -1)$ and $(x_2, y_2) = (2, 2)$

Solve each system of equations for problems 20–23.

20.
$x - y = 1$
$2x + y = -5$

21.
$x - 2y = -5$
$3x + y = -1$

22.
$x - 3y = 4$
$-3x + 2y = 7$

23.
$5x - 2y = -2$
$3x + 4y = 4$

Solve problems 24–30.

24. A late afternoon temperature of 21° decreases 27° by the next morning. What is the temperature on the next morning?

25. You can rent a boat from Rowers for a $50 fee plus $25 per hour or from Sinkers for a $100 fee plus $20 per hour. At what hour is the rental cost the same for both shops?

26. For revenue expression, $10x$, and the cost expression, $100 + 7.5x$, write and solve an inequality to determine when the revenue is greater than the cost. Then write and solve an inequality to determine when the profit is between $500 and $1,000.

27. Consider the revenue and cost functions:
    $R(x) = 7.5x$ and $C(x) = 5x + 60$
    Create a graph, and then determine the break-even point graphically and algebraically.

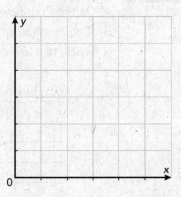

Continue on next page.

28. You earn a profit of $2,000 for selling 1,000 units, but you lose $200 if you only sell 40 units. Use these two points to determine a profit equation.

29. Determine the equation of the line that is perpendicular to the line $y = 2x - 1$ and passes through the point $(x_1, y_1) = (-1, 2)$.

30. A company makes two kinds of boats: A and B. To manufacture boat A, it takes 5 hours in assembly and 3 hour in finishing. To manufacture boat B, it takes 8 hours in assembly and 6 hours in finishing. The assembly department has 1,200 hours per week allocated, and the finishing department has 800 hours allocated. How many of each boat should be made in order to create as many boats as possible within the hours allocated?

- Check your answers in the *Solutions* section at the back of the book. Reading the solution for each problem will help you understand why the correct answers are right and will allow you to see each step of the solutions.
- On the chart below, circle the problem numbers that you did not solve correctly. If you answered more than one problem per lesson incorrectly, you should review that lesson before moving to the next unit.

Performance Analysis Chart

LESSON	PROBLEM NUMBER
1	1, 2, 3, 4, 24
2	5, 6, 7, 8, 25
3	9, 10, 11, 12, 26
4	13, 14, 27
5	15, 16, 17, 18, 19, 28, 29
6	20, 21, 22, 23, 30

UNIT 3 Exponential Models

In this unit, you will work with exponential expressions and equations. There are many real-world applications that involve exponential equations. For example, simple business applications dealing with compound interest and depreciation can be represented with equations like:

$$y = 5,000 \cdot (1.06)^x$$

and

$$y = 21,000 \cdot (0.85)^x$$

Solve Percent Equations

In this lesson, you will solve problems involving percent. Percents have many common usages and will help you understand the development of the exponential model later in the unit.

Consider the simple percent problem: 25% of 400 is 100, or $\frac{1}{4}(400) = 100$. The rate, R, is 25%. The base, B, is 400. The amount of the base, A, is 100.

Many percent problems can be solved using the percent equation:

$$Rate \cdot Base = Amount$$

$$R \cdot B = A$$

$$25\% \cdot 400 = 100$$

1.1 Solve for the Rate, *R*

The rate is the percent which is multiplied by the base to give the amount. When you know the base and the amount, you can solve for the rate, R. Consider the question: What percent of 50 is 20?

$$R \cdot B = A$$
$$R \cdot 50 = 20$$
$$R = \frac{20}{50} = \frac{40}{100} = 40\%$$

The percent equation shows that **20 is 40% of 50.**

EXAMPLES

Use the common fractions to help you estimate. Then compute with a calculator to the nearest percent.

a. **Of your business' annual $22,115 costs, $2,450 are spent on utilities. What percent of the total costs does your business spend on utilities?**

First, write a percent equation:

$$R \cdot B = A$$
$$R \cdot 22{,}115 = 2{,}450$$
$$R = \frac{2{,}450}{22{,}115}$$

Use mental math to estimate the rate:

$$\frac{2{,}450}{22{,}115} \approx \frac{2{,}000}{20{,}000} = 10\%$$

[**Mental Math**]

Since $\frac{2{,}450}{22{,}115}$ is more than $\frac{2{,}450}{24{,}500}$, the answer is probably closer to 11%.

Then compute the actual answer with a calculator and round to the nearest whole percent.

$$R = \frac{2,450}{22,115} \approx 11.08\% \approx 11\%$$

Utilities account for **approximately 11%** of your total costs.

b. There were 455,000 graduates statewide. Of those, 250,000 are expected to go to college immediately. What percent are expected to go to college immediately?

First, write a percent equation:

$$R \cdot B = A$$
$$R \cdot 455,000 = 250,000$$
$$R = \frac{250,000}{455,000}$$

Use mental math to estimate the rate:

$$\frac{250,000}{455,000} \approx \frac{250,000}{500,000} = 50\%$$

Then compute the actual answer with a calculator, and round up to the nearest whole number.

$$R = \frac{250,000}{455,000} \approx 54.95\% \approx 55\%$$

About 55% of the graduates statewide are expected to go to college immediately.

Try It 1.1

a. What percent of 90 is 50?

b. Of 4,096 employees, 544 are under contract. What percent of the employees are under contract?

c. Bill owns his own company. He takes home $3,525 from every $5,000 he makes. What percent is his take-home pay?

[Mental Math]

You know that $\frac{250,000}{500,000} = \frac{1}{2}$.

Since $\frac{250,000}{455,000}$ is more than $\frac{250,000}{500,000}$, you also know

that $\frac{250,000}{455,000}$ is more than $\frac{1}{2}$.

1.2 Solve for the Amount, A

When you know the rate and the base, you can solve for the part, A. Consider the problem:

$$33\frac{1}{3}\% \text{ of } 75 \text{ is what number?}$$

$$A = 33\frac{1}{3}\% \cdot 75$$

$$A = \frac{1}{3} \cdot 75$$

$$A = 25$$

The percent equation shows that **25 is $33\frac{1}{3}\%$ of 75.**

EXAMPLES

Use common fractions to estimate. Then compute with a calculator to the nearest part or amount.

a. **A manufacturer expects that 3.5% of 358 units produced will be defective. How many defective units are expected?**

Use mental math to estimate the part:

$$A = R \cdot B$$

$$A = 0.035 \cdot 358$$

$$A \approx \frac{1}{3}(36) = 12$$

[Mental Math]

Think 10% of 360 is 36, so 3.5% is about one third of 10%.

Then compute the actual answer with a calculator, and round to the nearest whole number.

$$A = 0.035 \cdot 358 = 12.53 \approx 13$$

The manufacturer expects that **about 13 units of every 358 units will be defective.**

b. **There are 75,125 people in Ingletown. A survey indicates that 41% of these people use the public bus route. How many use the public bus route?**

Use mental math to estimate the part:

$$A = R \cdot B$$

$$A = 0.41 \cdot 75{,}125$$

$$A \approx \frac{2}{5}(75) = 2(15) = 30 \text{ thousand} = 30{,}000$$

[Mental Math]

You can use 75 to represent 75,000. Then use 15 to represent 15,000. This means 30 represents 30,000.

Then compute the actual answer with a calculator, and round to the nearest whole number.

$$A = 0.41 \cdot 75{,}125 = 30{,}801.25 \approx 30{,}801.$$

About 30,801 people use the public bus route.

    a. 75% of 39 is what number?

    b. A school district anticipates that 15% of new teachers quit after the first year. If 212 new teachers are hired, how many are expected to quit?

    c. Ninety-five percent of homeowners move at least once. In Round Top there are 59,845 first time homeowners. How many of these first time homeowners are expected to move at least once?

1.3 Solve for the Base, *B*

When you know the rate and the amount, you can solve for the base *B*. Consider the problem:

$$6 \text{ is } 30\% \text{ of what number?}$$
$$R \cdot B = A$$
$$0.3 \cdot B = 6$$
$$B = \frac{6}{0.3} = 20$$

6 is 30% of 20.

EXAMPLES

Use common fractions to help you estimate. Then use a calculator to find the solution.

a. **In the city election, it is predicted that 65% of voters will vote early. If 69,176 voters vote early, how many are expected to vote altogether?**

Use mental math to estimate the base:	Then compute the actual answer with a calculator, and round to the nearest whole number.
$R \cdot B = A$ $0.65 \cdot B = 69{,}176$ $\frac{2}{3}B \approx 70$ $B \approx 70\left(\frac{3}{2}\right)$ $B \approx 35(3) = 105{,}000$	$0.65 \cdot B = 69{,}176$ $B = \dfrac{69{,}176}{0.65} \approx 106{,}425$

[Mental Math]

Remember that 65% is about the same as $\frac{2}{3}$.

About 106,425 voters are expected to vote early.

b. **52 is about 83% of what number?**

Use mental math to estimate the base:	Use a calculator to find the actual answer, and round to the nearest hundredth.
$R \cdot B = A$ $0.83 \cdot B = 52$ $\frac{4}{5}B \approx 52$ $B \approx 52\left(\frac{5}{4}\right)$ $B \approx 13(5) = 65$	$0.83 \cdot B = 52$ $B = \dfrac{52}{0.83} \approx 62.65$

[Mental Math]

Remember that 80% is about the same as $\frac{4}{5}$.

52 is about 83% of **62.65**.

Try It 1.3

a. For city council to fund a $21,500 park project, the city must charge a $\frac{1}{2}$% sales tax on all gas sales in the city. What must the total gas sales in the city be in order to fund the park project?

b. 217 is about 16% of what number?

CALCULATOR TIP

Solving Percent Problems

You can use a graphing calculator to find the common sales-tax percentage on several items by retrieving the previous line and editing.

Suppose you want to compute the 7.25% sales tax on the following prices.

$19.95

$4.35

$39.95

First convert the percent to a decimal: 7.25% is 0.0725. Then key in the first expression: 0.0725 · 19.95, and press ENTER. Pressing 2nd and ENTER will repeat the first expression. Then you can clear 19.95 and key in 4.35. Repeat with 39.95. Your screen will show:

```
.0725*19.95
              1.446375
.0725*4.35
               .315375
.0725*39.95
              2.896375
■
```

To round your answers to the nearest hundredth, or cent, press MODE and set the FLOAT section to 2. Quit that screen and enter the expressions again.

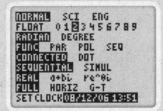

You can see that the sales tax is:

$1.45 for $19.95

$0.32 for $4.35

$2.90 for $39.95

In this lesson, you will solve problems involving percent increase and percent decrease. Percent increase and percent decrease have many common usages and lead to the development of the exponential models of growth and decay later in the unit.

Percent-increase examples include sales tax, tips, and money-growth funds. Percent-decrease examples include depreciation and discounts.

DEFINITION
Depreciation is the loss of or decrease in value.

Percent-increase and percent-decrease problems can be solved using the percent equation:

$$Rate \cdot Base = Amount$$

$$R \cdot B = A$$

2.1 Solve Percent-Increase Problems

Suppose you buy a car for $19,500 and then have to pay 5% sales tax. The 5% is called the percent increase. You can solve for the total price in two steps:

Step 1: Solve for sales tax.

[Mental Math]

To find 5% using mental math, use a percent that is easy to work with. Think of 5% as half of 10%. Since 10% of 19,500 is 1,950, then 5% is 975, or half of 1,950.

$$0.05(\$19,500) = \$975$$

Step 2: Add the tax to the price to get the total.

$$\$19,500 + \$975 = \textbf{\$20,475 total price}$$

You can also use the Distributive Property to compute the total in two steps by multiplying by 1 and by 0.05 and then adding. One is the whole (19,500), and 0.05 is the 5% tax.

$$\$19,500(1 + 0.05) = \$19,500 + \$975$$
$$= \textbf{\$20,475 total price}$$

The simplest way to find the total is with one operation.

$$\$19,500(1.05) = \textbf{\$20,475 total price}$$

Use r to represent the percent increase. In general, if r is the percent increase, then $R = 1 + r$, and the percent equation is:

$$Amount = Base \cdot Rate$$
$$A = B \cdot R$$
$$A = \$19{,}500(1 + 0.05)$$
$$A = \$19{,}500(1.05)$$
$$A = \$20{,}475$$

The amount of increase is $975.

EXAMPLES

Write and solve for the total amount, A. Then solve for the amount of increase.

a. **Ben put $5,000 in his savings account at the beginning of this year. His bank account pays him an annual interest rate of 6.125%. What is the value of Ben's savings at the end of the year? How much interest did his account earn?**

First, write the percent increase (r) as a decimal: $6.125\% = 0.06125$. Then find R. If $r = 0.06125$, then $R = 1.06125$.

[RECALL]

Remember that
$R = r + 1$.

$A = B \cdot R$	Use the percent equation.
$A = 5{,}000(1.06125)$	Substitute the known values and solve.
$A = 5{,}306.25$	This is the value of Ben's savings.

To find the interest, subtract the savings before interest from the savings after interest.

[Mental Math]

Since 6% of 5,000 is 300, you know that the answer makes sense.

$$\$5{,}306.25 - \$5{,}000 = \$306.25$$

The value of Ben's savings is **$5,306.25.** His account earned **$306.25** in interest.

b. **You buy a new television for $198.23. If the sales tax is 7.25%, what is the total cost? What is the tax?**

If $r = 0.0725$, then $R = 1.0725$.

$A = B \cdot R$	
$A = 198.23(1.0725)$	
$A = 212.60$	Round to the nearest cent.

The total cost is **$212.60**, and the tax is **$212.60 − $198.23 = $14.37.**

c. Your bill at a local restaurant is $53.98. If you leave a 15% tip, what will the total bill be? What is the tip?

If $r = 0.15$, then $R = 1.15$.

$$A = B \cdot R$$
$$A = 53.98(1.15)$$
$$A = 62.08 \qquad \text{Round to the nearest cent.}$$

The total bill is **$62.08**, and the tip is **$62.08 − $53.98 = $8.10.**

[Mental Math]

Round 53.98 to 54. Think of 15% as 10% and 5%. Since 10% of 54 is 5.40 and half of that is 5%, or 2.70, add the amounts to find the 15% tip.

5.40 + 2.70 = 8.10

The tip should be $8.10.

Try It 2.1

Write and solve for the total amount, A. Then solve for the amount of increase.

a. Kendra put $5,000 in her savings account at the beginning of last year. Her account pays her an annual interest rate of 4.75%. What is the value of her account at the end of the year? How much did her account earn?

b. Your dinner bill is $24.87. What is the total bill if you give a 20% tip? What is the tip?

c. Your new computer costs $895. What is the total cost if the sales tax is 6.75%? What is the sales tax?

2.2 Solve Percent-Decrease Problems

Suppose you buy a car for $19,500, and it depreciates 15% after the first year. What is the car's value after one year? You can solve for the value in two steps.

[Mental Math]

Round $19,500 to $20,000. Since 15% of 10,000 is 1,500, double that amount to find 15% of 20,000.

1,500 + 1,500 = 3,000

The depreciation amount should be about $3,000.

Step 1: Solve for the depreciation amount.

$$0.15(\$19,500) = \$2,925$$

Step 2: Subtract the depreciation amount from the original amount.

$$\$19,500 - \$2,925 = \$16,575$$

The value after one year is **$16,575.**

You can also use the Distributive Property to compute the total in one step.

$$\$19,500(1 - 0.15) = \$19,500 - \$2,925$$
$$= \$16,575$$

The simplest way to find the total is with one operation.

$$\$19,500(0.85) = \$16,575$$

Use r to represent the percent decrease. In general, if r is the percent decrease, then $R = 1 - r$, and the percent equation can be written as:

$$Amount = Base \cdot Rate$$
$$A = B \cdot R$$
$$A = \$19,500(1 - 0.15)$$
$$A = \$19,500(1.05)$$
$$A = \$16,575$$

The amount of decrease is $19,500 - $16,575 = $2,925.

Write and solve for the total amount, A. Then solve for the amount of decrease.

a. D'Wayne can take a 15% depreciation deduction on his taxes for his office equipment. If his equipment costs $12,500, what is his equipment worth after one year? What is his deduction?

If $r = 0.15$, then $R = 0.85$.

$$A = B \cdot R$$
$$A = \$12{,}500(0.85)$$
$$A = \$10{,}625$$

After one year, the equipment is worth **$10,625**. D'Wayne's tax deduction is **$12,500 − $10,625 = $1,875.**

b. An electronics store offers a 10% discount on its TVs. If the original price of a TV is $959, what is the reduced price? What is the discount?

If $r = 0.1$, then $R = 0.9$.

$$A = B \cdot R$$
$$A = \$959(0.9)$$
$$A = \$863.10$$

The reduced price is **$863.10,** and the discount is **$959 − $863.10 = $95.90.**

Try It 2.2

Write and solve for the total amount, A. Then solve for the amount of decrease.

a. Your $17,500 car will depreciate 20% after one year. What is it worth after one year, and what was the decrease in value?

b. The department store is offering 40% off of all last year's merchandise. What is the reduced price of a coat that originally cost $189? What is the discount?

c. What would be the total cost of the coat in problem **b** if the sales tax were 8%?

2.3 Solve for the Percent, *r*, or the Base, *B*

Suppose your house appreciates from $210,000 to $250,000. What is the percent increase? You can solve the problem in two steps.

Step 1: Solve for the increase.

$$\$250,000 - \$210,000 = \$40,000$$

Step 2: Determine the percent increase.

$$\frac{Increase}{Base} = \frac{40,000}{210,000} \approx \textbf{19\% increase}$$

You can also solve the equation $A = B \cdot R$ for R, and then subtract 1.

$$A = B \cdot R$$
$$250,000 = 210,000 \cdot R$$
$$\frac{250,000}{210,000} \approx 1.19 = R$$

Since $R = 1 + r$, then $r = R - 1$.

$$r = R - 1$$
$$r = 1.19 - 1$$
$$r = 0.19$$
$$r = 19\%$$

If the base, B, is unknown, then solve for B in the percent equation.

$$Amount = Base \cdot Rate$$
$$A = B \cdot R$$
$$B = \frac{A}{R}$$

a. **A $1,599 sound system is reduced to $1,199.25. What is the discount rate (percent decrease)?**

You know the base, $B = 1,599$ and the part, $A = 1,199.25$. Solve for R.

$$A = B \cdot R$$
$$1,199.25 = 1,599\,R$$
$$\frac{1,199.25}{1,599} = R$$
$$0.75 = R$$

For this percent decrease, $R = 1 - r$, so $r = 1 - R$.

$$r = 1 - 0.75$$
$$r = 0.25$$
$$r = 25\%$$

The discount rate is **25%**.

b. **You plan to spend a total of $50 on dinner. What is the most your bill can be if you plan to leave a 20% tip?**

You know that $50 is the total amount, A. You also know that $R = 1 + 0.20 = 1.2$.

$$A = B \cdot R$$
$$50 = B(1.2)$$
$$\frac{50}{1.2} = B$$
$$41.67 \approx B$$

Your bill has to be less than **$41.67**.

c. **A store is having a one-day sale, and everything is on sale for 25% off. Sales tax is 7%. If you spend $200 on sale merchandise, about how much would you have spent if the items were regularly priced?**

Here you have to deal with both percent decrease and percent increase. You know that $200 is the total amount, A. The two rates are $1 - 0.25 = 0.75$ and $1 + 0.07 = 1.07$. This means the overall rate is $R = 0.75(1.07)$.

$$A = B \cdot R$$
$$200 = B(0.75(1.07))$$
$$\frac{200}{0.75(1.07)} = B$$
$$249.22 \approx B$$

You would have spent **almost $250** if the merchandise were regularly priced.

CALCULATOR TIP

You can also find the discount rate by computing:

$$\frac{\text{Decrease}}{\text{Original Price}}$$

```
(1599-1199.25)/1
599
            .25
```

Write and solve an equation for each of the following.

a. Your $19,500 car will depreciate in value to $17,550 over the next year. What is the depreciation rate?

b. The department store is offering 40% off of all last year's merchandise. Your bill before tax is $82.50. How much would you have spent if the merchandise had been regularly priced?

c. You have $100 to spend on dinner for your family's dinner. How much can you order from the menu if sales tax is 6% and you want to leave a 15% tip?

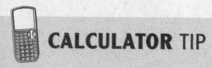

CALCULATOR TIP

Finding the Total Price

You can use a graphing calculator to compute the total price of several discounted items, including sales taxes.

Suppose you buy three items priced as:

$19.25
$299.00
$39.99

Suppose that when you check out, the items are on sale at 40% off and have a 7.25% sales tax. To calculate the final price of each item, first calculate the discounted price. Since you are taking 40% off, you want to find 60% of the original price, which is represented as 0.6. Then to find the tax for each item, multiply by 1.0725, which represents the total price plus tax. You can use the equation:

$$A = B \cdot R$$
$$A = B\,(0.6(1.0725))$$

To round your answers to the nearest hundredth, or cent, press MODE and set the rounding to 2 decimal places.

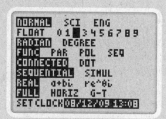

Quit the MODE screen and enter the expressions. Then key in the first expression: 19.95(0.6 · 1.0725), and press ENTER. Pressing 2nd and ENTER will repeat the first expression. Then you can clear 19.95 and key in 299.00. Repeat with 39.99. Your screen will show:

```
19.95(.6*1.0725)
              12.84
299(.6*1.0725)
             192.41
39.99(.6*1.0725)
              25.73
```

You can see that the total price of each item after the discount and including tax is:

$12.84 for $19.95
$192.41 for $299.00
$25.73 for $39.99

In this lesson, you will solve problems that involve simplifying exponential expressions. In the expression, 2^4, 2 is the **base** and 4 is the **exponent**. The expression, 2^4, is read "two to the fourth" and means the product of 4 factors of 2.

$$2^4 = 2 \cdot 2 \cdot 2 \cdot 2 = 16$$

In general, exponential expressions are written with base, x, and exponent, n.

$$x^n = \underbrace{x \cdot x \cdot x \cdot \ldots \cdot x}_{n \text{ factors of } x}$$

This is read "x raised to the nth power".

3.1 Evaluate Exponential Expressions

Using the definition of exponent, some of the exponential expressions for 2 are:

$$2^1 = 2 \qquad 2^2 = 2 \cdot 2 = 4 \qquad 2^3 = 2 \cdot 2 \cdot 2 = 8 \qquad 2^4 = 2 \cdot 2 \cdot 2 \cdot 2 = 16$$

By investigating patterns with exponential expressions, you can explore some important properties.

Explore It

Consider the pattern below:	
$2^4 = 16$ $2^3 = 8$ $2^2 = 4$ $2^1 = 2$ Note that 8 is half of 16, 4 is half of 8, and 2 is half of 4.	**1.** If you continue the pattern, what should 2^0 be? **2.** What should 2^{-1} be? **3.** What should 2^{-2} be? **4.** What is 2^{-4}? **5.** Explain why $(2 \cdot 3)^4 = 2^4 \cdot 3^4$.

When a and b are not equal to zero, the **properties of exponents** are:

1. $a^0 = 1$

2. $a^{-n} = \dfrac{1}{a^n}$

3. $(ab)^n = a^n b^n$

Note that expressions with negative exponents can be written as reciprocals with positive exponents. For example:

$$2^{-3} = \left(\frac{1}{2^3}\right) = \left(\frac{1}{8}\right) \text{ and } \left(\frac{1}{2}\right)^{-3} = \frac{1}{\left(\frac{1}{2}\right)^3} = 2^3 = 8$$

EXAMPLES

Use the properties of exponents to simplify each expression.

a. $(-4)^3 = (-4)(-4)(-4) = \mathbf{-64}$

b. $10^5 = 10 \cdot 10 \cdot 10 \cdot 10 \cdot 10 = \mathbf{100,000}$

Common Error!

$-3^4 \neq (-3)^4$

$-3^4 = -(3^4) = -81$

c. $(-3)^4 = (-3)(-3)(-3)(-3) = \mathbf{81}$

d. $\left(\frac{2}{3}\right)^3 = \frac{2}{3} \cdot \frac{2}{3} \cdot \frac{2}{3} = \frac{2^3}{3^3} = \mathbf{\frac{8}{27}}$

e. $10^{-5} = \frac{1}{10^5} = \frac{1}{100,000} = \mathbf{0.00001}$

f. $\left(\frac{2}{3}\right)^{-3} = \left(\frac{3}{2}\right)^3 = \frac{3^3}{2^3} = \mathbf{\frac{27}{8}}$

Try It 3.1

Use the properties of exponents to simplify each expression.

a. $(-2)^4 =$

b. $-5^2 =$

c. $10^{-3} =$

d. $10^3 =$

e. $\left(\frac{1}{3}\right)^4 =$

f. $\left(\frac{4}{3}\right)^{-2} =$

3.2 Apply Properties of Exponents

Use the powers of 2 to help you generalize other properties of exponents.

$2^1 = 2$	$2^2 = 4$	$2^3 = 8$	$2^4 = 16$
$2^5 = 32$	$2^6 = 64$	$2^7 = 128$	$2^8 = 256$

Explore It

For each of the following sets, look for a pattern and generalize a rule.

1. $2^2 \cdot 2^4 = (2 \cdot 2)(2 \cdot 2 \cdot 2 \cdot 2) = 2^?$

   $2^1 \cdot 2^6 = 2^?$

   $2^3 \cdot 2^8 = 2^?$

2. $\dfrac{2^5}{2^2} = \dfrac{2 \cdot 2 \cdot 2 \cdot 2 \cdot 2}{2 \cdot 2} = 2^?$

   $\dfrac{2^7}{2^6} = 2^?$

   $\dfrac{2^8}{2^3} = 2^?$

3. $(2^2)^3 = (2 \cdot 2)^3 = (2 \cdot 2)(2 \cdot 2)(2 \cdot 2)2^?$

   $(2^3)^4 = 2^?$

Use what you discovered about the expressions above to generalize the following properties.

When a is not equal to zero, the properties of exponents are:

1. $a^m a^n = a^{m+n}$

2. $\dfrac{a^m}{a^n} = a^{m-n}$

3. $\left(a^m\right)^n = a^{mn}$

When you use the properties, always write your answer with a positive exponent.
For example:

$$x^{-5} \cdot x^2 = x^{-5+2} = x^{-3} = \frac{1}{x^3}$$

Use the properties of exponents to simplify each expression. Write your answers with positive exponents.

a. $x^3x^4 = x^{3+4} = x^7$

b. $10^5 \cdot 10^{-7} = 10^{5+(-7)} = 10^{-2} = \dfrac{1}{10^2} = 0.01$

c. $\dfrac{(-3)^4}{-3} = (-3)^{4-1} = (-3)^3 = -27$

d. $\dfrac{x^{-7}}{x^{-5}} = x^{-7-(-5)} = x^{-2} = \dfrac{1}{x^2}$

e. $(x^{-2})^4 = x^{-2 \cdot 4} = x^{-8} = \dfrac{1}{x^8}$

f. $(ab^2)^3 = a^3b^6$

g. $\dfrac{ab^{-3}}{a^{-2}b^2} = (a^{1-(-2)})(b^{-3-2}) = a^3b^{-5} = \dfrac{a^3}{b^5}$

Try It 3.2

Use the properties of exponents to simplify each expression. Write your answers with positive exponents.

a. $x^3x^{-4} =$

b. $10^5 \cdot 10^7 =$

c. $\dfrac{(-2)^4}{-2} =$

d. $\dfrac{x^7}{x^{-5}} =$

e. $(x^{-3})^2 =$

f. $(a^4b^2)^3 =$

g. $\dfrac{a^{-1}b^3}{a^2b^2} =$

122 Unit 3: *Exponential Models*

CALCULATOR TIP

Checking Solutions

You can use a graphing calculator to store values for variables and to check that your expressions are equal.

Consider the following equation:

$$\frac{ab^{-3}}{a^{-2}b^2} = \frac{a^3}{b^5}$$

Pick any two values for the variables. For example, $a = 2$ and $b = 2$.

Use the store feature to input the values. See your calculator manual for specific instructions.

```
2→A
               2
3→B
               3
```

Then key in each expression using the variable you entered (A and B). Remember to use parentheses correctly. Check to see if both expressions have the same value.

```
(A*B^-3)/(A^-2*B
^2)
       .0329218107
(A^3)/(B^5)
       .0329218107
```

Since the expressions have the same value, the solution $\frac{a^3}{b^5}$ is correct.

Checkpoint

Write and solve a percent equation for each of the following.

1. What percent of 42 is 21?

2. 120 is about $66\frac{2}{3}\%$ of what number?

Write an equation, estimate, and then solve using a calculator.

3. Your dinner costs $35.62. You decide to give a 15% tip. How much is the tip?

4. A $21,500 car is discounted $2,580. The new price is $18,920. By what percent was the car discounted?

5. Once a new car is driven off the sales lot, the resale value is only 85% of its original value. If the resale value is $15,360, what was its original value?

Write and solve a percent equation for problems 6–10.

6. A $599 purchase is discounted $33\frac{1}{3}\%$. What is the reduced price? What is the discount?

7. James gave all of his employees a 5.5% raise at the end of the year. Juan made $12.50 per hour this year. How much will he make per hour next year?

8. A $2,500 engagement ring is discounted to $2,200. What is the discount rate?

9. You saved $15,000 last year. At the end of the year, your savings is worth $15,600. What is the annual interest rate on your savings account?

10. A store is having a 20% off sale on all goods. The sales tax is 8%. If you spend $450 on sale-priced merchandise, what would you have spent if the merchandise had been regularly priced?

Use the properties of exponents to simplify each expression. Write all answers with positive exponents.

11. $-10^{-4} =$

12. $\left(\frac{1}{3}\right)^0 =$

13. $(-5)^{-2} =$

14. $10^5 \cdot 10^{-9} =$

15. $(x^5)^{-2} =$

Check your answers in the *Solutions* section at the back of the book. If you missed more than one answer from problems 1 to 5, review lesson 1. If you missed more than one answer from problems 6 to 10, review lesson 2. If you missed more than one answer from problems 11 to 15, review lesson 3.

Write and Evaluate Exponential-Growth Functions·

FOCUS	Write and evaluate exponential-growth functions and solve compound-interest problems

In this lesson, you will solve problems involving exponential growth. Population growth and money growth are two of the most common examples. You will learn that applying a percent increase repeatedly will give an **exponential function**.

For example, your financial advisor could tell you that every $1 you deposit into your retirement account will double every decade. The table at right shows the growth of your dollar.

After 4 decades (40 years) your dollar is worth $16.

Decade	Amount ($)
0	1
1	2
2	4
3	8
4	16

[RECALL]

The **powers** of 2 are products of the integer 2 multiplied by itself a certain number of times.

You probably observed that the data in the table are the powers of 2. The most elementary example of exponential growth is the doubling function, $y = 2^x$. Below is a table and a graph the represent $y = 2^x$. The table and graph show the growth.

Decade (x)	Amount (y = 2^x)	Ordered Pair (x, y)
0	$y = 2^0 = 1$	(0, 1)
1	$y = 2^1 = 2$	(1, 2)
2	$y = 2^2 = 4$	(2, 4)
3	$y = 2^3 = 8$	(3, 8)
4	$y = 2^4 = 16$	(4, 16)

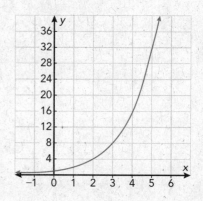

Exponential growth functions increase from left to right.
The initial value ($1) occurs at time 0 since $2^0 = 1$.

Now think about $100 doubling every decade.

Decade	Amount ($)
0	$100 = 100 \cdot 2^0$
1	$200 = 100 \cdot 2^1$
2	$400 = 100 \cdot 2^2$
3	$800 = 100 \cdot 2^3$
4	$1,600 = 100 \cdot 2^4$

This situation can be modeled with the equation:

$$y = 100 \cdot 2^x$$

The initial value ($100) occurs at time 0. Note the equation below.

$$100 \cdot 2^0 = 100 \cdot 1 = 100$$

In general, the **exponential-growth function** can be written as:

$$y = a \cdot b^x$$

Where a is the initial value at $x = 0$, and $b > 1$.

4.1 Graph Exponential Functions

Recall from Lesson 3 that $y = 2^{-1} = \frac{1}{2}$ and that $y = 2^{-2} = \frac{1}{2^2} = \frac{1}{4}$. You can sketch a complete graph for an exponential function by including negative x-values.

EXAMPLES

Complete the table and the graph for each exponential function.

a. $y = 2^x$

First evaluate the function for the given x-values. Then plot the points on the coordinate plane.

x	$y = 2^x$
-2	$y = 2^{-2} = \frac{1}{4}$
-1	$y = 2^{-1} = \frac{1}{2}$
0	$y = 2^0 = 1$
1	$y = 2^1 = 2$
2	$y = 2^2 = 4$
3	$y = 2^3 = 8$

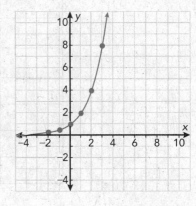

> **NOTE**
>
> *Each point is plotted using an ordered pair made up of one x-value from the table and the corresponding y-value. Note that the first ordered pair in the table is $(-2, \frac{1}{4})$, and there is a point plotted at $(-2, \frac{1}{4})$.*

b. $y = 10 \cdot 2^x$

First evaluate the function for the given x-values. Then plot the points on the coordinate plane.

x	$y = 10 \cdot 2^x$
-2	$y = 10 \cdot 2^{-2} = 2.25$
-1	$y = 10 \cdot 2^{-1} = 5$
0	$y = 10 \cdot 2^0 = 10$
1	$y = 10 \cdot 2^1 = 20$
2	$y = 10 \cdot 2^2 = 40$
3	$y = 10 \cdot 2^3 = 80$

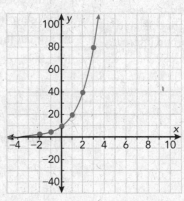

Try It 4.1

Complete the table for each exponential function, and then graph each ordered pair.

a. $y = 3^x$

x	$y = 3^x$
-2	
-1	
0	
1	
2	
3	

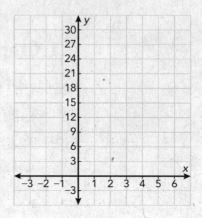

b. $y = 4 \cdot 3^x$

x	$y = 4 \cdot 3^x$
-2	
-1	
0	
1	
2	
3	

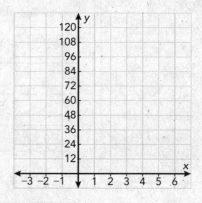

4.2 Write and Evaluate Annual Compound-Interest Functions

Compound-interest functions are one example of an exponential-growth function. You have seen how to compute the value of a bank account by using percent increase. Suppose you buy a $5,000 seven-year Certificate of Deposit (CD) from your bank at an annual interest rate of 6%. You can compute the value after one year by multiplying by 1.06.

$$A = 5,000(1.06)$$
$$A = 5,300$$

After one year, you have **$5,300.**

Explore It

Consider the $5,000 seven-year CD with an annual interest rate of 6%. After one year, it will be worth $5,300.

1. How much will the CD be worth after 2 years?

2. How much will the CD be worth after 3 years?

3. Explain how you can use an exponential model to determine the value of the CD after 7 years.

CALCULATOR TIP

Use 2nd Enter on a graphing calculator to retrieve and edit the last line you entered. This is helpful when you are evaluating functions that are similar because you can edit the last line you entered rather than creating a new entry.

```
5000*1.06^2
            5618
5000*1.06^3
          5955.08
5000*1.06^7
      7518.151295
■
```

Annual compound interest involves applying the interest rate to interest you have already earned. Below is a chart to show how compound interest affects the information from the Explore It.

Year (x)	Amount (y)
0	$y = 5,000$
1	$y = 5,000(1.06) = 5,000(1.06)^1 = 5,300$
2	$y = 5,000(1.06)(1.06) = 5,000(1.06)^2 = 5,618$
3	$y = 5,000(1.06)(1.06)(1.06) = 5,000(1.06)^3 = 5,955.08$
7	$y = 5,000(1.06)^7 \approx 7,518.15$

Look at year 2 in the chart. From year 1 to year 2, you earned $318 in interest, which is $18 more than the $300 you earned the first year. This is the effect of compounding, or earning interest on your interest. This situation can be modeled with the exponential function:

$$y = 5,000 \cdot 1.06^x$$

Note that the initial value (5,000) occurs at time zero because:

$$y = 5,000 \cdot 1.06^0 = 5,000 \cdot 1 = 5,000$$

Write an exponential function, and then solve for the total amount, A.

a. You bought a three-year $5,000 CD from your bank at an annual interest rate of 6.125%. What is the value of your CD after three years?

First assign a variable to each amount: $a = 5{,}000$ and $b = 1.06125$. Then write the exponential function when $x = 3$, and substitute for the known values.

$$y = a \cdot b^x$$
$$y = 5{,}000 \cdot (1.06125)^3 \approx 5{,}976.17$$

After 3 years, your CD is worth **$5,976.17**.

b. You buy a five-year $2,500 CD from your bank at an annual interest rate of 4.75%. What is the value of your CD after five years?

First assign a variable to each amount: $a = 2{,}500$ and $b = 1.0475$. Then write the exponential function when $x = 5$, and substitute for the known values.

$$y = a \cdot b^x$$
$$y = 2{,}500 \cdot (1.0475)^5 \approx 3{,}152.90$$

After 5 years, your CD is worth **$3,152.90**.

Try It 4.2

Write an exponential function for each problem, and then solve for the total amount, A.

a. You bought a two-year $1,000 CD from your bank at an annual interest rate of 5%. What is the value of your CD after two years?

b. You bought a five-year $5,000 CD from your bank at an annual interest rate of 3.25%. What is the value of your CD after five years?

[TIP]

The value of x will vary based on the number of years.

4.3 Write and Evaluate Exponential-Growth Functions

There are many real-world examples of exponential growth. Population growth and other kinds of growth, including business applications, are often modeled with exponential functions.

EXAMPLES

Write an exponential function, and then evaluate it for the given x-values.

a. **The elk population in a national park is expected to grow at an annual rate of 7%. The population now is 2,250. What is the projected population after 5 years?**

Assign variables to the values: $a = 2{,}250$ and $b = 1.07$ Then solve the exponential-growth function when $x = 5$.

$$y = a \cdot b^x$$
$$y = 2{,}250 \cdot (1.07)^5 \approx \mathbf{3{,}155}$$

[TIP]

With population data; be sure to round to the nearest whole unit.

b. **Your business is projecting 25% growth in revenue each year for the next four years. If your revenue this year was \$75,000, what is the projected revenue for each of the next four years?**

Assign variables to the values: $a = 75{,}000$ and $b = 1.25$. Then write the exponential-growth function and substitute the known values. Use a table to show each function value.

$$y = a \cdot b^x$$
$$y = 75{,}000 \cdot (1.25)^x$$

Year (x)	Revenue $(y = 75{,}000 \cdot (1.25)^x)$
0	$y = 75{,}000 \cdot (1.25)^0 = 75{,}000$
1	$y = 75{,}000 \cdot (1.25)^1 = 93{,}750$
2	$y = 75{,}000 \cdot (1.25)^2 = 117{,}188$
3	$y = 75{,}000 \cdot (1.25)^3 = 146{,}484$
4	$y = 75{,}000 \cdot (1.25)^4 = 183{,}105$

When you are working with dollar amounts, it sometimes makes sense to round to the nearest dollar. Note that with a 25% compound-interest rate, the revenue nearly doubles after 3 years. Your projected revenue after four years is over \$180,000.

■ **Try It 4.3**

Write an exponential function, and then evaluate it for the given *x*-values.

a. The population of a town is projected to grow at an annual rate of 3.5%. The current population is 16,450. What is the projected population after 10 years?

b. Your business plans for a 5% annual inflation rate. If the costs this year were $140,000, what are the projected costs for each of the next three years?

Year (x)	Projected Cost (y)
0	
1	
2	
3	

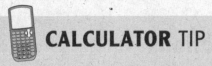

CALCULATOR TIP

Build a Table for an Exponential Function

You can use a graphing calculator to build a table of values for an exponential function. Consider the projected revenue function $y = 75{,}000 \cdot (1.25)^x$. Use a calculator to find the projected revenue after 4 years.

Type the function rule into Y=. Remember to include x as the exponent.

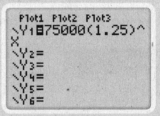

Set the table to start at 0.

Review the table on screen, and find the revenue at year 4.

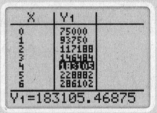

Your projected revenue after four years is $183,105.

Write and Evaluate Exponential-Decay Functions

| FOCUS | Write and evaluate exponential-decay functions |

In this lesson, you will solve problems involving exponential decay. A quantity that decreases by a fixed percent is subject to exponential decay. Population decline and depreciation are among the more common examples. You will see that applying percent decrease repeatedly creates an exponential-decay function.

[RECALL]

Remember that $\frac{1}{2} = 2^{-1}$.

Your friend told you that every \$1 you spend on computer equipment loses half its value each year. The table at right shows the depreciation of your dollar. Each following amount is half of the amount from the previous year.

After 4 years, every \$1 you spent on computer equipment investment is only worth about 6¢.

Year (x)	Value (\$) (y)
0	1
1	$1 \cdot \frac{1}{2} = \frac{1}{2} = 0.50$
2	$\frac{1}{2} \cdot \frac{1}{2} = \frac{1}{4} = 0.25$
3	$\frac{1}{4} \cdot \frac{1}{2} = \frac{1}{8} = 0.125$
4	$\frac{1}{2} \cdot \frac{1}{8} = \frac{1}{16} = 0.0625$

You can see that the data in the table above are the negative powers of 2. The most basic example of exponential decay is the halving function, $y = \left(\frac{1}{2}\right)^x$ or $y = 2^{-x}$. You can use what you know about exponents to build a table and a graph for $y = 2^x$. The starting amount is 1. Each following amount is half of the amount from the previous year. The table and graph below show this decay.

[RECALL]

Remember that $a^{-n} = \left(\frac{1}{a}\right)^n$.

Year (x)	Value (\$) (y)	(x, y)
0	$y = 2^{-x} = \left(\frac{1}{2}\right)^x \cdot 1$	$(0, 1)$
1	$y = 2^{-1} = \frac{1}{2} = 0.5$	$\left(1, \frac{1}{2}\right)$
2	$y = 2^{-2} = \frac{1}{2^2} = \frac{1}{4} = 0.25$	$\left(2, \frac{1}{4}\right)$
3	$y = 2^{-3} = \frac{1}{2^3} = \frac{1}{8} = 0.125$	$\left(3, \frac{1}{8}\right)$
4	$y = 2^{-4} = \frac{1}{2^4} = \frac{1}{16} = 0.0625$	$\left(4, \frac{1}{16}\right)$

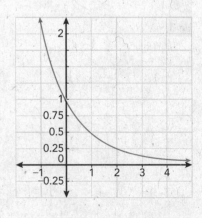

Exponential-decay functions decrease from left to right. The initial value (\$1) for expression $y = 2^x$ occurs at time 0 since $2^{-0} = 2^0 = 1$.

In general, the **exponential-decay function** can be written as

$$y = a \cdot b^x$$

Where *a* is the initial value when $x = 0$ and $0 < b < 1$.

5.1 Graph Exponential-Decay Functions

For the exponential-decay function $y = 2^{-x}$, note that if $x = -2$, then $y = 2^{-(-2)} = 2^2 = 4$. You can sketch a complete graph by including negative *x*-values.

EXAMPLES

Create a table for each exponential function, and then graph the results for exponential function.

a. $y = 2^{-x}$

x	$y = 2^{-x}$
-2	$y = 2^{-(-2)} = 2^2 = 4$
-1	$y = 2^{-(-1)} = 2^1 = 2$
0	$y = 2^{-0} = 1$
1	$y = 2^{-1} = \dfrac{1}{2}$
2	$y = 2^{-2} = \dfrac{1}{4}$
3	$y = 2^{-3} = \dfrac{1}{8}$

The values in the first column of the table represent the *x*-values. The values in the second column represent the corresponding *y*-values. These values create ordered pairs, such as (−2, 4), which can be plotted on the graph below.

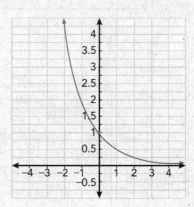

b. $y = 100 \cdot 2^{-x}$

x	$y = 100 \cdot 2^{-x}$
-2	$y = 100 \cdot 2^{-(-2)} = 100 \cdot 4 = 400$
-1	$y = 100 \cdot 2^{-(-1)} = 100 \cdot 2 = 200$
0	$y = 100 \cdot 2^{-(0)} = 100$
1	$y = 100 \cdot 2^{-1} = 100 \cdot \frac{1}{2} = 50$
2	$y = 100 \cdot 2^{-2} = 100 \cdot \frac{1}{4} = 25$
3	$y = 100 \cdot 2^{-3} = 100 \cdot \frac{1}{8} = 12.5$

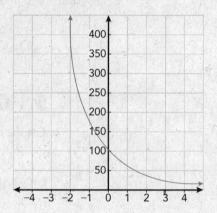

Note that the initial value at $x = 0$ is 100 because $100 \cdot 2^{-0} = 100 \cdot 2^{0} = 100 \cdot 1 = 100$.

Try It 5.1

Complete the table for each exponential function, and then graph the results.

a. $y = 3^{-x}$

x	$y = 3^{-x}$
-2	
-1	
0	
1	
2	
3	

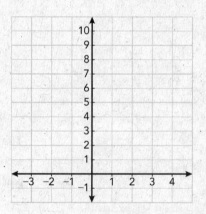

b. $y = 20 \cdot 2^{-x}$

x	$y = 20 \cdot 2^{-x}$
-2	
-1	
0	
1	
2	
3	

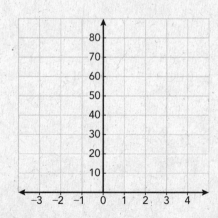

5.2 Write and Evaluate Exponential-Decay Functions

You have learned how to find the value of equipment that depreciates 50% each year. Population decline can also be modeled with exponential-decay functions. You can use the idea of percent decrease to build an exponential function.

Explore It

Suppose an endangered species of 300 eagles is predicted to decline by 10% each year. Answer the three following questions.

1. How many eagles are there after one year?

2. How many eagles are there after two years?

3. How many eagles are there after three years?

Since you need to find the population that is remaining, subtract 10% from 100% and convert to a decimal. This number will represent the percentage of eagles left each year.

$$100\% - 10\% = 90\%$$
$$1 - 0.1 = 0.9$$

You can compute the population by repeatedly applying the percent-decrease factor as shown in the table below.

Year (x)	Population (x)
0	$y = 300$
1	$y = 300(0.9) = 300(0.9)^1 = 270$
2	$y = 300(0.9) = 300(0.9)(0.9) = 300(0.9)^2 = 243$
3	$y = 300(0.9) = 300(0.9)(0.9)(0.9) = 300(0.9)^3 \approx 219$

After one year, there are **270 eagles.** After two years, there are **243 eagles.** By the third year, the population has declined to about **219 eagles.**

This situation can be modeled with the exponential-decay function:

$$y = 300 \cdot (0.9)^x$$

Note that the initial value, 300, occurs at time 0 because $y = 300 \cdot 0.09^0 = 300 \cdot 1 = 300$.

[RECALL]

Remember that you can use 2nd Enter on a graphing calculator to retrieve and edit the last line you entered. This is helpful when you are evaluating functions that are similar because you can edit the last line you entered rather than creating a new entry. This allows you to make multiple computations more easily.

```
300*.9
            270
300*.9^2
            243
300*.9^3
          218.7
```

Write an exponential function for each situation, and then evaluate it for the given *x*-values.

a. **The population in a rural town is expected to decrease at an annual rate of 5%. The population now is 3,250. What is the population expected to be after 5 years?**

First assign a variable to each amount: $a = 3,250$ and $b = 1 - 0.05 = 0.95$. Then write the exponential function and substitute the values, including $x = 5$, and substitute for the known values.

$$y = a \cdot b^x$$
$$y = 3,250 \cdot (0.95)^5 \approx 2,515$$

After 5 years, the population of the town would be **2,515.**

b. **The value of a car that costs $21,000 depreciates at a rate of 15% each year. Create a table to show how the value decreases over the first four years.**

Assign variables to the values: $a = 21,000$ and $b = 1 - 0.15 = 0.85$. Then write the exponential function. Use a table to show each function value.

$$y = a \cdot b^x$$
$$y = 21,000 \cdot (0.85)^x$$

Year (x)	Value ($) ($y = 21,000 \cdot (0.85)^x$)
0	$y = 21,000 \cdot (0.85)^0 = 21,000$
1	$y = 21,000 \cdot (0.85)^1 = 17,850$
2	$y = 21,000 \cdot (0.85)^2 = 15,173$
3	$y = 21,000 \cdot (0.85)^3 = 12,897$
4	$y = 21,000 \cdot (0.85)^4 = 10,962$

After four years, your car will only be worth **$10,962,** which is a little less than $11,000.

Try It 5.2

Write an exponential function for each situation, and then evaluate it for the given *x*-values.

a. The current population of trout in the lake 1,200. A scientist predicts the trout population will decline at a rate of 12% per year. What is the predicted population after 5 years?

b. Sam purchased $79,000 of equipment for his automotive shop. He expects that the equipment will depreciate by 10% each year. Complete the table below to show the value of the equipment over the next three years.

Year (x)	Value ($) (y)
0	
1	
2	
3	

CALCULATOR TIP

Build a Table for an Exponential-Decay Function

You can use a graphing calculator to build a table of values for an exponential function. Consider the exponential-decay function $y = 3,250 \cdot (0.95)^x$. Use a calculator to find the value after 5 years.

Key the function rule into Y=.

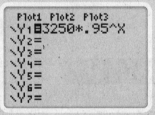

Set the table to start at 0.

Review the table on screen, and find the revenue at year 5.

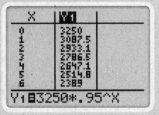

After 5 years, the initial value of 3,250 decreases to about 2,515.

LESSON 6 Solve Exponential Applications

In this lesson, you will solve problems involving exponential models, or functions that are exponential. You will learn to determine an exponential model from a table and to write and solve simple exponential growth and decay problems using the guess-and-check method.

[RECALL]

Remember that exponential functions are of the form $y = ab^x$, where a is the initial value when $x = 0$.

Your bank tells you that if you invest $1,000 in an account, your money will grow as shown in the table at right. How can you determine the interest rate?

Year (x)	Amount (y)
0	$1,000.00
1	$1,080.00
2	$1,166.40
3	$1,259.71

To determine the interest rate, first divide.

$$\frac{1,080}{1,000} = 1.08$$

Divide the year 2 amount by the year 1 amount.

$$1.08 - 1 = 0.08 = 8\%$$

Then subtract 1.
The interest rate is 8%.

Check:

$$\frac{1,166.40}{1,080} = 1.08$$

You can check your answer by dividing the year 2 amount by the year 1 amount.

$$1.08 - 1 = 0.08 = 8\%$$

Then subtract the whole. The answer is correct.

6.1 Solve Exponential-Growth Problems

[TIP]

When you are dividing successive outputs, you are dividing the second number by the first, the third number by the second, and so on.

To determine the values of a and b in an exponential-growth model ($y = ab^x$), you must find the value of b by dividing successive outputs and then determine the initial value, a.

EXAMPLES

Determine an exponential function for each situation, and then solve each problem.

a. **Consider the problem in the introduction. In which year would you have at least $1,500 in your account?**

In the table above, you can see that the initial value of $a = 1,000$ when $x = 0$. To find the value of b, solve for the exponential model, $y = ab^x$ by dividing year 2 by year 1:

$$\frac{1,080}{1,000} = 1.08 = b$$

The exponential function is:

$$y = 1,000 \cdot 1.08^x$$

To determine the year in which you have at least $1,500 in your account, you can extend the table from page 140.

You can see that in **year 6** you have at least $1,500 in your account.

Year (x)	Amount($) (y)
4	$y = 1{,}000 \cdot 1.08^4 = 1{,}360.49$
5	$y = 1{,}000 \cdot 1.08^5 = 1{,}469.33$
6	$y = 1{,}000 \cdot 1.08^6 = 1{,}586.87$

b. **The census bureau uses an exponential model to predict the population growth of a city. This data is shown in the table below. When will the population be at least 90,000?**

Year (x)	Population (y)
0	75,300
1	78,312
2	81,444

First determine the exponential model. For the exponential model $y = ab^x$, you find b, by dividing year 1 by year 0. You can check the value by dividing year 2 by year 1. They will have the same value.

$$\frac{78{,}312}{75{,}300} = 1.04 \qquad\qquad \frac{81{,}444}{78{,}312} = 1.04$$

The value of b is 1.04. The initial value of $a = 75{,}300$ when $x = 0$, so the exponential function is:

$$y = 75{,}300 \cdot 1.04^x$$

To determine when the population reaches at least 90,000, you can evaluate for other x-values using guess and check. You can see from the y-values in the table that it is not likely that year 3 will be at least 90,000. Using the guess-and-check method, you can guess that the x-value will be year 4 or 5. Check both years to see if your guess is correct.

$$y = 75{,}300 \cdot 1.04^4 = 88{,}090$$
$$y = 75{,}300 \cdot 1.04^5 = 91{,}614$$

You can see that in **year 5** the population will be at least 90,000.

c. A wildlife biologist predicts the population growth of a buffalo herd using an exponential model. The data is displayed in the table below. What is the projected population after 5 years?

Year (x)	Population (y)
1	2,430
2	2,624
3	2,834

First determine the exponential model. For the exponential model $y = ab^x$, you find the value of b by dividing $\frac{2,624}{2,430} = 1.08$. To find the value of a, solve the equation:

$$a\,(1.08) = 2,430$$

$$a = \frac{2,430}{1.08} = 2,250$$

This means the exponential function is $y = 2,250 \cdot 1.08^x$. To determine the population after 5 years, evaluate the function when $x = 5$.

$$y = 2,250 \cdot 1.08^5 = 3,306$$

After 5 years, the population is predicted to be **3,306 buffalo.**

Try It 6.1

Determine an exponential function for each situation, and then solve each problem.

a. The city manager uses an exponential model to predict population growth of a city. The data is shown in the table below. In what year will the population be at least 140,000?

Year (x)	Population (y)
0	125,300
1	129,059
2	132,931

b. The projected return on a $5,000 investment is shown in the table below. What is the annual interest rate? When will the investment be worth at least $7,000?

Year (x)	Amount (y)
0	$5000
1	$5,300
2	$5,618

c. A scientist predicts the population of field mice using an exponential model. What is the projected population after 7 years?

Year (x)	Population (y)
1	4,300
2	4,730
3	5,203

6.2 Solve Exponential-Decay Problems

As with exponential growth, to determine an exponential-decay model when $y = ab^x$, you can determine the value of b by dividing successive outputs and then determine the initial value, a.

EXAMPLES

Determine an exponential function and solve each problem.

a. **The depreciated value of a truck that originally cost $26,000 is shown in the table at right. What is the depreciation rate? What is the first year that the truck will be worth less than $10,000?**

Year (x)	Value (y)
0	$26,000
1	$21,320
2	$17,482

First determine the exponential model. For the exponential model $y = ab^x$, you find b, by dividing:

$$b = \frac{21,320}{26,000} = 0.82$$

The depreciation rate is $1 - 0.82 = 0.18 = 18\%$ per year.

From the table, you can see that the initial value of $a = 26,000$ when $x = 0$, so the exponential function is:

$$y = 26,000 \cdot 0.82^x$$

To determine the first year that the truck is worth less than $10,000, evaluate the function for additional x-values. You can see from the pattern of y-values in the table that year 3 is not likely to be less than $10,000, so you can guess and check years 4 and 5.

$$y = 26,000 \cdot 1.04^4 = 11,755$$
$$y = 26,000 \cdot 1.04^5 = 9,639$$

The first year that the truck is worth less than $10,000 is **year 5.**

b. A scientist uses an exponential-decay model to predict the population of an endangered species of fish in a polluted lake. What is the first year that the fish population will drop below 600?

Year (x)	Population (y)
1	1,530
2	1,377
3	1,239

[Mental Math]

$1 - 0.9 = 0.1 = 10\%$

First determine the exponential model. For the exponential model $y = ab^x$, you can find the value of b, by dividing: $\dfrac{1,377}{1,530} = 0.9$. The population is decreasing by about 10% each year.

To find the value of a, solve the equation:

$$a(0.9) = 1,530$$

$$a = \frac{1,530}{0.9} = 1,700$$

You have enough information to write the exponential function:

$$y = 1,700 \cdot 0.9^x$$

To determine when the population drops below 600, you can evaluate the function for different values of x. Based on the patterns of y-values in the table, you can tell that year 4 is not likely to be the first year the population is below 600. Using the guess-and-check method, you can guess that the x-value will be year 9 or 10. Check both years to see if your guess is correct.

$$y = 1,700 \cdot 0.9^9 = 659$$
$$y = 1,700 \cdot 0.9^{10} = 593$$

You can see that when $x = 10$ years the population drops to 593, which is the first year it is below 600.

Try It 6.2

Determine an exponential function, and then solve each problem.

a. The projected depreciated value of a company's computer equipment is shown in the table. What is the first year that the equipment will be worth less than $2,000?

Year (x)	Amount (y)
0	$40,000
1	$24,000
2	$14,400

b. A city's population is projected to decrease as shown in the table. What is the first year that the population will drop below 140,000?

Year (*x*)	Population (*y*)
1	190,000
2	180,500
3	171,475

CALCULATOR TIP

Build a Table for an Exponential Function

You can use a graphing calculator to build a table of values for an exponential function. Consider the exponential-decay function $y = 26{,}000 \cdot 0.82^x$ from example *a* in section 6.2. You determined that the solution was year 5. Use a calculator to create a table to check your solution. In what year will the truck be worth less than $10,000?

Key the function into Y=.

Set the table to start at 0.

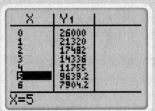

View the table. Check to see if year 5 is correct. You can see that your solution was correct—the depreciated value of the truck is less than $10,000 in **year 5**.

Self-Evaluation

Write and solve a percent equation for problems 1–10.

1. 15 is what percent of 75?

2. 27 is 30% of what number?

3. Your dinner costs $29.68. You leave a 20% tip. What is the amount of the tip in dollars?

4. A car that originally cost $31,500 is discounted by $3,100. The new price is $28,400. What is the percent discount?

5. When you drive your new car off the lot, the resale value decreases to only 82% of its retail value. If the resale value is $25,300, what was its retail value?

6. Susie makes $14.50 an hour. Next month she will receive a 3.5% raise. What will her new hourly rate be?

7. Your $30,000 salary increases to $30,600. What is the percent increase?

8. A computer is regularly priced $2,500, but today it is discounted to $2,400. What is the discount rate as a percent?

9. What is the total price of a $1,250 sound system plus a 7.5% sales tax?

10. Today your favorite store is offering a 30% discount on all goods. The sales tax is 6%. You spend exactly $300 at the store. How much would you have spent if the items had been regularly priced?

Use the properties of exponents to simplify each expression in problems 11–15. Write your answers with positive exponents.

11. $x^{-3} x^3 =$

12. $(x^{-3})^{-2} =$

13. $\dfrac{x^{-6}}{x^7} =$

14. $\dfrac{a^{-4} b^3}{a^2 b^3} =$

15. $\dfrac{(3a^{-1})^2 b^{-2}}{a^{-3}(2b)^2} =$

Complete the table, and then graph each exponential function for problems 16 and 17.

16. $y = 3 \cdot 2^x$

x	$y = 3 \cdot 2^x$
−2	
−1	
0	
1	
2	
3	

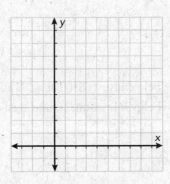

Continue on next page.

17. $y = 2 \cdot 3^x$

x	$y = 2 \cdot 3^x$
-2	
-1	
0	
1	
2	
3	

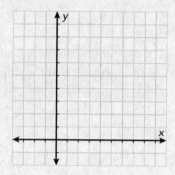

Evaluate each compound-interest problem for the indicated value.

18. A five-year $1,000 investment at 3.5%

19. A two-year $10,000 investment at 6%

Solve problems 20–27.

20. Your company sets a goal to increase revenue by 5% each year. The revenue now is $325,000. Write an exponential function to represent this goal, and then determine the projected revenue for years 1, 2, and 3.

21. A scientist predicts the population of prairie dogs in a certain area will increase 7.5% each year. The population now is 1,220. Write an exponential function to represent this growth, and then determine the projected population in ten years.

22. Felipe invests $500 at a 5% annual interest rate. Write an exponential function to represent Felipe's investment, and then determine the amount in the account in ten years.

23. The census bureau predicts that a city with a population of 200,000 will decline each year at a rate of 4.5%. Write an exponential function to represent this decline, and then determine the projected population in ten years.

24. Based on data she collects, a wildlife biologist predicts that a wolf population of 1,500 will decrease 6.5% each year. Write an exponential function to represent the wolf population decline, and then determine the projected population in five years.

25. A car that originally cost $37,000 will depreciate at a rate of 12% per year. Write an exponential function to represent this depreciation, and then determine the value of the car after three years.

26. In a community, the housing market is expected to decline 6% each year. Write an exponential function to represent a $220,000 house in this market, and then determine the value of that house after four years.

27. A computer depreciates at a rate of 50% per year. Write an exponential function to represent this situation, and then determine the value after three years of a computer that originally cost $3,000.

Write an exponential model using form $y = ab^x$ to represent the situations in problems 28–30.

28. A bank account grows as shown in the table. Determine the first year in which the account will be at least $20,000.

Year (x)	Amount (y)
0	$15,000.00
1	$15,825.00
2	$16,695.38

Continue on next page.

29. The population of a town is projected to grow as shown in the table. Determine the first year that the population will be at least 4,000.

Year (x)	Population (y)
1	2,750
2	3,025
3	3,328

30. A new car is expected to depreciate as shown in the table. Determine the first year that the value will fall below $4,000.

Year (x)	Value (y)
1	$18,500.00
2	$14,800.00
3	$11,840.00

ARE YOU READY TO GO ON ?

- Check your answers in the *Solutions* section at the back of the book. Reading the solution for each problem will help you understand why the correct answers are right and will allow you to see each step of the solutions.
- On the chart below, circle the problem numbers that you did not solve correctly. If you answered more than one problem per lesson incorrectly, you should review that lesson before moving to the next unit.

Performance Analysis Chart

LESSON	PROBLEM NUMBER
1	1, 2, 3, 4, 5
2	6 ,7, 8, 9, 10
3	11, 12, 13, 14, 15
4	16, 17, 18, 19
5	20, 21, 22, 23, 24, 25, 26, 27
6	28, 29, 30

UNIT 4 Polynomial Models

In this unit, you will work with quadratic equations. There are many real-world applications that involve quadratic equations. For example, simple science and business applications dealing with maximum height and maximum revenue could be written as:

$$h(t) = 112t - 16t^2$$
and
$$R(x) = -18x^2 + 540x + 18,000$$

LESSON 1 Multiply Polynomials

In this lesson, you will multiply **polynomial expressions**. Polynomial expressions in one variable (such as x) contain one or more terms with x raised to a non-negative integer power. For example, $4x^2 - 8x - 14$ is a three-term polynomial called a **trinomial**. The value of the greatest exponent is called the degree. The **degree of the polynomial** $4x^2 - 8x - 14$ is 2 because it is the greatest exponent. The **leading coefficient**, the coefficient of the highest degree term, of $4x^2 - 8x - 14$ is 4, and the constant term is -14. A constant term has no variable.

1.1 Multiply by a Monomial

A one-term polynomial, such as $4x^2$, is called a **monomial**. You can use the Distributive Property to multiply by a monomial. You can use either left distribution, $a(b + c) = ab + ac$, or right distribution, $(b + c)a = ba + ca$. You have already used the Distributive Property to simplify expressions. The following example shows how to use left distribution:

$$2(3x - 5) = 2 \cdot 3x - 2 \cdot 5 \qquad \text{Use left distribution.}$$

$$= 6x - 10 \qquad \text{Simplify.}$$

EXAMPLES

Find each product using the Distributive Property when necessary.

a. $(-2x) \cdot (3x^2)$

[TIP]

Note that
$x \cdot x^2 = x^{1+2} = x^3$.

$$(-2x) \cdot (3x^2) = (-2 \cdot 3)(x \cdot x^2) \qquad \text{Regroup and then simplify.}$$

$$= -6x^3$$

b. $4x(x^2 + 2x - 5)$

$$4x(x^2 + 2x - 5) = (4x \cdot x^2) + (4x \cdot 2x) - (4x \cdot 5) \quad \text{Use the Distributive Property.}$$

$$= 4x^3 + 8x^2 - 20x \qquad \text{Simplify.}$$

c. $(4x - 1)(-5x)$

$$(4x - 1)(-5x) = 4x(-5x) - 1(-5x) \qquad \text{Use right distribution.}$$

$$= -20x^2 + 5x \qquad \text{Simplify.}$$

One way to check your work is to substitute any number for x into the original expression and the simplified expression to see if they have the same value. On the next page, you can see how to check example **c** using $x = 10$.

$$(4x - 1)(-5x) = (4 \cdot 10 - 1)(-5 \cdot 10) \qquad -20x^2 + 5x = -20 \cdot 10 + 5 \cdot 10$$

$$= 39(-50) \qquad\qquad\qquad = -2{,}000 + 50$$

$$= -1{,}950 \qquad\qquad\qquad = -1{,}950$$

Since both expressions yield $-1{,}950$, you simplified the original expression correctly.

Try It 1.1

Find each product using the Distributive Property where necessary.

a. $(-5x) \cdot (-4x^2)$

b. $2x(3x^2 - x + 5)$

c. $(-3x + 2)(-4x)$

1.2 Multiply Binomials

A two-term polynomial, such as $2x - 1$, is called a binomial. You can also use the Distributive Property to multiply binomials. Sometimes you may use the Distributive Property more than once when you are multiplying binomials.

EXAMPLES

Find each product using the Distributive Property.

a. $(x + 5)(x + 3)$

$$(x + 5)(x + 3) = x(x + 3) + 5(x + 3) \qquad \text{Use right distribution.}$$

$$= x \cdot x + x \cdot 3 + 5x + 5 \cdot 3 \qquad \text{Use left distribution.}$$

$$= x^2 + 3x + 5x + 15 \qquad \text{Combine like terms: } 3x + 5x = 8x$$

$$= x^2 + 8x + 15$$

You simplified to show that $(x + 5)(x + 3) = x^2 + 8x + 15$.

b. $(x + 3)(x - 2)$

$$(x + 3)(x - 2) = x(x - 2) + 3(x - 2) \qquad \text{Use right distribution.}$$

$$= (x \cdot x) - (x \cdot 2) + 3x - (3 \cdot 2) \quad \text{Use left distribution.}$$

$$= x^2 - 2x + 3x - 6 \qquad\qquad \text{Combine like terms:}$$

$$\qquad\qquad\qquad\qquad\qquad\qquad -2x + 3x = -1x$$

$$= x^2 - x - 6$$

You simplified to show that $(x + 3)(x - 2) = x^2 - x - 6$.

You may use the "box" method to check your answer or as an alternate way to multiply.

	x	-2
x	x^2	$-2x$
$+3$	$3x$	-6

The top row shows the product $x(x-2) = x^2 - 2x$.

The bottom row shows the product $3(x-2) = 3x - 6$.

The answer checks:

$$(x+3)(x-2) = x^2 - 2x + 3x - 6$$

$$= x^2 - x - 6$$

c. $(2x - 1)(3x - 2)$

$$(2x - 1)(3x - 2) = 2x(3x - 2) - 1(3x - 2)$$
Use right distribution.

$$= 2x \cdot 3x - 2x \cdot 2 - 1 \cdot 3x - 1(-2)$$
Use left distribution.

$$= 6x^2 - 4x - 3x + 2$$
Combine like terms: $-4x + 3x$.

$$= 6x^2 - 7x + 2$$

NOTE

Notice that:

$-1(-2) = -(-2) = 2$

You simplified to show that **$(2x - 1)(3x - 2) = 6x^2 - 7x + 2$.**

Try It 1.2

Simplify each expression using the Distributive Property.

a. $(x + 1)(x + 6)$

b. $(x - 2)(x + 7)$

c. $(4x - 2)(x - 5)$

1.3 Multiply Binomials Using Special Products

You can use the Distributive Property to derive two important special products: the trinomial square and the difference of two squares.

Consider the expression $(2x+3)^2$ when $a = 2x$ and $b = 3$. Below you can see how to simplify the expression with the known values and then with the variables only.

$$(2x+3)^2 = (2x+3)(2x+3) \qquad\qquad (a+b)^2 = (a+b)(a+b)$$

$$= 2x(2x+3) + 3(2x+3) \qquad\qquad = a(a+b) + b(a+b)$$

$$= 2x(2x) + 2x(3) + 3(2x) + 3(3) \qquad\qquad = aa + ab + ba + bb$$

$$= 4x^2 + 12x + 9 \qquad\qquad = a^2 + 2ab + b^2$$

The second equation shows that $(a+b)^2 = a^2 + 2ab + b^2$. The expression $a^2 + 2ab + b^2$ is called a **perfect-square trinomial**, which is the product of a binomial multiplied by itself. You can use the trinomial square to multiply more quickly. Note that the first and last terms in the product are the squares of the first and last terms of the original binomial. The middle term is twice the product of the terms in the binomial. Below you can see how the trinomial square is used to simplify the expression $(2x+3)^2$.

$$(2x+3)^2 = (2x)^2 + 2(2x)(3) + 3^2$$
$$= 4x^2 + 12x + 9$$

For the expression $(a-b)^2$, you can also use the formula $a^2 - 2ab + b^2$ as the trinomial square.

Now consider the expression $(2x+3)(2x-3)$ when $a = 2x$ and $b = 3$. Below you can see how to simplify the expression with the known values and then with the variables only.

$$(2x+3)(2x-3) = 2x(2x-3) + 3(2x-3) \qquad\qquad (a+b)(a-b) = a(a-b) + b(a-b)$$

$$= 2x(2x) - 2x(3) + 3(2x) - 3(3) \qquad\qquad = aa - ab + ba - bb$$

$$= 4x^2 - 6x + 6x - 9 \qquad\qquad = a^2 - ab + ab - b^2$$

$$= 4x^2 - 9 \qquad\qquad = a^2 - b^2$$

The second equation shows that $(a+b)(a-b) = a^2 - b^2$, which is the **difference of two squares.** You can use the difference of two squares formula to multiply quickly. The product is the first term squared minus the second term squared. Below you can see how the difference of two squares is used to simplify the expression $(2x+3)(2x-3)$.

$$(2x+3)(2x-3) = (2x)^2 - 3^2$$

$$= 4x^2 - 9$$

[TIP]

You can model a trinomial square graphically with an area model.

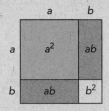

The area of the outer square is the product of its length and width:
$(a+b)(a+b) = (a+b)^2$

The area of the outer square is also the sum of the four smaller areas:
$a^2 + ab + ab + b^2 =$
$a^2 + 2ab + b^2$

This means that:
$(a+b)^2 = (a+b)(a+b)$
$= a^2 + 2ab + b^2$

Find each product using one of the special products: a trinomial square or a difference of two squares.

a. $(x-5)^2$

Use the trinomial square formula: $(a-b)^2 = a^2 - 2ab + b^2$ when $a = x$ and $b = 5$. You can see that the middle term is twice the product of a and $-b$.

$$(x-5)^2 = x^2 - 2(x)(5) + 5^2$$
$$= x^2 - 10x + 25$$

b. $(3x+4)^2$

Use the trinomial square formula: $(a+b)^2 = a^2 + 2ab + b^2$ when $a = 3x$ and $b = 4$.

$$(3x+4)^2 = (3x)^2 + 2(3x)(4) + 4^2$$
$$= 9x^2 + 24x + 16$$

c. $(x+4)(x-4)$

Use the difference of two squares formula $(a-b)^2 = a^2 - 2ab + b^2$ when $a = x$ and $b = 4$.

$$(x+4)(x-4) = x^2 - 4^2$$
$$= x^2 - 16$$

d. $(2x+1)(2x-1)$

Use the difference of two squares formula $(a-b)^2 = a^2 - 2ab + b^2$ when $a = 2x$ and $b = 1$.

$$(2x+1)(2x-1) = (2x)^2 - 1^2$$
$$= 4x^2 - 1$$

Try It 1.3

Find each product using one of the special products: a trinomial square or a difference of two squares.

a. $(x+6)^2$ 　　　　　　　　　　　　　　**b.** $(4x-3)^2$

c. $(x - 3)(x + 3)$

d. $(2x - 5)(2x + 5)$

CALCULATOR TIP

Checking Products

You can check the solution to the equality $(2x - 1)(3x - 2) = 6x^2 - 7x + 2$ by building a table on your graphing calculator.

Enter each expression to show it is equal to Y.

```
Plot1 Plot2 Plot3
\Y1■(2X-1)(3X-2)

\Y2■6X²-7X+2
\Y3=
\Y4=
\Y5=
\Y6=
```

Check to be sure that your table is set to start at 0. Then show the table, and verify that the expressions have the same values in the table. If the y-values agree, then the product $6x^2 - 7x + 2$ is correct.

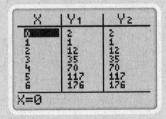

You can see that the y-values agree, so your product is correct.

In this lesson, you will use your knowledge about multiplication to factor polynomial expressions. Factoring involves "undoing" the multiplication by identifying the factors that were multiplied to create the given expression.

When you factor, it will be useful to recall the prime numbers. A **prime number** has exactly two factors: itself and 1. Listed below are the first 5 prime numbers.

$$\{2, 3, 5, 7, 11...\}$$

Sometimes you will write a number using prime factorization, which involves writing a number as a product of only prime numbers. Below is the prime factorization of 36. Note that 2 and 3 are both prime numbers.

$$36 = 4 \cdot 9$$
$$= 2 \cdot 2 \cdot 3 \cdot 3$$

2.1 Factor Using the GCF

In Lesson 3.1, you learned that:

$$2(3x - 5) = (2 \cdot 3x) - (2 \cdot 5) = 6x - 10$$

To factor the expression $6x - 10$, you first identify the greatest common factor (GCF) of $6x$ and 10. The **greatest common factor** of two or more numbers is the largest natural number that evenly divides them. Since 2 is the only common factor of $6x$ and 10, you can work backward to show the prime factorization of each term:

$$2 \cdot 3x = 6x \quad \text{and} \quad 2 \cdot 5 = 10$$

Then you can use a procedure called "factoring out" the 2. Substitute the alternate values (or factors) of $6x$ and 10, and then factor out the GCF.

$$6x - 10 = (2 \cdot 3x) - (2 \cdot 5)$$
$$= 2(3x - 5)$$

EXAMPLES

Find the GCF, and then factor each expression.

a. $12x^2 - 9x$

$$12x^2 = 2 \cdot 2 \cdot 3 \cdot x \cdot x$$
$$9x = 3 \cdot 3 \cdot x$$

Use prime factorization to find the GCF, which is $3x$.

$$12x^2 = 3x \cdot 4x$$
$$9x = 3x \cdot 3$$

Then write each term as a product of the GCF and another factor.

$$12x^2 - 9x = (3x \cdot 4x) - (3x \cdot 3)$$
$$= 3x(4x - 3)$$

Substitute the expressions from the previous step, and factor out $3x$.

$$3x(4x - 3) = 12x^2 - 9x$$

Check by multiplying. The solution should be the original expression.

The GCF is **$3x$**, and $12x^2 - 9x = \mathbf{3x(4x - 3)}$.

[TIP]

To find the other factor for $12x^2 = 2 \cdot 2 \cdot 3 \cdot x \cdot x$, you can identify the remaining factors after removing the GCF $3x$. The other factor is $4x$:

$$2 \cdot 2 \cdot x = 4x$$

b. $24x^3 + 8x^2 - 20x$

$$24x^3 = 2 \cdot 2 \cdot 2 \cdot 3 \cdot x \cdot x \cdot x$$
$$8x^2 = 2 \cdot 2 \cdot 2 \cdot x \cdot x$$
$$20x = 2 \cdot 2 \cdot 5 \cdot x$$

Use prime factorization to find the GCF, which is $4x$.

$$24x^3 = 4x \cdot 6x^2$$
$$8x^2 = 4x \cdot 2x$$
$$20x = 4x \cdot 5$$

Then write each term as a product of the GCF and another term.

$$24x^3 + 8x^2 - 20x = 4x \cdot 6x^2 + 4x \cdot 2x - 4x \cdot 5$$
$$= 4x(6x^2 + 2x - 5)$$

Substitute the expressions from the previous step, and factor out $4x$.

$$4x(6x^2 + 2x - 5) = 24x^3 + 8x^2 - 20x$$

Check by multiplying.

The GCF is **$4x$**, and $24x^2 + 8x^2 - 20x = \mathbf{4x(6x^2 + 2x - 5)}$.

c. $-6x^3 - 12x^2$

$$-6x^3 - 12x^2 = -1(6x^3 + 12x^2)$$
$$6x^3 = 2 \cdot 3 \cdot x \cdot x \cdot x$$
$$12x^2 = 2 \cdot 2 \cdot 3 \cdot x \cdot x$$

Since both terms are negative, factor out -1. Then find the GCF, which is $2 \cdot 3 \cdot x \cdot x = 6x^2$.

> **[HINT]**
>
> When both terms in an expression are negative, you should factor out -1 before finding the GCF.

$$6x^3 = 6x^2 \cdot x$$
$$12x^2 = 6x^2 \cdot 2$$

Write each term as a product of the GCF and another term.

$$-6x^3 - 12x^2 = -1(6x^3 + 12x^2)$$
$$= -1(6x^2 \cdot x + 6x^2 \cdot 2)$$
$$= -6x^2(x + 2)$$

Substitute the expressions from the previous step.
Remember to factor out -1, and then factor out $6x^2$.

$$-6x^2(x + 2) = -6x^3 - 12x^2$$

Check by multiplying.

The GCF is **$6x^2$**, and $-6x^3 - 12x^2 = \mathbf{-6x^2(x + 2)}$.

Try It 2.1 ···

Find each product using the GCF.

a. $15x^2 - 20x$

b. $6x^3 - 9x^2 - 3x$

c. $-16x^3 - 24x^2$

2.2 Factor Polynomials of the Form $x^2 + bx + c$

Degree two polynomials of the form $x^2 + bx + c$ are called quadratic polynomials. In the last lesson, you learned to multiply polynomials:

$$
\begin{aligned}
(x + 5)(x + 3) &= x(x + 3) + 5(x + 3) \\
&= x^2 + 3x + 5x + 15 \\
&= x^2 + 8x + 15
\end{aligned}
$$

Notice that the coefficients of x, 3 and 5, are also factors of 15 and that $3x + 5x = 8x$. To factor $x^2 + 8x + 15$, you must find the factors that have a product of 15 (3 and 5) and a sum of 8.

$x^2 + 8x + 15 = x^2 + 3x + 5x + 15$	Write 8x as 3x + 5x.
$= x(x + 3) + 5(x + 3)$	Factor x from the first two terms, and factor 5 from the last two terms.
$= x(\underline{x + 3}) + 5(\underline{x + 3})$	Note that (x + 3) is a common factor.
$= (x + 5)(x + 3)$	Factor (x + 3) from the remaining terms.

Note that in the last step you factor out to the right.

Factor each polynomial.

a. $x^2 + 4x + 3$

To factor $x^2 + 4x + 3$, find the factors with a product of 3 (1 and 3) and a sum of 4. Begin by writing $4x$ as $1x + 3x$.

$$\begin{aligned} x^2 + 4x + 3 &= x^2 + x + 3x + 3 \\ &= x(x + 1) + 3(x + 1) \\ &= x(x + 1) + 3(x + 1) \\ &= (x + 3)(x + 1) \end{aligned}$$

Factor x from the first two terms, and factor 3 from the last two terms.

Note that $(x + 1)$ is a common factor.

Factor $(x + 1)$ from the remaining terms.

This means $x^2 + 4x + 3 = (x + 3)(x + 1)$.

b. $x^2 + x - 6$

To factor $x^2 + x - 6$, find the factors that have a product of -6 (-2 and 3) and a sum of 1. Begin by writing x as $-2x + 3x$.

$$\begin{aligned} x^2 + x - 6 &= x^2 - 2x + 3x - 6 \\ &= x(x - 2) + 3(x - 2) \\ &= x(x - 2) + 3(x - 2) \\ &= (x + 3)(x - 2) \end{aligned}$$

Factor x from the first two terms, and factor 3 from the last two terms.

Note that $(x - 2)$ is a common factor.

Factor $(x - 2)$ from the remaining terms.

This means $x^2 + x - 6 = (x - 2)(x + 3)$.

c. $2x^2 - 12x + 72$

Begin by factoring out the GCF, 2:
$$2x^2 - 12x + 18 = 2(x^2 - 6x + 9)$$

Now factor the new expression, $x^2 - 6x + 9$. Find factors that have a product of 9 (-3 and -3) and a sum of -6. Begin by writing $-6x$ as $-3x - 3x$.

$$\begin{aligned} 2x^2 - 12x + 18 &= 2(x^2 - 6x + 9) \\ &= 2(x^2 - 3x - 3x + 9) \\ &= 2(x(x - 3) - 3(x - 3)) \\ &= 2(x(x - 3) - 3(x - 3)) \\ &= 2(x - 3)(x - 3) \end{aligned}$$

Factor out the GCF, 2.

Factor x from the first two terms,

and factor -3 from the last two terms.

Note that $(x - 3)$ is a common factor.

Factor $(x - 3)$ from the remaining terms.

This means $2x^2 - 12x + 18 = 2(x - 3)(x - 3)$.

d. $x^2 - 36$

Notice that this is a difference of two squares, which is a special product. Use $(a + b)(a - b) = a^2 - b^2$ to factor.

$$x^2 - 36 = (x + 6)(x - 6)$$

■ **Try It 2.2** ···

Factor each polynomial.

a. $x^2 + 2x + 1$

b. $x^2 - 2x - 8$

c. $3x^2 - 15x + 18$

d. $x^2 - 100$

2.3· Factor Polynomials of the Form $ax^2 + bx + c$

Polynomials of the form $ax^2 + bx + c$ are another type of quadratic polynomial. In the last lesson you learned to multiply polynomials:

$$(2x + 3)(x + 4) = 2x^2 + 8x + 3x + 12$$
$$= 2x^2 + 11x + 12$$

Notice that the coefficients of x, 8 and 3, are also factors of 24, which is the product of the leading coefficient, 2, and the constant term, 12. Note also that $8x + 3x = 11x$.

To factor $2x^2 + 11x + 12$, you must find the factors that have a product of $2 \cdot 12 = 24$ (8 and 3) and a sum of 11.

$2x^2 + 11x + 12 = 2x^2 + 8x + 3x + 12$	Begin by writing 11x as 8x + 3x.
$= 2x(x + 4) + 3(x + 4)$	Factor 2x from the first two terms, and factor 3 from the last two terms.
$= 2x(\underline{x + 4}) + 3(\underline{x + 4})$	Note that (x + 4) is a common factor.
$= (2x + 3)(x + 4)$	Factor (x + 4) from the remaining terms.

This is often called the "*ac*" method since you start with $ax^2 + bx + c$ by looking at factors of ac whose sum is b.

EXAMPLES

a. **Factor: $6x^2 + 13x + 5$**

To factor $6x^2 + 13x + 5$, find the factors that have a product of $6 \cdot 5 = 30$ and a sum of 13. Since $10 \cdot 3 = 30$ and $10 + 3 = 13$, you can begin by writing $13x$ as $10x + 3x$.

$6x^2 + 13x + 5 = 6x^2 + 10 + 3x + 5$	Factor 2x from the first two terms,
$= 2x(3x + 5) + 1(3x + 5)$	and factor 1 from the last two terms.
$= 2x(\underline{3x + 5}) + 1(\underline{3x + 5})$	Note that (3x + 5) is a common factor.
$= (2x + 1)(3x + 5)$	Factor (3x + 5) from the remaining terms.

This means $6x^2 + 13x + 5 = (2x + 1)(3x + 5)$.

You can make a list of the factors of 84. Then look for a difference of 8.

$1 \cdot 84 = 84$
$2 \cdot 42 = 84$
$3 \cdot 28 = 84$
$4 \cdot 21 = 84$
$6 \cdot 14 = 84$

Use a positive and a negative number to create a product of -84 and a sum of 8.

$14 + (-6) = 8$

b. Factor: $4x^2 + 8x - 21$

To factor $4x^2 + 8x - 21$, find the factors that have a product of $4(-21) = -84$ and a sum of 8. Since $14(-6) = -84$ and $14 + (-6) = 8$, you can begin by writing $8x$ as $14x - 6x$.

$$4x^2 + 8x - 21 = 4x^2 + 14x - 6x - 21$$

$$= 2x(2x + 7) - 3(2x + 7)$$

$$= 2x(2x + 7) - 3(2x + 7)$$

$$= (2x - 3)(2x + 7)$$

Factor $2x$ from the first two terms, and factor -3 from the last two terms.

Note that $(2x + 7)$ is a common factor.

Factor $(2x + 7)$ from the remaining terms.

This means **$4x^2 + 8x - 21 = (2x - 3)(2x + 7)$**.

c. Factor: $2x^2 + 3x + 6$

To factor $2x^2 + 3x + 6$, you must find the factors that have a product of $2 \cdot 6 = 12$ and a sum of 3. The factors of 12 are 1, 2, 3, 4, 6, and 12. No two factors whose product is 12 have a sum of 5.

This means the polynomial **$2x^2 + 3x + 6$ cannot be factored.**

This last example shows how the "*ac*" method is the best method for factoring. You may have learned a multiplication method called FOIL in another course. With the FOIL method, you guess and check to try to find the right factors. With the "*ac*" method, there is no guessing.

Try It 2.3

Factor each polynomial.

a. $2x^2 + 7x + 6$

b. $4x^2 - 10x - 3$

c. $4x^2 + 3x - 10$

CALCULATOR TIP

Check Factoring

As with multiplication, you can check factoring by building tables on your graphing calculator. Use the following method to check this equation:

$$4x^2 + 8x - 21 = (2x - 3)(2x + 7),$$

Enter each expression so that it is equal to Y.

```
Plot1 Plot2 Plot3
\Y1◼4X²+8X-21
\Y2◻(2X-3)(2X+7)

\Y3=
\Y4=
\Y5=
\Y6=
```

Be sure that the table is set to start at 0. Then verify that the expressions have the same values in the table.

```
 X   | Y1   | Y2
 0   | -21  | -21
 1   | -9   | -9
 2   | 11   | 11
 3   | 39   | 39
 4   | 75   | 75
 5   | 119  | 119
 6   | 171  | 171
Y2◻(2X-3)(2X+7)
```

Since the values are the same, you know that the solution is correct.

LESSON 3 Simplify Radicals

FOCUS   Compute square roots, simplify radicals, and solve right triangle problems

In this lesson, you will simplify **radical expressions**, which involve using the radical symbol, $\sqrt{\ }$. As a simple example, you know that $5^2 = 25$. This is read as "5 squared is 25." This means 5 is the **square root** of 25. The radical symbol $\sqrt{\ }$ represents the positive or principal square root of a number. You would read $\sqrt{25} = 5$ as "The principal square root of 25 is 5." The expression, 25, under the radical is called the **radicand**. Square roots are used to solve real world problems, including right triangle problems.

Every positive number has two square roots. The negative square root of 25 is -5 because $(-5)^2 = 25$, but the radical symbol only returns the positive root. Note that the negative square root is the opposite of the **principal square root**. The symbol $-\sqrt{\ }$ represents the negative square root.

The **perfect squares** are numbers that have a positive integer as a square root. They are:

$$1, 4, 9, 16, 25, \ldots$$

You can represent square numbers geometrically. The 3×3 square below has an area of 9 square units.

$$3^2 = 9$$

Table of Principal Square Roots

$\sqrt{1} = 1$	$\sqrt{36} = 6$	$\sqrt{121} = 11$
$\sqrt{4} = 2$	$\sqrt{49} = 7$	$\sqrt{144} = 12$
$\sqrt{9} = 3$	$\sqrt{64} = 8$	$\sqrt{169} = 13$
$\sqrt{16} = 4$	$\sqrt{81} = 9$	$\sqrt{196} = 14$
$\sqrt{25} = 5$	$\sqrt{100} = 10$	$\sqrt{225} = 15$

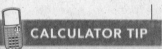

CALCULATOR TIP

You can approximate the square roots of numbers that are not square using a calculator.

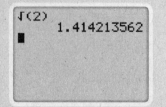

$\sqrt{(2)}$
     1.414213562

You can quickly determine that $\sqrt{1} = 1$, $\sqrt{4} = 2$, $\sqrt{9} = 3$, and so on. The principal square root of a whole number that is not a square number is called an **irrational number** and can only be approximated. For example, $\sqrt{2} \approx 1.414$.

3.1 Compute Square Roots

You can quickly find the square root of a square number. For example, to find the square root of 121, ask yourself, "What number times itself is 121?" You know that $\sqrt{121} = 11$ because $11^2 = 121$.

To find the approximate square root of a number that is not a square number, you can estimate the square root by determining which two square numbers your number lies between. For example, to estimate the principal square root of 30, note that 30 is between the square numbers 25 and 36: $25 < 30 < 36$. This means that the square root of 30 is between 5 and 6: $5 < \sqrt{30} < 6$. You can estimate that $\sqrt{30} \approx 5.5$.

[TIP]

You can estimate the square root of 110 by comparing it to the nearest two square numbers:

$$10^2 = 100$$
and
$$11^2 = 121$$

You can see that the square root of 110 will be between 10 and 11.

EXAMPLES

Compute or estimate each square root.

a. $\sqrt{144} = 12$

$\sqrt{144} = 12$ because $12^2 = 144$.

b. $\sqrt{400} = 20$

$\sqrt{400} = 20$ because $20^2 = 400$.

c. $\sqrt{110} \approx 10.5$

$\sqrt{110} \approx 10.5$ because $100 < 110 < 121$.

d. $\sqrt{75} \approx 8.7$

$\sqrt{75} \approx 8.7$ because $64 < 75 < 81$.

Try It 3.1

Compute or estimate each square root.

a. $\sqrt{169}$

b. $\sqrt{900}$

c. $\sqrt{57}$

d. $\sqrt{212}$

3.2 Simplify Radicals

You often have to simplify radicals in order to solve problems involving right triangles or quadratic equations. You need to know the important properties of radicals as shown by the examples below.

Common Error!

$\sqrt{4 + 9} \neq \sqrt{4} + \sqrt{9}$ because
$\sqrt{4 + 9} = \sqrt{13}$ and
$\sqrt{4} + \sqrt{9} = 2 + 3 = 5$.

$$\sqrt{4 \cdot 9} = \sqrt{4}\sqrt{9}$$
$$= 2 \cdot 3 \qquad \text{You can see this is correct because}$$
$$= 6 \qquad \sqrt{4 \cdot 9} = \sqrt{36} = 6$$

In general, for positive numbers a and b, $\sqrt{a \cdot b} = \sqrt{a} \cdot \sqrt{b}$.

Simplifying radicals sometimes involves factoring out the greatest square number.

$$\sqrt{32} = \sqrt{16 \cdot 2} \qquad \text{Factor 32.}$$
$$= \sqrt{16} \cdot \sqrt{2} \qquad \text{16 is the greatest square factor.}$$
$$= 4\sqrt{2} \qquad \sqrt{ab} = \sqrt{a} \cdot \sqrt{b}$$

Another property involves multiplying a radical by itself.

$$\sqrt{5} \cdot \sqrt{5} = \sqrt{25}$$
$$= 5$$

In general, for positive number a,
$\sqrt{a \cdot a} = \sqrt{a^2} = a.$

The last property is called **rationalizing the denominator**. Consider the expression $\frac{2}{\sqrt{3}}$.

To rationalize the denominator, you multiply the denominator by itself because $\sqrt{3} \cdot \sqrt{3} = 3$, which is a rational number.

$$\frac{2}{\sqrt{3}} = \frac{2}{\sqrt{3}} \cdot \frac{\sqrt{3}}{\sqrt{3}}$$

Multiply by $1 = \frac{\sqrt{3}}{\sqrt{3}}$.

$$= \frac{2\sqrt{3}}{3}$$

$\sqrt{3} \cdot \sqrt{3} = 3$

[TIP]

In the denominator, you multiply to simplify:

$$\sqrt{3} \cdot \sqrt{3} = \sqrt{9} = 3$$

EXAMPLES

Simplify each radical expression.

[HINT]

Factor out the greatest square number.

a. $\sqrt{50}$

$$\sqrt{50} = \sqrt{25 \cdot 2}$$

$$= \sqrt{25} \cdot \sqrt{2}$$

$$= 5\sqrt{2}$$

b. $\sqrt{1{,}200}$

$$\sqrt{1{,}200} = \sqrt{400 \cdot 3}$$

$$= \sqrt{400} \cdot \sqrt{3}$$

$$= 20\sqrt{3}$$

[HINT]

Rationalize the denominator.

c. $\frac{4}{\sqrt{2}}$

$$\frac{4}{\sqrt{2}} = \frac{4}{\sqrt{2}} \cdot \frac{\sqrt{2}}{\sqrt{2}}$$

Multiply by $1 = \frac{\sqrt{2}}{\sqrt{2}}$.

$$= \frac{4\sqrt{2}}{2}$$

$\sqrt{2} \cdot \sqrt{2} = 2$

$$= 2\sqrt{2}$$

Divide by the denominator: $\frac{4}{2} = 2$.

Try It 3.2

Simplify each radical expression.

a. $\sqrt{32}$

b. $\sqrt{125}$

c. $\frac{6}{\sqrt{5}}$

3.3 Solve Right Triangle Problems

In the previous sections, you learned some of the properties of radicals. In this section, you will apply the properties of radicals to solve right triangle problems.

The **Pythagorean Theorem** states that for a right triangle, the sum of the squares of sides a and b is equal to the square of the hypotenuse c, which is the side opposite the right angle.

Pythagorean Theorem:

$$a^2 + b^2 = c^2$$

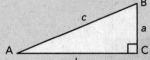

[RECALL]

A right angle forms a corner and measures 90°. A right triangle is a triangle with a right angle.

Note that when $a = 3$, $b = 4$, and $c = 5$, then $3^2 + 4^2 = 5^2$ because $9 + 16 = 25$.

The numbers 3-4-5 form a **Pythagorean Triple**, which is a group of three positive integers that satisfy the equation $a^2 + b^2 = c^2$.

Another property you can use involves multiplying a radical by itself.

$$\sqrt{5} \cdot \sqrt{5} = \sqrt{25}$$
$$= 5$$

In general, for positive numbers,
$\sqrt{a \cdot a} = \sqrt{a^2} = a.$

EXAMPLES

Use the Pythagorean Theorem to solve for the missing side in each right triangle.

a. If $a = 5$ and $c = 10$, determine b.

$$a^2 + b^2 = c^2$$
$$5^2 + b^2 = 10^2 \qquad \text{Substitute 5 for } a \text{ and 10 for } c.$$
$$25 + b^2 = 100 \qquad \text{Find the squares of 5 and 10.}$$
$$b^2 = 100 - 25 \qquad \text{Solve for } b^2.$$
$$b^2 = 75$$
$$b = \sqrt{75} \qquad \text{Solve for } b.$$
$$b = \sqrt{25 \cdot 3} \qquad \text{Factor out the greatest square number.}$$
$$\mathbf{b = 5\sqrt{3}} \qquad \text{Simplify.}$$

[TIP]

You can check the value of b by substituting into the original equation.

b. If $a = 9$ and $b = 12$, determine c.

$$a^2 + b^2 = c^2$$
$$9^2 + 12^2 = c^2 \qquad \text{Substitute 9 for } a \text{ and 12 for } b.$$
$$81 + 144 = c^2 \qquad \text{Find the squares of 9 and 12.}$$
$$225 = c^2 \qquad \text{Solve for } c^2.$$
$$\mathbf{15 = c} \qquad \text{Check the values: } 15^2 = 225.$$

NOTE

The numbers 9-12-15 form a Pythagorean Triple.

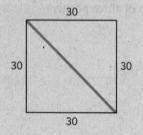

c. If $a = b$ and $c = 4$, determine a and b.

$$a^2 + b^2 = c^2$$
$$a^2 + a^2 = 4^2 \qquad \text{Substitute } a \text{ for } b \text{ and 4 for } c.$$
$$2a^2 = 16 \qquad \text{Simplify both sides.}$$
$$a^2 = 8 \qquad \text{Solve for } a^2.$$
$$a = \sqrt{8} \qquad \text{Solve for } a.$$
$$a = \sqrt{4 \cdot 2} \qquad \text{Factor out the greatest square number.}$$
$$\mathbf{a = 2\sqrt{2}} \qquad \text{Simplify.}$$
$$\mathbf{b = 2\sqrt{2}} \qquad \text{Substitute for } b \text{ since } a = b.$$

d. **A farmer plants an orchard so that the rows are 30 feet apart and the trees in the rows are 30 feet apart. To be sure that the orchard is square, the farmer can use the Pythagorean Theorem to check the diagonal length between two trees. What should the diagonal length be?**

$$a^2 + b^2 = c^2$$
$$30^2 + 30^2 = c^2 \qquad \text{Substitute 30 for } a \text{ and } b.$$
$$900 + 900 = c^2 \qquad \text{Find the square of 30.}$$
$$c^2 = 1,800 \qquad \text{Solve for } c^2.$$
$$c = \sqrt{1,800} \qquad \text{Solve for } c.$$
$$c = \sqrt{900 \cdot 2} \qquad \text{Factor out the greatest square number.}$$
$$c = 30\sqrt{2} \qquad \text{Simplify.}$$
$$\mathbf{c \approx 30 \cdot 1.414 \approx 42.4} \qquad \text{Use a calculator to estimate.}$$

The diagonal length between two trees should be about $42\frac{1}{2}$ feet.

Try It 3.3

Use the Pythagorean Theorem to solve for the missing side in each right triangle.

a. If $a = 4$ and $c = 12$, determine b.

b. If $a = 5$ and $b = 12$, determine c.

c. A 100-foot vertical pole is anchored to the ground by a guy wire that is 10 feet from the base of the pole. The pole forms a 90° angle with the ground. How long is the guy wire?

CALCULATOR TIP

Checking Solutions

You can check your solutions using your graphing calculator and substitution. Suppose you're told that $a = 5$ and $c = 10$ and you determine that $b = 5\sqrt{3}$. You can substitute all the values into the Pythagorean Theorem $(a^2 + b^2 = c^2)$ to check your solution.

```
5²+(5√(3))²
                    100
▪
```

Since $c^2 = 10^2 = 100$, your solution is correct: $b = 5\sqrt{3}$.

You can also find the value of b^2 by finding the square of $5\sqrt{3}$:

$$b^2 = (5\sqrt{3})^2$$
$$= (5\sqrt{3})(5\sqrt{3})$$
$$= 5 \cdot 5 \cdot \sqrt{3} \cdot \sqrt{3}$$
$$= 5^2 \cdot (\sqrt{3})^2$$
$$= 25 \cdot 3$$
$$= 75$$

Find each product.

1. $-3x(x^2 - 3x - 2)$

2. $(x + 2)(x + 4)$

3. $(4x - 2)(x - 5)$

4. $(x - 7)^2$

5. $(2x - 5)(2x + 5)$

Factor each polynomial.

6. $4x^3 - 12x^2 + 24x$

7. $x^2 - 5x - 6$

8. $2x^2 - 50$

9. $x^2 - 15x + 50$

10. $3x^2 - 4x - 4$

Compute or estimate.

11. $\sqrt{64}$

12. $\sqrt{150}$

13. Simplify $\dfrac{6}{\sqrt{3}}$.

Use the Pythagorean Theorem to solve problems 14 and 15. Simplify radicals as needed.

14. If $a = 4$, and $b = 12$, determine c.

15. If $b = 15$, and $c = 12$, determine a.

Check your answers in the *Solutions* section at the back of the book. If you missed more than one answer from problems 1 to 5, review lesson 1. If you missed more than one answer from problems 6 to 10, review lesson 2. If you missed more than one answer from problems 11 to 15, review lesson 3.

LESSON 4 Solve Quadratic Equations

Solve quadratic equations by factoring, by completing the square, and with the quadratic formula

In this lesson, you will use factoring to learn new techniques to solve **quadratic equations**. The **standard form of quadratic equations** is $ax^2 + bx + c = 0$.

One important property used to solve quadratic equations is the Zero Product Property. This property states that if the product of two numbers is zero, then the first or second number must be zero.

If $ab = 0$, then $a = 0$ or $b = 0$.

To understand the Zero Property, consider the factored quadratic equation:

$$(x + 5)(x - 3) = 0$$

To solve this quadratic equation, set each factor equal to zero.

$$(x + 5)(x - 3) = 0$$
$$x + 5 = 0 \text{ or } x - 3 = 0$$
$$x = -5 \text{ or } x = 3$$

The solutions $x = -5$ or $x = 3$ are the **zeros of the quadratic equation**. They are the x values that when substituted into the original equation yield zero.

DEFINITION
The zeros of a quadratic equation are also called the "roots."

$$(x + 5)(x - 3) = (-5 + 5)(x - 3) \qquad (x + 5)(x - 3) = (x + 5)(3 - 3)$$
$$= 0 \cdot (x - 3) = 0 \qquad\qquad = (x + 5) \cdot 0 = 0$$

4.1 Solve Quadratic Equations by Factoring

To solve quadratic equations, sometimes you can use special products or the "ac" method that you learned in Lesson 2. The "ac" method says that a quadratic will factor if you can find factors of ac with the equation $a + c = b$.

EXAMPLES

Use the factoring method and the Zero Product Property to solve each quadratic equation.

a. $x^2 + x - 6 = 0$

$$
\begin{array}{ll}
x^2 + x - 6 = 0 & \\
(x + 3)(x - 2) = 0 & \text{Factor the left side.} \\
x + 3 = 0 \text{ or } x - 2 = 0 & \text{Set each factor equal to zero.} \\
x = -3 \text{ or } x = 2 & \text{Solve both equations.}
\end{array}
$$

Check by substituting each solution into the original equation.

$$x^2 + x - 6 = 0 \qquad\qquad x^2 + x - 6 = 0$$
$$(-3)^2 + (-3) - 6 \overset{?}{=} 0 \qquad (2)^2 + (2) - 6 \overset{?}{=} 0$$
$$9 - 3 - 6 = 0 \qquad\qquad 4 + 2 - 6 = 0$$

[TIP]

Notice that this is a difference of two squares. You can use $a^2 - b^2 = (a + b)(a - b)$ to factor.

b. $4x^2 - 9 = 0$

$$4x^2 - 9 = 0$$
$$(2x + 3)(2x - 3) = 0 \qquad \text{Factor the left side.}$$
$$2x + 3 = 0 \text{ or } 2x - 3 = 0 \qquad \text{Set each factor equal to zero.}$$
$$x = -\frac{3}{2} \text{ or } x = \frac{3}{2} \qquad \text{Solve both equations.}$$

Check by substituting each solution into the original equation.

$$4x^2 - 9 = 0 \qquad\qquad 4x^2 - 9 = 0$$
$$4\left(-\frac{3}{2}\right)^2 - 9 \overset{?}{=} 0 \qquad 4\left(\frac{3}{2}\right)^2 - 9 \overset{?}{=} 0$$
$$4\left(\frac{9}{4}\right) - 9 \overset{?}{=} 0 \qquad 4\left(\frac{9}{4}\right) - 9 \overset{?}{=} 0$$
$$9 - 9 = 0 \qquad\qquad 9 - 9 = 0$$

[TIP]

Use the *ac* method. Find two factors of −30 whose sum is 13.

$$-2 \cdot 15 = -30$$
and
$$-2 + 15 = 13$$

c. $6x^2 + 13x - 5 = 0$

$$6x^2 + 13x - 5 = 0$$
$$6x^2 - 2x + 15x - 5 = 0 \qquad \text{Factor by grouping.}$$
$$2x(3x - 1) + 5(3x - 1) = 0$$
$$(2x + 5)(3x - 1) = 0$$
$$2x + 5 = 0 \text{ or } (3x - 1) = 0 \qquad \text{Set each factor equal to zero.}$$
$$x = -\frac{5}{2} \text{ or } x = \frac{1}{3} \qquad \text{Solve both equations.}$$

Check by substituting each solution into the original equation.

$$6x^2 + 13x - 5 = 0 \qquad\qquad 6x^2 + 13x - 5 = 0$$
$$6\left(-\frac{5}{2}\right)^2 + 13\left(-\frac{5}{2}\right) - 5 \overset{?}{=} 0 \qquad 6\left(\frac{1}{3}\right)^2 + 13\left(\frac{1}{3}\right) - 5 \overset{?}{=} 0$$
$$6\left(\frac{25}{4}\right) - \frac{65}{2} - 5 \overset{?}{=} 0 \qquad 6\left(\frac{1}{9}\right) + \frac{13}{3} - 5 \overset{?}{=} 0$$
$$\frac{75}{2} - \frac{65}{2} - \frac{10}{2} \overset{?}{=} 0 \qquad \frac{2}{3} + \frac{13}{3} - \frac{15}{3} \overset{?}{=} 0$$
$$\frac{10}{2} - \frac{10}{2} = 0 \qquad\qquad \frac{15}{3} - \frac{15}{3} = 0$$

Try It 4.1 ⋯⋯⋯⋯⋯⋯⋯⋯⋯⋯⋯⋯⋯⋯⋯⋯⋯⋯⋯⋯⋯⋯⋯⋯⋯⋯⋯⋯⋯⋯⋯⋯⋯⋯⋯⋯⋯

Use the factoring method and the Zero Product Property to solve each quadratic equation. Check your solutions using the substitution method.

a. $x^2 + 7x + 12 = 0$

b. $4x^2 + 20x + 25 = 0$

c. $4x^2 + 4x - 3 = 0$

4.2 Solve Quadratic Equations by Completing the Square

To solve quadratic equations, you can sometimes use a method called completing the square. To **complete the square**, you must construct a **perfect-square trinomial**. Examples of common trinomial squares are listed below.

$$(x + 1)^2 = x^2 + 2x + 1 \qquad (x - 1)^2 = x^2 - 2x + 1$$
$$(x + 2)^2 = x^2 + 4x + 4 \qquad (x - 2)^2 = x^2 - 4x + 4$$
$$(x + 3)^2 = x^2 + 6x + 9 \qquad (x - 3)^2 = x^2 - 6x + 9$$
$$(x + 4)^2 = x^2 + 8x + 16 \qquad (x - 4)^2 = x^2 - 8x + 16$$
$$(x + 5)^2 = x^2 + 10x + 25 \qquad (x - 5)^2 = x^2 - 10x + 25$$

Notice that in $x^2 + 10x + 25$, 25 is half the coefficient of x squared:

$$\left(\frac{10}{2}\right)^2 = 5^2 = 25$$

Taking half of that coefficient and squaring it is the key to completing the square for quadratic equations.

Before you can complete the square, it is important to know how to solve simple quadratic equations like $x^2 = 4$. There are two solutions, 2 or -2, because $2^2 = 4$ and $(-2)^2 = 4$. The solution can also be written as ± 2, "plus or minus two". The general method is shown below.

$$x^2 = 4$$
$$x = \pm\sqrt{4}$$
$$x = \pm 2$$

Sometimes the solutions are irrational numbers.

$$x^2 = 18$$
$$x = \pm\sqrt{18}$$
$$x = \pm\sqrt{9 \cdot 2}$$
$$x = \pm 3\sqrt{2}$$

To complete the square, you must create a trinomial square using the first and second terms of the quadratic equation. For example, if the first two terms are $x^2 - 6x$, you would complete the square by dividing the coefficient of x by 2:

$$\left(\frac{-6}{2}\right)^2 = (-3)^2 = 9$$

Then add 9 to the first two terms and factor:

$$x^2 - 6x + 9 = (x - 3)^2$$

EXAMPLES

Complete the square to solve each quadratic equation.

a. $x^2 + 6x - 1 = 0$

$x^2 + 6x - 1 = 0$	
$x^2 + 6x = 1$	Add 1 to both sides.
$x^2 + 6x + 9 = 1 + 9$	Add $\left(\frac{6}{2}\right)^2 = 3^2 = 9$ to both sides.
$(x + 3)^2 = 10$	Take the square root of both sides.
$x + 3 = \pm\sqrt{10}$	Use $\pm$ for $\sqrt{10}$.
$x = -3 \pm \sqrt{10}$	Solve for x.

Check by substituting each solution into the original equation.

$$(-3 + \sqrt{10})^2 + 6(-3 + \sqrt{10}) - 1 \overset{?}{=} 0$$
$$9 - 6\sqrt{10} + 10 - 18 + 6\sqrt{10} - 1 \overset{?}{=} 0$$
$$19 - 19 = 0$$

$$(-3 - \sqrt{10})^2 + 6(-3 - \sqrt{10}) - 1 \overset{?}{=} 0$$
$$9 + 6\sqrt{10} + 10 - 18 - 6\sqrt{10} - 1 \overset{?}{=} 0$$
$$19 - 19 = 0$$

b. $x^2 + 3x + 2 = 0$

$$x^2 + 3x + 2 = 0$$

$$x^2 + 3x = -2 \qquad \text{Subtract 2 from both sides.}$$

$$x^2 + 3x + \frac{9}{4} = -2 + \frac{9}{4} \qquad \text{Add } \left(\frac{3}{2}\right)^2 = \frac{9}{4} \text{ to both sides.}$$

$$\left(x + \frac{3}{2}\right)^2 = -\frac{8}{4} + \frac{9}{4} \qquad \text{Factor.}$$

$$x + \frac{3}{2} = \pm\sqrt{\frac{1}{4}}$$

$$x = -\frac{3}{2} \pm \frac{1}{2} \qquad \text{Solve both equations for } x.$$

$$x = -\frac{3}{2} + \frac{1}{2} = -\frac{2}{2} = -1$$

$$x = -\frac{3}{2} - \frac{1}{2} = -\frac{4}{2} = -2$$

Check by substituting each solution into the original equation.

$x^2 + 3x + 2 \overset{?}{=} 0$	$x^2 + 3x + 2 \overset{?}{=} 0$
$(-1)^2 + 3(-1) + 2 \overset{?}{=} 0$	$(-2)^2 + 3(-2) + 2 \overset{?}{=} 0$
$1 - 3 + 2 = 0$	$4 - 6 + 2 = 0$

c. $2x^2 - 16x - 7 = 0$

$$2x^2 - 16x - 7 = 0$$

$$2x^2 - 16x = 7 \qquad \text{Add 7 to both sides.}$$

$$2(x^2 - 8x) = 7 \qquad \text{Factor out 2.}$$

$$x^2 - 8x = \frac{7}{2} \qquad \text{Divide both sides by 2.}$$

$$x^2 - 8x + 16 = \frac{7}{2} + 16 \qquad \text{Add } \left(\frac{8}{2}\right)^2 = 4^2 = 16 \text{ to both sides.}$$

$$(x - 4)^2 = \frac{39}{2} \qquad \text{Factor.}$$

$$x - 4 = \pm\sqrt{\frac{39}{2}} \qquad \text{Solve for } x.$$

$$x = 4 \pm \frac{\sqrt{78}}{2}$$

Check by substituting each solution into the original equation.

$2x^2 - 16x - 7 = 0$	$2x^2 - 16x - 7 = 0$
$2\left(4 + \frac{\sqrt{78}}{2}\right)^2 - 16\left(4 + \frac{\sqrt{78}}{2}\right) - 7 \overset{?}{=} 0$	$2\left(4 - \frac{\sqrt{78}}{2}\right)^2 - 16\left(4 - \frac{\sqrt{78}}{2}\right) - 7 \overset{?}{=} 0$
$2\left(16 + 4\sqrt{78} + \frac{78}{4}\right) - 64 - 8\sqrt{78} - 7 \overset{?}{=} 0$	$2\left(16 - 4\sqrt{78} + \frac{78}{4}\right) - 64 + 8\sqrt{78} - 7 \overset{?}{=} 0$
$32 + 8\sqrt{78} + 39 - 71 - 8\sqrt{78} \overset{?}{=} 0$	$32 - 8\sqrt{78} + 39 - 71 + 8\sqrt{78} \overset{?}{=} 0$
$71 - 71 = 0$	$71 - 71 = 0$

Try It 4.2

Complete the square to solve each quadratic equation.

a. $x^2 + 10x - 3 = 0$

b. $x^2 + 5x + 2 = 0$

c. $3x^2 + 18x - 4 = 0$

4.3 Solve Quadratic Equations Using the Quadratic Formula

Look at the steps in Example **c** from the last section. You can use those same steps to derive the quadratic formula for solving the general quadratic $ax^2 + bx + c = 0$.

$$ax^2 + bx + c = 0$$

$$ax^2 + bx = -c \qquad \text{Subtract } c \text{ from both sides.}$$

$$a\left(x^2 + \frac{b}{a}x\right) = -c \qquad \text{Factor out } a.$$

$$x^2 + \frac{b}{a}x = \frac{-c}{a} \qquad \text{Divide both sides by } a.$$

$$x^2 + \frac{b}{a}x + \left(\frac{b}{2a}\right)^2 = \frac{-c}{a} + \frac{b^2}{4a^2} \qquad \text{Add } \left(\frac{b}{2a}\right)^2 = \frac{b^2}{4a^2} \text{ to both sides.}$$

$$\left(x + \frac{b}{2a}\right)^2 = \frac{b^2 - 4ac}{4a^2} \qquad \text{Factor.}$$

$$x + \frac{b}{2a} = \pm\sqrt{\frac{b^2 - 4ac}{4a^2}} \qquad \text{Solve for } x.$$

$$x = -\frac{b}{2a} \pm \frac{\sqrt{b^2 - 4ac}}{2a}$$

$$x = \frac{-b \pm \sqrt{b^2 - 4ac}}{2a} \qquad \text{Simplify.}$$

[TIP]

To convert $\frac{-c}{a}$ to the same denominator as $\frac{b^2}{4a^2}$, multiply by $1 = \frac{4a}{4a}$.

$$\frac{-c}{a} \cdot \frac{4a}{4a} = \frac{-4ac}{4a^2}$$

Then you can add with like denominators.

$$\frac{-4ac}{4a^2} + \frac{b^2}{4a^2} = \frac{b^2 - 4ac}{4a^2}$$

Compare these steps to those used to solve Example **c** in the last section. You can see that you can solve any quadratic equation in form $ax^2 + bx + c = 0$ using the formula:

$$x = \frac{-b \pm \sqrt{b^2 - 4ac}}{2a}$$

EXAMPLES

Use the quadratic formula to solve each quadratic equation.

a. $x^2 + 6x - 1 = 0$

$$x = \frac{-b \pm \sqrt{b^2 - 4ac}}{2a} \qquad \text{Write the formula.}$$

$$x = \frac{-6 \pm \sqrt{(6)^2 - 4(1)(-1)}}{2(1)} \qquad \text{Substitute } a = 1, b = 6, c = -1$$

$$x = \frac{-6 \pm \sqrt{36 + 4}}{2} \qquad \text{Simplify the radical.}$$

$$x = \frac{-6 \pm 2\sqrt{10}}{2} \qquad \text{Divide by 2.}$$

$$x = -3 \pm \sqrt{10}$$

NOTE

Note that this example is the same as Example a in section 4.2 so that you can compare each method.

[HINT]

To simplify $\sqrt{40}$, factor out the greatest square factor.

$$\sqrt{40} = \sqrt{4} \cdot \sqrt{10}$$
$$= 2\sqrt{10}$$

Check by substituting each solution into the original equation.

$(-3 + \sqrt{10})^2 + 6(-3 + \sqrt{10}) - 1 \overset{?}{=} 0$	$(-3 - \sqrt{10})^2 + 6(-3 - \sqrt{10}) - 1 \overset{?}{=} 0$
$9 - 6\sqrt{10} + 10 - 18 + 6\sqrt{10} - 1 \overset{?}{=} 0$	$9 + 6\sqrt{10} + 10 - 18 - 6\sqrt{10} - 1 \overset{?}{=} 0$
$19 - 19 = 0$	$19 - 19 = 0$

b. $4x^2 - 16x - 9 = 0$

$$x = \frac{-b \pm \sqrt{b^2 - 4ac}}{2a}$$ Write the formula.

$$x = \frac{-(-16) \pm \sqrt{(-16)^2 - 4(4)(-9)}}{2(4)}$$ Substitute $a = 4$, $b = -16$, $c = -9$.

$$x = \frac{16 \pm \sqrt{256 + 144}}{8}$$ Simplify.

$$x = \frac{16 \pm \sqrt{400}}{8}$$

$$x = \frac{16 \pm 20}{8}$$ Divide by 4.

$$x = \frac{4 \pm 5}{2}$$

$$x = \frac{4 + 5}{2} = \frac{9}{2} \text{ or } x = \frac{4 - 5}{2} = -\frac{1}{2}$$

[RECALL]

Remember that $\sqrt{400} = 20$.

[HINT]

If you get a rational solution, you know that you could have factored using the *ac* method.

Check by substituting each solution into the original equation.

$4x^2 - 16x - 9 = 0$	$4x^2 - 16x - 9 = 0$
$4\left(\frac{9}{2}\right)^2 - 16\left(\frac{9}{2}\right) - 9 \overset{?}{=} 0$	$4\left(-\frac{1}{2}\right)^2 - 16\left(-\frac{1}{2}\right) - 9 \overset{?}{=} 0$
$4\left(\frac{81}{4}\right) - 72 - 9 \overset{?}{=} 0$	$4\left(\frac{1}{4}\right) + 8 - 9 \overset{?}{=} 0$
$81 - 72 - 9 = 0$	$1 + 8 - 9 = 0$

Try It 4.3

Use the quadratic formula to solve each quadratic equation.

a. $x^2 - 7x - 1 = 0$

b. $4x^2 - 8x - 21 = 0$

CALCULATOR TIP

Checking Solutions to Quadratic Equations

To check your quadratic equation solutions, you can use the STO key to store a solution in x. Type in the quadratic equation to see if the result of the substitution is zero. Consider the quadratic equation:

$$x^2 + 6x - 1 = 0$$

The first solution is $x = -3 + \sqrt{10}$. Begin by storing $-3 + \sqrt{10}$ in x using the STO key.

```
-3+√(10)→X
        .1622776602
```

Now type in the quadratic in x to see that the substitution results in a zero.

```
-3+√(10)→X
        .1622776602
X²+6X-1
              0
■
```

Now you can check the second solution, which is $-3 - \sqrt{10}$.

```
-3-√(10)→X
        -6.16227766
X²+6X-1
          1ᴇ-12
```

Notice the rounding error. This number is $10^{-12} = \frac{1}{10^{12}}$ which is very small and very close to zero. This indicates that the solution is correct.

LESSON 5 Graph Quadratic Functions

In this lesson, you will graph quadratic functions. **Quadratic functions** are of the form $y = f(x) = ax^2 + bx + c$, which is called the **standard form of quadratic functions**. The simplest quadratic function is the **parent function** $y = f(x) = x^2$. The table and graph for this function are shown below.

x	$y = f(x) = x^2$	(x, y)
-3	$f(-3) = (-3)^2 = 9$	$(-3, 9)$
-2	$f(-2) = (-2)^2 = 4$	$(-2, 4)$
-1	$f(-1) = (-1)^2 = 1$	$(-1, 1)$
0	$f(0) = (0)^2 = 0$	$(0, 0)$
1	$f(1) = (1)^2 = 1$	$(1, 1)$
2	$f(2) = (2)^2 = 4$	$(2, 4)$
3	$f(3) = (3)^2 = 9$	$(3, 9)$

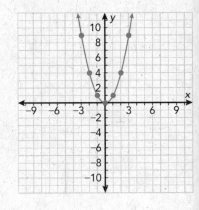

The graph of a quadratic function is called a **parabola**. For the parabola shown above, the vertical line $x = 0$ is called the **axis of symmetry**. This means you can fold the parabola in half across the y-axis or along the line $x = 0$, and the points will match up. On this parabola, the point $(0, 0)$ is called the **vertex of the parabola**.

DEFINITION
The **vertex** is the lowest or highest point on the parabola, which gives the minimum or maximum y-value of the function.

Notice also that $x = 0$ is a zero of the quadratic function. A **zero of a function** is an x-value that yields a y-value equal to zero. To find zeros of quadratic functions, set the function rule equal to zero, and then solve for x.

$$x^2 = 0$$
$$x = \pm\sqrt{0}$$
$$x = 0$$

DEFINITION
The x-intercept and y-intercept are the points where a given line crosses the x-axis and y-axis.

5.1 Graph Quadratic Functions

You can graph quadratic functions by locating the zeros (x-intercepts), the y-intercept, and the vertex. Notice that the parabola above is a zero at $x = 0$ and the y-intercept is also zero.

◼ Explore It

Consider the function $y = f(x) = x^2 + 2x - 3$.

1. Complete the table on page 184 by evaluating the function for each x-value, and then graph the ordered pairs. Connect the points to form a parabola.

x	$y = f(x) = x^2 + 2x - 3$	(x, y)
−4	$f(-4) = (-4)^2 + 2(-4) - 3 = 5$	
−3	$f(-3) = (-3)^2 + 2(-3) - 3 = $ ___	
−2		
−1		
0		
1		
2		

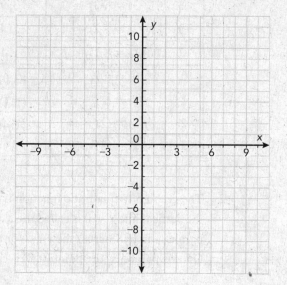

2. What is the vertex? What is the axis of symmetry?

3. What x-values are the zeros?

4. Solve the quadratic equation $x^2 + 2x - 3 = 0$, and then compare with the zeros you found on the graph.

5. Which x-value determines the y-intercept?

6. Compute the value $x = -\dfrac{b}{2a}$. How will that value help you determine the vertex?

When you graph the function $y = f(x) = x^2 + 2x - 3$, you discover some interesting things about quadratic functions. The zeros -3 and 1 are determined by solving the quadratic equation $x^2 + 2x - 3 = 0$. The y-intercept is $y = f(0) = 0^2 + 2 \cdot 0 - 3 = -3$. The vertex x-value can be found by computing $x = -\dfrac{b}{2a} = \dfrac{2}{2(1)} = -1$. The x-value of the vertex is also the axis of symmetry, $x = -1$.

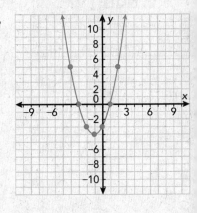

Use the axis of symmetry to find the y-value of the vertex:

$$f(-1) = (-1)^2 + 2(-1) - 3 = -4$$

Notice also that the line of the vertex x-value ($x = -1$) is halfway between the zeros -3 and 1. This makes sense if you rewrite the quadratic formula $x = \dfrac{-b \pm \sqrt{b^2 - 4ac}}{2a}$ as $x = \dfrac{-b}{2a} \pm \dfrac{\sqrt{b^2 - 4ac}}{2a}$, where the zeros are $\pm \dfrac{\sqrt{b^2 - 4ac}}{2a}$ from $\dfrac{-b}{2a}$.

EXAMPLES

For each function, determine all intercepts, the vertex, and the axis of symmetry. Then sketch the parabola.

a. $f(x) = x^2 + 4x - 5$

The y-intercept is:

$$f(0) = 0^2 + 4 \cdot 0 - 5 = \mathbf{-5}$$

To find the zeros, solve for the x-intercepts:

$$x^2 + 4x - 5 = 0$$
$$(x + 5)(x - 1) = 0$$
$$x = \mathbf{-5} \text{ or } x = \mathbf{1}$$

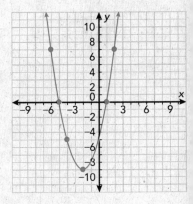

To find the vertex x-value, compute:

$$x = -\frac{4}{2(1)} = -2$$

To find the vertex y-value, evaluate:

$$f(-2) = (-2)^2 + 4 \cdot (-2) - 5 = 4 - 8 - 5 = -9$$

The vertex is $(\mathbf{-2, -9})$, and the line of symmetry is $x = \mathbf{-2}$.

[HINT]

$-b = -4$
and
$2a = 2(1) = 2$

b. $f(x) = x^2 - 6x + 9$

The y-intercept is:

$$f(0) = 0^2 - 6 \cdot 0 + 9 = 9$$

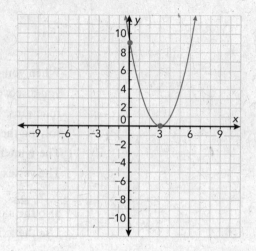

To find the zeros, solve for the x-intercepts:

$$x^2 - 6x + 9 = 0$$

$$(x - 3)^2 = 0$$

$$x = 3$$

To find the vertex x-value, compute:

$$x = -\frac{(-6)}{2(1)} = \frac{6}{2} = 3$$

To find the vertex y-value, evaluate:

$$f(3) = 3^2 - 6 \cdot 3 + 9 = 0$$

The vertex is $(3, 0)$, and the line of symmetry is $x = 3$.

c. $f(x) = 2x^2 + 5x + 1$

The y-intercept is:

$$f(0) = 2(0)^2 + 5(0) + 1 = 1$$

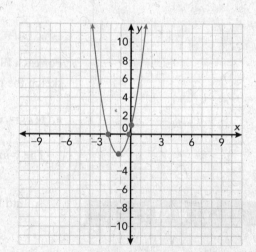

To find the zeros, use the quadratic equation:

$$x = \frac{-b \pm \sqrt{b^2 - 4ac}}{2a}$$

$$x = \frac{-5 \pm \sqrt{(5)^2 - 4(2)(1)}}{2(2)}$$

$$x = \frac{-5 \pm \sqrt{17}}{4}$$

Use a calculator to estimate the zeros:

$$x = \frac{-5 \pm \sqrt{17}}{4} \approx -0.219 \text{ or } x = \frac{-5 - \sqrt{17}}{4} \approx -2.28$$

To find the vertex x-value, compute:

$$x = -\frac{5}{2(2)} = -\frac{5}{4} = -1.25$$

To find the vertex y-value, evaluate:

$$f\left(-\frac{5}{4}\right) = 2\left(-\frac{5}{4}\right)^2 + 5\left(-\frac{5}{4}\right) + 1 = -2.125$$

The vertex is $(-1.25, -2.125)$, and the line of symmetry is $x = -1.25$.

> **NOTE**
>
> *A trinomial square will have only one zero.*

> **CALCULATOR TIP**
>
> You can use a calculator to estimate and to find the y-value of the vertex.

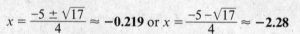

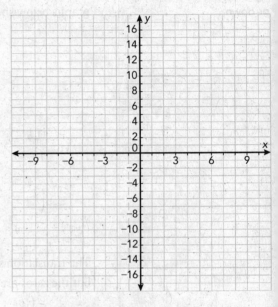

Try It 5.1

For each function, determine all intercepts, the vertex, and the axis of symmetry. Then sketch the parabola.

a. $f(x) = 2x^2 + 3x + 1$

b. $f(x) = x^2 - 9$

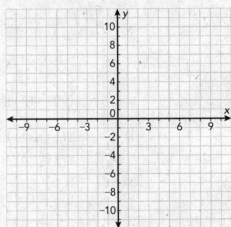

c. $f(x) = x^2 - 3x - 1$

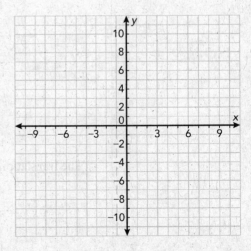

5.2 Transform Quadratic Functions

Transformations involve changing the parent function $y = f(x) = x^2$ into a quadratic in the form $y = f(x) = a(x - h)^2 + k$. A **translation** of a parabola is sometimes called a *slide* because it is a horizontal or vertical shift (or both) of a parabola on a graph. The graphs below show the parent function $y = x^2$ with the translation given by $y = x^2 - 2$.

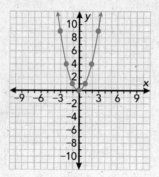
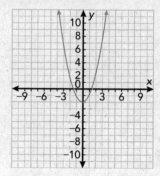

The translation shifts the graph vertically –2 units. The axis of symmetry is still $x = 0$ but the zeros are now:

$$x^2 - 2 = 0$$

$$x^2 = 2$$

$$x = \pm\sqrt{2}$$

Note also that the translated vertex is $(0, -2)$.

The graphs below show the parent function $y = x^2$ along with the translation given by $y = (x - 3)^2$ from Exercise 2 in the last section.

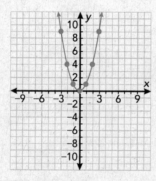
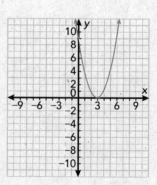

The translation shifts the parabola horizontally 3 units. The axis of symmetry is $x = 3$.

When you apply both the vertical and horizontal shifts, you have the translated function $y = (x - 3)^2 - 2$.

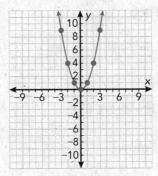
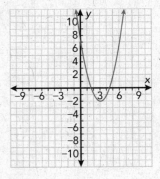

The translation shifts the parabola vertically −2 units and horizontally 3 units. The axis of symmetry is $x = 3$, the vertex is $(3, -2)$ but the zeros are now:

$$(x - 3)^2 - 2 = 0$$

$$(x - 3)^2 = 2$$

$$x = 3 \pm \sqrt{2}$$

In general, for the function $y = f(x) = a(x - h)^2 + k$, the parent function is shifted horizontally h units and vertically k units. The vertex is (h, k). The line $x = h$ is the line of symmetry. The function $y = f(x) = a(x - h)^2 + k$ is sometimes called the **vertex form of the quadratic function**.

Another type of transformation is called a **reflection**, or mirror image. The graphs below show the parent function $y = x^2$ along with the transformation given by $y = -x^2$. On the graphs below you can see that the point $(\mathbf{2, 4})$ is reflected to the point $(\mathbf{2, -4})$.

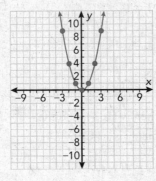
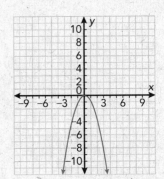

EXAMPLES

For each transformed function, determine all intercepts, the vertex, and the axis of symmetry. Then sketch the parabola. Then write the function in the form $y = f(x) = a(x - h)^2 + k$.

a. $f(x) = (x + 4)^2 - 9$

The y-intercept is:

$$f(0) = (0 - 4)^2 - 9 = 7$$

To find the zeros, solve:
$$(x + 4)^2 - 9 = 0$$
$$(x + 4)^2 = 9$$
$$x = -4 \pm 3$$
$$x = -1 \text{ or } x = -7$$

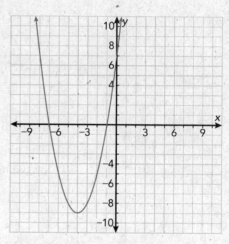

From the original function, you already know the vertex y-value, or k, is -9. To determine h, think $x + 4 = x - (-4)$, so the vertex x-value, or h, is -4. The vertex then is $(-4, -9)$, and the line of symmetry is $x = -4$.

To write in the form $y = f(x) = ax^2 + bx + c$, expand the function:
$$f(x) = (x + 4)^2 - 9$$
$$= x^2 + 8x + 16 - 9$$
$$= x^2 + 8x + 7$$

b. $f(x) = -(x - 1)^2 + 3$

The y-intercept is:

$$f(0) = -(0 - 1)^2 + 3 = 2$$

To find the zeros, solve:
$$-(x - 1)^2 + 3 = 0$$
$$-(x - 1)^2 = -3$$
$$(x - 1)^2 = 3$$
$$x = 1 \pm \sqrt{3}$$
$$x \approx 2.732 \text{ or } x \approx -0.732$$

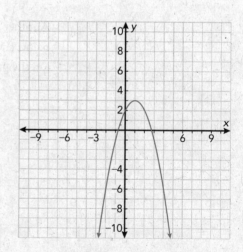

The vertex then is $(1, 3)$, and the line of symmetry is $x = 1$.

To write in the form $y = f(x)\, ax^2 + bx + c$, expand the function:
$$f(x) = -(x - 1)^2 + 3$$
$$= -(x^2 - 2x + 1) + 3$$
$$= -x^2 + 2x + 2$$

> **NOTE**
>
> *The y-intercept, 7, is also the constant term.*

> **NOTE**
>
> *The y-intercept, 2, is also the constant term.*

Try It 5.2

For each transformed function, determine all intercepts, the vertex, and the axis of symmetry. Then sketch each parabola. Then write the function in the form $y = f(x) = a(x - h)^2 + k$.

a. $f(x) = -(x - 3)^2 + 16$

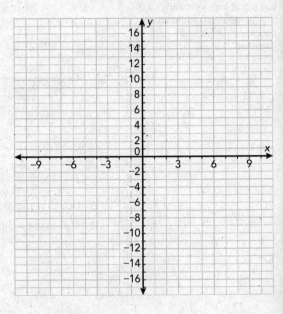

b. $f(x) = (x - 3)^2 - 2$

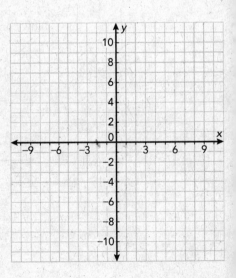

5.3 Solve Quadratic Equations with Complex Zeros

Sometimes parabolas do not have points on the x-axis. Consider the translation of the parent function $y = x^2$ given by $y = x^2 + 1$.

[TIP]

You can visulaize transformations better if you use a graphics calculator by graphing the parent function and the transformed function together.

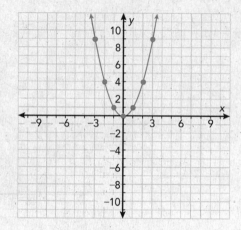
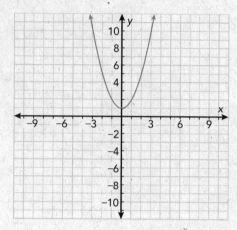

Notice that the graph does not intercept the x-axis. When you solve for zeros, you get the following solutions:

$$x^2 + 1 = 0$$
$$x^2 = -1$$
$$x = \pm\sqrt{-1}$$

There is no real number that squares to yield −1, so $\sqrt{-1}$ is represented as i and is called an **imaginary number**.

Now consider the function $y = -(x - 3)^2 - 2$, and compare to the parent function.

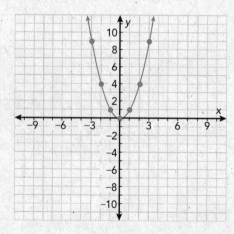
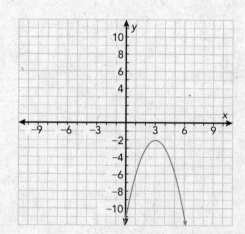

After a reflection across the x-axis, the translation shifts the graph vertically -2 units and horizontally 3 units. The axis of symmetry is now $x = 3$, the vertex is $(3, -2)$, but the zeros are not **real numbers.** They are now:

$$-(x - 3)^2 - 2 = 0$$
$$(x - 3)^2 = -2$$
$$x = 3 \pm \sqrt{-2}$$
$$x = 3 \pm \sqrt{2}\sqrt{-1}$$
$$x = 3 \pm \sqrt{2} \cdot i$$

The zero $x = 3 \pm \sqrt{2} \cdot i$ is called a **complex number**. It consists of a real number, 3, plus an imaginary number, $\sqrt{2} \cdot i$.

In general, complex numbers are of the form $a \pm bi$. The square of an imaginary number is the original negative number. This means $i^2 = \left(\sqrt{-1}\right)^2 = -1$.

EXAMPLES

For each function determine the complex zeros, and then check by substitution.

a. $f(x) = (x + 4)^2 + 9$

$(x + 4)^2 + 9 = 0$	Check your answer with the first or
$(x + 4)^2 = -9$	second solution.
$x + 4 = \pm\sqrt{-9}$	$(x + 4)^2 + 9 \overset{?}{=} 0$
$x = -4 \pm \sqrt{9}\sqrt{-1}$	$(-4 + 3i + 4)^2 + 9 \overset{?}{=} 0$
$\boldsymbol{x = -4 \pm 3i}$	$(3i)^2 + 9 \overset{?}{=} 0$
	$9(-1) + 9 = 0$

b. Use the quadratic formula to solve: $f(x) = x^2 - 2x + 4$

$$x = \frac{-b \pm \sqrt{b^2 - 4ac}}{2a}$$

$$x = \frac{-(-2) \pm \sqrt{(-2)^2 - 4(1)(4)}}{2(1)}$$

$$x = \frac{2 \pm \sqrt{-12}}{2}$$

$$x = \frac{2 \pm 2\sqrt{-3}}{2}$$

$$\boldsymbol{x = 1 \pm \sqrt{3} \cdot i}$$

To check your solution, use what you know about binomial multiplication to square the complex numbers.

$$(1 + i\sqrt{3})^2 - 2(1 + i\sqrt{3}) + 4 \overset{?}{=} 0$$

$$(1 + i\sqrt{3})(1 + i\sqrt{3}) - 2(1 + i\sqrt{3}) + 4 \overset{?}{=} 0$$

$$1 + 2\sqrt{3}i - 3 - 2 - 2\sqrt{3}i + 4 \overset{?}{=} 0$$

$$-4 + 4 = 0$$

[**RECALL**]

Remember that the square of an imaginary number is negative.

$$(3i)^2 = 3^2 \cdot i^2$$
$$= 9\,(-1)$$
$$= -9$$

NOTE

When you check the first solution, notice that

$$\left(1 + \sqrt{3i}\right)^2$$
$$= \left(1 + \sqrt{3i}\right)\left(1 + \sqrt{3i}\right)$$
$$= 1\left(1 + \sqrt{3i}\right)$$
$$\quad + \sqrt{3i}\left(1 + \sqrt{3i}\right)$$
$$= 1 + \sqrt{3i} + \sqrt{3i} + \sqrt{3i} \cdot \sqrt{3i}$$
$$= 1 + 6\sqrt{3i} - 3$$

because the square of an imaginary number is the original negative number.

Try It 5.3

For each function determine the complex zeros, and then check by substitution.

a. $f(x) = (x-3)^2 + 4$

b. $f(x) = x^2 + 3x + 5$

CALCULATOR TIP

Checking Solutions

You can use a graphing calculator to estimate the zeros of a quadratic function. Consider the function $f(x) = 2x^2 + 5x + 1$.

Method 1:

Type the function into $Y=$, and graph it. TRACE just to the left of the first zero.

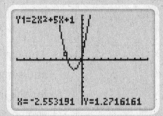

Under 2nd TRACE (CALC), choose zero. Press ENTER to choose the left bound. This is any point just to the left of the zero.

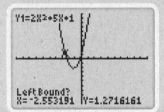

Then right arrow past the zero, and press ENTER to choose the right bound. This is any point just to the right of the zero

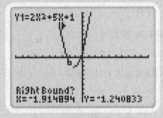
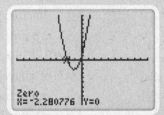

Repeat to find the other zero.

Method 2:

You can also check complex solutions using the i key. Consider the function $f(x) = x^2 - 2x + 4$ with solution $x = 1 \pm \sqrt{3} \cdot i$.

First store the solution in x, and then type in the function rule. The i symbol is usually shown above the decimal point. Use the 2nd key to access it.

In this lesson, you will solve quadratic applications. There are many applications in the physical sciences and in business that can be modeled with quadratic functions using domain and range. Recall that a function is a rule that assigns to each input x one and only one output y. The **domain** is simply the set of inputs (x) for which the function is defined, and the **range** is the set of outputs (y).

You can often determine the domain and range from a graph. For example, for the linear function $f(x) = 2x + 1$ shown on the graph, the inputs consist of all possible numbers and so do the outputs. For this graph, the domain is the set of all real numbers, and the range is also the set of all real numbers.

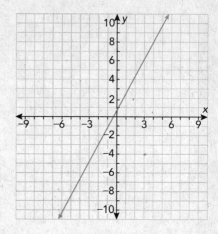

The domain and range are different for vertical and horizontal lines. For the function $y = 3$, or $y = 0 \cdot x + 3$, each x is paired with one and only one output, 3. The slope is 0. The domain is the set of all real numbers since any number can be multiplied by zero, but the range will always be $y = 3$, the only output value.

The equation $x = -5$ is not a function because the one and only x-value is paired with all y-values. It is a vertical line through the point $x = -5$.

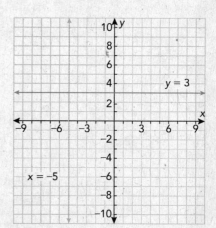

6.1 Determine the Domain and Range of Quadratic Functions

The vertex of a quadratic function can be used to determine the range.

Consider again the quadratic parent function $y = f(x) = x^2$. Since you can square any number, the domain is the set of all real numbers, but the range consists of all positive numbers or zero.

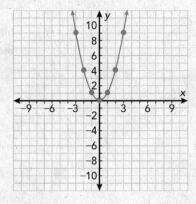

The range is given by the inequality $y \geq 0$ because all the y-values are greater than or equal to zero.

Now consider again the function $y = f(x) = x^2$ and its translation $y = (x - 3)^2 - 2$. The domain is the set of all real numbers, but the range is determined by the vertex $(3, -2)$. The range is given by the inequality $y \geq -2$ because all the y-values are greater than or equal to -2.

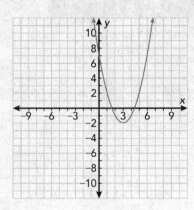

EXAMPLES

Graph each quadratic function, and determine the domain and range.

a. $f(x) = x^2 + 4x - 5$

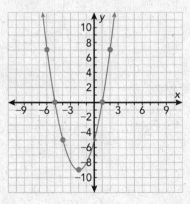

To find the vertex x, compute:

$$x = -\frac{b}{2a} = -\frac{4}{2(1)} = -2$$

To find the vertex y-value, evaluate:

$$f(-2) = (-2)^2 + 4 \cdot (-2) - 5 = 4 - 8 - 5 = -9$$

The domain is all real numbers, and the range is given by the inequality $y \geq -9$.

b. $f(x) = -(x - 1)^2 + 3$

Note that the negative sign shows this is a reflection. The parabola turns down instead of up. You can see the vertex is $(1, 3)$. **The domain is the set of all real numbers, but the range is given by the inequality** $y \leq 3$.

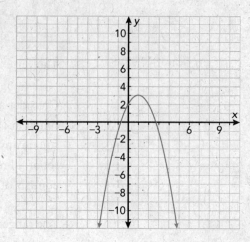

Try It 6.1

Graph each quadratic function, and determine the domain and range.

a. $f(x) = -(x - 3)^2 + 16$

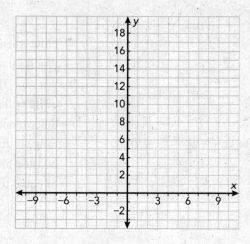

[TIP]

Use a calculator to help you visualize the range.

b. $f(x) = x^2 - 9$

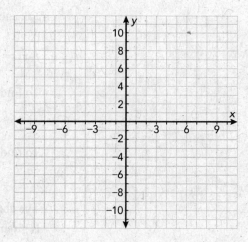

c. $f(x) = x^2 - 3x - 1$

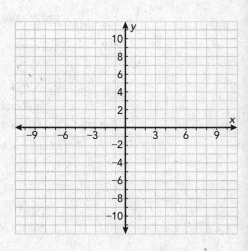

6.2 Solve Physics Applications

NOTE

In Physics, the variable t is used instead of x.

As you know, objects fall because of gravity. A simple example involves dropping a ball from a height of 200 feet. The height of the object is given by the function $h(t) = 200 - 16t^2$ where t is time in seconds. The term $-16t^2$ indicates the effect of gravity on the object.

At one second, or when $t = 1$, the ball is $h(1) = 200 - 16(1)^2 = 184$ feet from the ground.

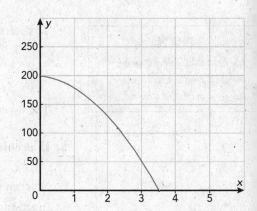

At two seconds, or when $t = 2$, the ball is $h(2) = 200 - 16(2)^2 = 136$ feet from the ground.

NOTE

While the domain of $h(t) = 200 - 16t^2$ is all real numbers, when you solve real-world problems, you will only consider the "restricted" domain. This consists of only the t-values that make sense in the problem. You will only consider the positive square root.

To determine when the ball hits the ground, you can solve the equation $200 - 16t^2 = 0$ for t. This is the time when the height is zero.

$$200 - 16t^2 = 0$$
$$-16t^2 = -200$$
$$t^2 = \frac{-200}{-16}$$
$$t = \sqrt{\frac{200}{16}} \approx 3.54 \text{ seconds}$$

The ball **hits the ground just after 3.5 seconds.**

Solve each problem. Use a graphing calculator or sketch a graph to verify your solution.

a. **A rocket that is shot straight up from the ground with an initial speed (also called the instantaneous velocity) of 112 feet per second can be modeled with the function, $h(t) = 112t - 16t^2$. Determine the maximum height of the rocket and how long it takes to reach the ground again.**

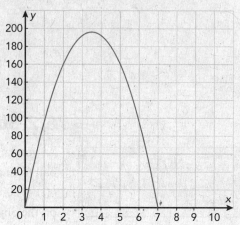

To find the vertex, rewrite the function as $h(t) = -16t^2 + 112t$. Then to find the vertex x-value, compute:

$$t = -\frac{b}{2a} = -\frac{112}{2(-16)} = 3.5$$

To find the vertex y-value, evaluate:

$$h(3.5) = -16(3.5)^2 + 112(3.5)$$
$$= 196 \text{ feet}$$

The rocket reaches a maximum height of **196** feet after 3.5 seconds.

To determine how long it takes the rocket to hit the ground, solve the equation:

$$112t - 16t^2 = 0$$
$$16t(7 - t) = 0$$
$$t = 0 \text{ or } t = 7$$

NOTE

The first solution t = 0 simply indicates that the rocket is on the ground at zero seconds.

The rocket **hits the ground in 7 seconds.**

b. **If an object is dropped from a height of 64 feet, when does it hit the ground?**

You can model this problem with the function $h(t) = 64 - 16t^2$. To determine when the ball hits the ground you can solve the equation $64 - 16t^2 = 0$ for t, the time when the height is zero.

$$64 - 16t^2 = 0$$
$$-16t^2 = -64$$
$$t^2 = \frac{-64}{-16}$$
$$t^2 = 4$$
$$t = 2$$

The ball **hits the ground in 2 seconds.**

■ **Try It 6.2** ....

Solve each problem. Use a graphing calculator or sketch a graph to verify your solution.

a. A rocket that shot straight up from the ground with an initial speed of 96 feet per second can be modeled with the function $h(t) = 96t - 16t^2$. Determine the maximum height of the rocket and how long it takes to return to the ground.

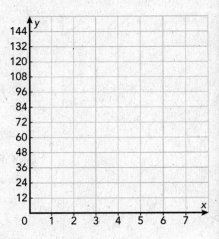

b. If an object is dropped from a height of 100 feet, when does it hit the ground?

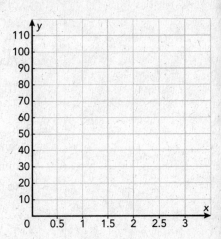

6.3 Solve Business Applications

Revenue functions in business can sometimes be modeled with quadratic functions. Suppose an electonics manufacturer uses the price equation $P(x) = 2000 - 50x$ to set the price of a TV, where x is in thousands. This means that if they can sell 3,000 televisions, then the price is $P(3) = 2,000 - 50(3) = 1,850$, or \$1,850 per television.

Remember that revenue is the number of units multiplied by the price per unit:

$$R(x) = x \cdot P(x)$$
$$= x(2,000 - 50x)$$

The revenue is a quadratic function.

$$R(x) = 2,000x - 50x^2$$

For example, if the company sells 3,000 televisions, the revenue will be:

$$R(3) = 2,000(3) - 50(3)^2$$
$$= 5,550 \text{ thousand dollars}$$

The revenue would be 5,550(1,000) = $5,550,000. This is a restricted domain problem since the zeros make no sense.

$$R(40) = 2,000(40) - 50(40)^2$$
$$= 0$$

The company would not want to generate $0 in revenue if they sell 40,000 units. They need to determine the number of units and price needed to bring in revenue.

EXAMPLES

a. Consider the revenue function $R(x) = 2,000x - 50x^2$ in the previous example, where x is number of units in thousands. Find the number of units that would create maximum revenue, and then find the maximum revenue and determine the price per television.

The maximum revenue is the **maximum of the function**, or the y-value of the highest point on the graph of the function. This means the maximum will occur at the vertex of the parabola.

To find the vertex, rewrite the function as $R(x) = -50x^2 + 2,000x$.

To find the vertex x-value, compute:

$$x = -\frac{b}{2a} = \frac{-2,000}{2(-50)} = 20$$

Since x is in thousands of units, the number of televisions that must be sold to maximize revenue is:

$$20 \cdot 1,000 = 20,000$$

To find the vertex y-value, evaluate:

$$R(20) = -50(20)^2 + 2,000(20)$$
$$= 20,000$$

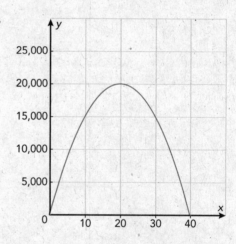

Since x is in thousand of units, the revenue is $20,000 \cdot 1,000 =$ **$20,000,000**, and the number of units that would maximize revenue is **20,000**.

To find the price per television, substitute 20 into the price function.

$$P(x) = 2,000 - 50x$$
$$P(20) = 2,000 - 50(20)$$
$$= 1,000$$

At $1,000 per television, the company can sell 20,000 TVs and generate a revenue of $20 million.

b. A hotel has 300 rooms. The manager determines that if she charges $60 per night she will rent all rooms for 300 · 60 = $18,000 in revenue. For each $3 increase in the room rate, she determined that she will rent 6 fewer rooms. For example, if she adds the $3 increase to the original room rate four times, then the room rate is $60 + $3(4) = $72, but she will only rent 300 − 6(4) = 276 rooms. This means her revenue is:

$$\text{Number of rooms} \cdot \text{Cost per room} = \text{Revenue}$$
$$(300 - 6(4))(60 + 3(4)) = 276 \cdot 72$$
$$= \$19,872$$

You can see that her revenue goes up when fewer rooms are rented. You can generalize this with the revenue function where x is the number of $3 increases in the room rate:

$$\text{Revenue} = \text{Number of rooms} \cdot \text{Cost per room}$$
$$R(x) = (300 - 6x)(60 + 3x)$$

How many $3 increments maximize the revenue, and what is the maximum revenue? How much should she charge to maximize the revenue? How many rooms must be rented to maximize the revenue?

To find the maximum revenue, you have to find the vertex. First multiply the two factors:

$$\text{Revenue} = \text{Number of rooms} \cdot \text{Cost per room}$$
$$R(x) = (300 - 6x)(60 + 3x)$$
$$R(x) = 300(60 + 3x) - 6x(60 + 3x)$$
$$R(x) = 18,000 + 900x - 360x - 18x^2$$
$$R(x) = -18x^2 + 540x + 18,000$$

Find the vertex x-value:

$$x = -\frac{b}{2a} = \frac{-540}{2(-18)} = 15$$

You can see it takes **15 three-dollar increases** to reach maximum revenue.

The number of rooms is 300 − 6(15) = 210.

The cost per room is 60 + 3(15) = 105.

The maximum revenue is 210(105) = 22,050.

Check your work by evaluating the revenue function for $x = 15$.
$$R(15) = -18(15)^2 + 540(15) + 18,000$$
$$= 22,050$$

a. Rosa uses the price equation $P(x) = 50 - x$ to set the price for a dozen roses where x represents hundreds of orders. Write a revenue function, and then determine the maximum revenue, the number of orders needed to reach maximum revenue, and the price per order. Complete the graph for this function.

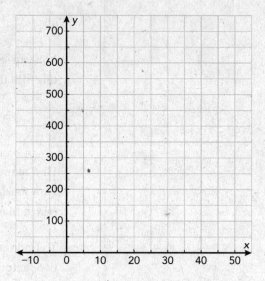

b. A theatre has 1,000 seats. All seats will be sold if the each ticket costs $20. For every $2 increase in price, 5 fewer seats will be sold. What is the maximum revenue possible, and how many seats are sold? Complete the graph for this function.

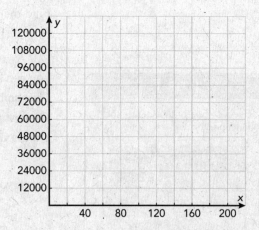

CALCULATOR TIP

Using a Table and a Graph

You can use a table and a graph to help you solve quadratic applications. Consider the function $h(t) = 112t - 16t^2$. Type the function into Y=, and set the table to show increments of 0.5.

View the table and scroll down.

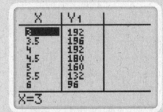
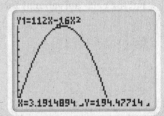

You can see the symmetry in the table since 192 is the y-value on either side of the vertex is at (3.5, 196), with 196 as the maximum value.

Use the table to set the window for the graph. Trace to the left of the vertex.

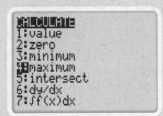
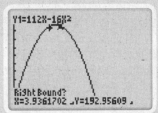

To find the maximum, choose maximum under 2ⁿᵈ TRACE (CALC). Press ENTER to choose the left bound, which is any x-value just to the left of the maximum. Then use the right arrow to scroll past the zero, and press ENTER to choose the right bound, which is any x-value just to the right of the maximum.

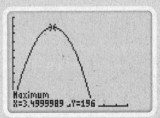

Note the rounding error, 3.4999989. The maximum value is $y = 196$ and occurs at $x = 3.5$.

Find each product for problems 1–5.

1. $-5x(-x^2 - 3x + 7)$ **2.** $(x - 2)(x + 4)$

3. $(3x - 2)(x - 6)$ **4.** $(4x - 1)^2$

5. $(3x - 2)(3x + 2)$

Factor each polynomial for problems 6–10.

6. $x^2 - 8x + 16$ **7.** $x^2 - 2x - 15$

8. $8x^2 - 18$ **9.** $2x^2 + 13x + 6$

10. $2x^2 - 13x - 7$

Simplify problems 11 and 12.

11. $\dfrac{2}{\sqrt{2}}$

12. $\dfrac{5}{\sqrt{3}}$

Use the Pythagorean Theorem to solve problems 13–15. Simplify radicals as needed.

13. If $a = 6$ and $b = 8$, determine c.

14. If $a = 15$ and $c = 20$, determine b.

15. A 20-foot ladder is leaning against a wall. If the bottom of the ladder is 3 feet from the wall, how high up the wall does the ladder reach?

Continue on next page.

Solve problems 16–20 using the method of your choice.

16. $x^2 - 8x - 1 = 0$

17. $2x^2 - 18 = 0$

18. $4x^2 - 4x + 1 = 0$

19. $5x^2 - 2x + 1 = 0$

20. $12x^2 + 2x - 2 = 0$

For each function in problems 21–24, determine all zeros.

21. $f(x) = x^2 + 4x - 5$

22. $f(x) = 2x^2 + x - 1$

23. $f(x) = 2x^2 + 3x + 6$

24. $f(x) = 16x^2 - 1$

For each function in problems 25 and 26, determine all intercepts, the vertex, and the axis of symmetry. Then sketch each parabola, and write the function in the form: $y = f(x) = a(x - h)^2 + k$.

25. $f(x) = -(x + 1)^2 - 2$

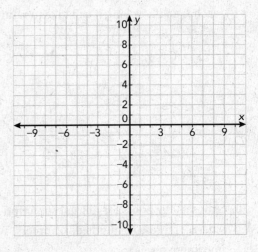

26. $f(x) = (x - 3)^2 - 1$

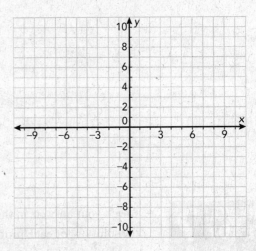

Determine the domain and the range for each function in problems 27 and 28.

27. $f(x) = -(x - 1) - 3$

28. $f(x) = x^2 + 3x - 1$

Continue on next page.

Solve each application in problems 29 and 30.

29. A rocket shot straight up from the ground with an initial speed of 144 feet per second can be modeled with the function $h(t) = 144t - 16t^2$. Determine the maximum height the rocket reaches and how long it will take to return to the ground.

30. Sam sets the prices for journal subscriptions. He uses the price equation $P(x) = 75 - 3x$ where x represents hundreds of orders. Write a revenue function, and then determine the maximum revenue.

ARE YOU READY TO GO ON ?

- Check your answers in the Solutions section at the back of the book. Reading the solution for each problem will help you understand why the correct answers are right and will allow you to see each step of the solutions.
- On the chart below, circle the problem numbers that you did not solve correctly. If you answered more than one problem per lesson incorrectly, you should review that lesson before moving to the next unit.

Performance Analysis Chart

LESSON	PROBLEM NUMBER
4.1	1, 2, 3, 4, 5
4.2	6, 7, 8, 9, 10
4.3	11, 12, 13, 14, 15
4.4	16, 17, 18, 19, 20
4.5	21, 22, 23, 24, 25, 26
4.6	27, 28, 29, 30

UNIT 5 Other Models

In this unit, you will work with other models. The main focus is on the concepts and skills necessary to be proficient with absolute values, logarithms, and rational and radical expressions and equations. These models can be applied in the sciences and social sciences, in areas such as population growth, learning, and aviation.

LESSON 1 Solve Absolute-Value Equations

FOCUS Solve and graph absolute-value equations

DEFINITION
Absolute-value equations contain at least one absolute-value expression.

In this lesson, you will graph and solve absolute-value equations. The *parent* absolute-value function is $y = f(x) = |x|$. Recall from Unit 2 that the absolute value of an integer is its distance from the origin, which is at 0. Absolute values are always positive. For example, $|-4| = 4$. This is read as the absolute value of -4 is 4.

In general, the absolute value of a number x is defined as:

$$|x| = x \text{ if } x \geq 0$$

$$|x| = -x \text{ if } x < 0$$

The table and graph of the absolute-value function $y = f(x) = |x|$ are shown below.

x	$f(x) = |x|$	(x, y)
-3	$f(-3) = |-3| = 3$	$(-3, 3)$
-2	$f(-2) = |-2| = 2$	$(-2, 2)$
-1	$f(-1) = |-1| = 1$	$(-1, 1)$
0	$f(0) = |0| = 0$	$(0, 0)$
1	$f(1) = |1| = 1$	$(1, 1)$
2	$f(2) = |2| = 2$	$(2, 2)$
3	$f(3) = |3| = 3$	$(3, 3)$

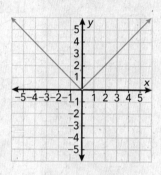

Notice that the graph has a V shape and, like the quadratic parent function, has a vertex at the origin, $(0, 0)$.

NOTE
There is no solution to the equation $|x| = -4$ because absolute values are always positive.

You can use graphs to display absolute-value equations. The graph at the right shows the points of intersection when $y = |x|$, or $y = 4$. The x-values are solutions to the equation $|x| = 4$. They are 4 or -4.

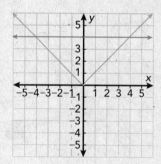

1.1 Solve Absolute-Value Equations

In general, when a is positive, the solution for $|x| = a$ is $x = a$ or $x = -a$. This is shown as $x = \pm a$. You can use graphs to show the solutions to simple absolute-value equations. In the examples that follow, remember that a horizontal shift is of the form $y = f(x) = |x - h|$.

EXAMPLES

Solve each absolute-value equation.

a. $|x - 3| = 2$

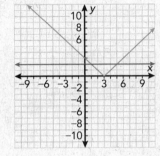

This equation is shown on the graph at right. Notice that the vertex is shifted 3 units right from where the vertex of the parent function would be. You can see that when $y = 2$, then $x = 1$ or 5. These are the solutions. Check by solving algebraically:

$$|x - 3| = 2$$
$$x - 3 = \pm 2$$
$$x - 3 = 2 \text{ or } x - 3 = -2$$
$$\boldsymbol{x = 5 \text{ or } x = 1}$$

[RECALL]

Remember that shifts occur when the vertex is not located at (0, 0).

b. $|x + 4| = 3$

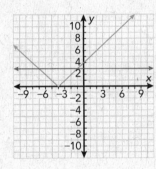

Notice the horizontal shift of -4 units because $|x + 4| = |x - (-4)|$. You can see from the points of intersection of the two lines that the solutions are -7 or -1. Check by solving algebraically:

$$|x + 4| = 3$$
$$x + 4 = \pm 3$$
$$x + 4 = 3 \text{ or } x + 4 = -3$$
$$\boldsymbol{x = -1 \text{ or } x = -7}$$

[RECALL]

$x - h$ shifts the graph h units. If h is positive, it is a right shift. If h is negative, it is a left shift.

c. $2|x - 1| = 7$

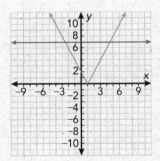

Notice the horizontal shift of 1 unit. You can see from the points of intersection that the solutions are -2.5 or 4.5. Check by solving algebraically:

$$2|x - 1| = 7$$
$$|x - 1| = \frac{7}{2}$$
$$|x - 1| = \pm\frac{7}{2}$$
$$x - 1 = \frac{7}{2} \text{ or } x - 1 = -\frac{7}{2}$$
$$x = \frac{2}{2} + \frac{7}{2} = \frac{9}{2} \text{ or } x = \frac{2}{2} - \frac{7}{2} = -\frac{5}{2}$$
$$\boldsymbol{x = 4.5 \text{ or } x = -2.5}$$

Solve each absolute-value equation.

a. $|x - 4| = 1$

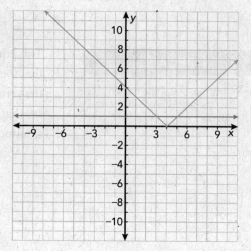

b. $|x + 2| = 4$

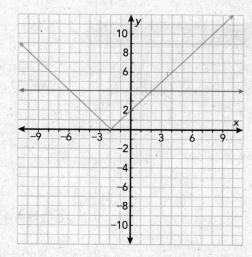

c. $3|x + 2| = 5$

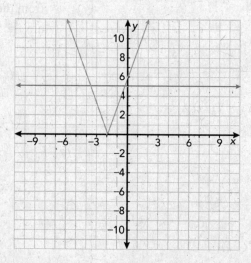

1.2 Graph Absolute-Value Equations

You can use your knowledge of transformations to graph absolute-value functions of the form $y = f(x) = a|x - h| + k$. Remember that transformations shift the parent function horizontally h units and vertically k units, and the vertex is at (h, k). If a is negative, you begin with a reflection in the x-axis. The graph below shows the parent function before the reflection across the x-axis and the transformation given by $y = f(x) = -|x - 1| + 2$.

CALCULATOR TIP

Use a graphing calculator to show the graph of each equation. This will allow you to see the intercepts.

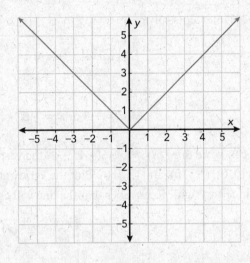 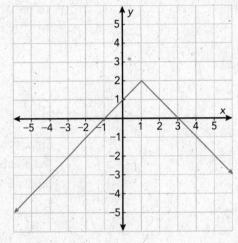

The translation shifts the graph vertically 2 units and horizontally 1 unit after the reflection. Note also that the translated vertex is $(1, 2)$. To find the y-intercept, x must be equal to 0. The y-intercept is:

$$f(0) = -|0 - 1| + 2$$
$$= -1 + 2$$
$$= 1$$

[RECALL]

Just as with quadratic functions the horizontal and vertical shifts determine the vertex of the absolute-value function.

You can see that the graph passes through point $(0, 1)$.

To find the x-intercepts, or zeros, y must be equal to 0. The x-intercepts are:

$$-|x - 1| + 2 = 0$$
$$-|x - 1| = -2$$
$$|x - 1| = 2$$
$$x - 1 = \pm 2$$
$$x - 1 = 2 \text{ or } x - 1 = -2$$
$$x = -1 \text{ or } x = 3$$

You can see that these points were plotted as $(-1, 0)$ and $(3, 0)$. This is similar to the way you found the zeros for quadratic functions.

EXAMPLES

For each function, determine all intercepts and the vertex, and then sketch the graph.

a. $f(x) = |x + 4| - 1$

The y-intercept is $f(0) = |0 + 4| - 1 = \mathbf{3}$.

To find the x-intercepts solve:

$$|x + 4| - 1 = 0$$
$$|x + 4| = 1$$
$$x + 4 = \pm 1$$
$$\mathbf{x = -3 \text{ or } x = -5}$$

Since you can write this $f(x) = |x - (-4)| - 1$, the vertex is $(\mathbf{h, k}) = (\mathbf{-4, -1})$. Plot the points $(0, 3)$, $(-3, 0)$, and $(-5, 0)$. Plot the vertex at $(-4, -1)$. Then connect the points from left to right. Remember that the line will change direction at the vertex.

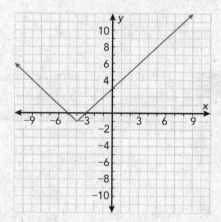

b. $f(x) = -|x - 3| + 5$

The y-intercept is $f(0) = -|0 - 3| + 5 = \mathbf{2}$.

To find the x-intercepts solve:

$$-|x - 3| + 5 = 0$$
$$-|x - 3| = -5$$
$$|x - 3| = 5$$
$$x - 3 = \pm 5$$
$$\mathbf{x = -2 \text{ or } x = 8}$$

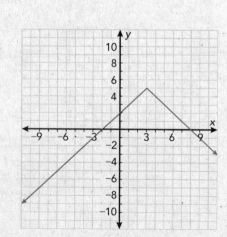

The vertex is $(\mathbf{3, 5})$. Then graph the points.

For each function, determine all intercepts and the vertex, and then sketch the graph.

a. $f(x) = |x - 3| + 5$

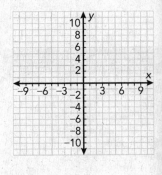

b. $f(x) = -|x + 1| + 3$

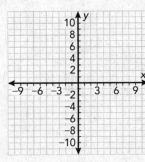

CALCULATOR TIP

Finding the Vertex

You can find the vertex of absolute-value functions with a graphing calculator. Consider the function $f(x) = -|x - 3| + 5$. The absolute-value notation is found under the MATH menu. Choose NUM and then choose *abs*, which is the absolute value. Then key in the expression. Remember that you're looking for the negative of the absolute value.

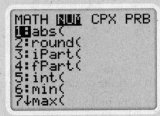

Then plot and view the graph. You can see that the vertex is at **(3, 5).**

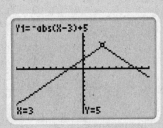

LESSON 2 Simplify Rational Expressions

In this lesson, you will use your knowledge of multiplication and factoring to simplify rational expressions. **Rational expressions** are algebraic fractions whose numerators and denominators are polynomials. One example is $\frac{x^2 - 1}{x + 1}$. The expression is undefined when $x = -1$ since that would make the denominator zero. Knowing this allows you to simplify the expression by factoring the numerator.

[TIP]

Division by zero is not defined, so a fraction can never have a denominator of 0. For example, when the denominator is $x + 1$, x cannot be -1.

$$\frac{x^2 - 1}{x + 1} = \frac{(x + 1)(x - 1)}{x + 1}$$ Factor the numerator.

$$= \frac{(x + 1)(x - 1)}{x + 1}$$ Divide out the common factor $x + 1$.

$$= x - 1$$ $\frac{x^2 - 1}{x + 1} = x - 1$ when $x \neq -1$.

2.1 Add or Subtract Rational Expressions

You have to find common denominators to add or subtract rational expressions just as you did with fractions.

EXAMPLES

Find a common denominator and add or subtract.

a. $\dfrac{3}{2} + \dfrac{4}{2x - 3}$

Note that the expression is undefined when the denominator is zero, so the denominator $2x - 3$ cannot equal zero. This means you must first set the denominator equal to 0 and then solve for the value x. This will give you the value that x cannot equal.

$$2x - 3 \neq 0$$
$$2x \neq 3$$
$$x \neq \frac{3}{2}$$

A simple method to find the common denominator is to multiply the denominators: $2(2x - 3)$. Begin by multiplying the first term of the expression by $\frac{2x - 3}{2x - 3}$ and the second term by $\frac{2}{2}$. This will produce the same denominator.

$$\frac{3}{2} + \frac{4}{2x - 3} = \frac{3}{2} \cdot \frac{2x - 3}{2x - 3} + \frac{4}{2x - 3} \cdot \frac{2}{2}$$ Convert to common denominator.

$$= \frac{6x - 9}{4x - 6} + \frac{8}{4x - 6}$$ Add.

$$= \frac{6x - 1}{4x - 6}$$

This means $\dfrac{3}{2} + \dfrac{4}{2x - 3} = \dfrac{6x - 1}{4x - 6}$ when $x \neq \dfrac{3}{2}$.

b. $\dfrac{x+1}{2x+1} - \dfrac{4}{x-5}$

[HINT]

Set the first denominator not equal to zero, and solve.

$$2x + 1 \neq 0$$
$$2x \neq -1$$
$$x \neq -\dfrac{1}{2}$$

Since the expression is undefined when either denominator is zero, $x \neq -\dfrac{1}{2}$ and $x \neq 5$. The common denominator is the product of the denominators: $(2x + 1)(x - 5)$. Begin by multiplying the first term of the expression by $\dfrac{x-5}{x-5}$ and the second term by $\dfrac{2x+1}{2x+1}$.

$$\dfrac{x+1}{2x+1} - \dfrac{4}{x-5} = \dfrac{x+1}{2x+1} \cdot \dfrac{x-5}{x-5} - \dfrac{4}{x-5} \cdot \dfrac{2x+1}{2x+1} \qquad \text{Multiply to convert to a common denominator.}$$

$$= \dfrac{x^2 - 4x - 5}{(2x+1)(x-5)} - \dfrac{8x+4}{(2x+1)(x-5)}$$

$$= \dfrac{x^2 - 4x - 5 - 8x - 4}{(2x+1)(x-5)} \qquad \text{Subtract.}$$

$$= \dfrac{x^2 - 12x - 9}{2x^2 - 9x - 5} \qquad \text{Combine like terms.}$$

This means $\dfrac{x+1}{2x+1} - \dfrac{4}{x-5} = \dfrac{x^2 - 12x - 9}{2x^2 - 9x - 5}$ when $x \neq -\dfrac{1}{2}$, $x \neq 5$.

c. $\dfrac{x-1}{12x^2 - 3} + \dfrac{5}{12x + 6}$

Begin by factoring the denominators:

$$12x^2 - 3 = 3(4x^2 - 1) = 3(2x + 1)(2x - 1)$$

$$12x + 6 = 6(2x + 1) = 2 \cdot 3(2x + 1)$$

Since the expression is undefined when either denominator is zero, $x \neq -\dfrac{1}{2}$ and $x \neq \dfrac{1}{2}$. The LCD contains the common factors $3(2x + 1)$ and the remaining factors $2(2x - 1)$, so the LCD is:

$$3(2x + 1) \cdot 2(2x - 1) = 6(4x^2 - 1) = 24x^2 - 6$$

Multiply the first term by $\dfrac{2}{2}$ to get the LCD: $(12x^2 - 3) \cdot 2 = 24x^2 - 6$.

Multiply the second term by $\dfrac{2x-1}{2x-1}$ to get the LCD: $(12x + 6)(2x - 1) = 24x^2 - 6$.

$$\dfrac{x}{12x^2 - 3} + \dfrac{5}{12x + 6} = \dfrac{x}{12x^2 - 3} \cdot \dfrac{2}{2} + \dfrac{5}{12x + 6} \cdot \dfrac{2x-1}{2x-1} \qquad \text{Find LCD.}$$

$$= \dfrac{2x}{24x^2 - 6} + \dfrac{10x - 5}{24x^2 - 6} \qquad \text{Add.}$$

$$= \dfrac{12x - 5}{24x^2 - 6} \qquad \text{Combine like terms.}$$

This means $\dfrac{x}{12x^2 - 3} + \dfrac{5}{12x + 6} = \dfrac{12x - 5}{24x^2 - 6}$ when $x \neq -\dfrac{1}{2}$, $x \neq \dfrac{1}{2}$.

Try It 2.1

Find a common denominator and add or subtract.

a. $\dfrac{1}{4} + \dfrac{5}{x-1}$

b. $\dfrac{x-1}{x-3} - \dfrac{x}{x+2}$

c. $\dfrac{x-1}{3x-6} + \dfrac{x+3}{x^2-4x+4}$

2.2 Multiply or Divide Rational Expressions

You can multiply or divide rational expressions using the same method that you learned for fractions in Unit 1—factor the numerators and denominators and divide out common factors.

$$\frac{24}{25} \cdot \frac{35}{36} = \frac{2 \cdot 2 \cdot 2 \cdot 3}{5 \cdot 5} \cdot \frac{5 \cdot 7}{2 \cdot 2 \cdot 3 \cdot 3}$$

$$= \frac{2}{5} \cdot \frac{7}{3}$$

$$= \frac{14}{15}$$

EXAMPLES

Divide out common factors. Then multiply or divide.

a. $\dfrac{x^2 + 4x + 3}{4x^2} \cdot \dfrac{6x}{x + 3}$

$$\frac{x^2 + 4x + 3}{4x^2} \cdot \frac{6x}{x + 3} = \frac{(x + 3)(x + 1)}{2 \cdot 2 \cdot x \cdot x} \cdot \frac{2 \cdot 3 \cdot x}{x + 3} \qquad \text{Factor.}$$

$$= \frac{(x + 3)(x + 1)}{2 \cdot 2 \cdot x \cdot x} \cdot \frac{2 \cdot 3 \cdot x}{x + 3} \qquad \text{Divide common factors.}$$

$$= \frac{x + 1}{2x} \cdot \frac{3}{1} \qquad \text{Multiply.}$$

$$= \frac{3x + 3}{2x}$$

b. $\dfrac{x^2 - 4}{x + 1} \div \dfrac{x^2 + x - 2}{x^2 - 1}$

$$\frac{x^2 - 4}{x + 1} \div \frac{x^2 + x - 2}{x^2 - 1} = \frac{x^2 - 4}{x + 1} \cdot \frac{x^2 - 1}{x^2 + x - 2} \qquad \text{Multiply by the reciprocal.}$$

$$= \frac{(x + 2)(x - 2)}{x + 1} \cdot \frac{(x + 1)(x - 1)}{(x + 2)(x - 1)} \qquad \text{Factor.}$$

$$= \frac{(x + 2)(x - 2)}{x + 1} \cdot \frac{(x + 1)(x - 1)}{(x + 2)(x - 1)} \qquad \text{Divide common factors.}$$

$$= x - 2$$

■ **Try It 2.2** ....

Divide out common factors. Then multiply or divide.

a. $\dfrac{x^2 - 4x - 5}{6x} \cdot \dfrac{3x^2}{2x - 10}$

b. $\dfrac{x^2 + 5x + 6}{x - 2} \div \dfrac{x^2 - 9}{x^2 - 4}$

CALCULATOR TIP

Checking Algebra

You can check your algebra by building tables with a graphing calculator.

Consider the equation $\dfrac{x}{12x^2 - 3} + \dfrac{5}{12x + 6} = \dfrac{12x - 5}{24x^2 - 6}$. Under the Y= menu, enter the left side of the equation as Y₁ and the right side as Y₂. Then view the table.

```
Plot1 Plot2 Plot3
\Y1▓X/(12X²-3)+5
/(12X+6)
\Y2█(12X-5)/(24X
²-6)
\Y3=▮
\Y4=
\Y5=
```

```
X     | Y1     | Y2
------|--------|-------
0     | .83333 | .83333
1     | .38889 | .38889
2     | .21111 | .21111
3     | .14762 | .14762
4     | .11376 | .11376
5     | .09259 | .09259
6     | .07809 | .07809
Y2█(12X-5)/(24X...
```

Since the *y*-values for each *x*-value are the same, you know the solution is correct.

LESSON 3 Simplify Radical Expressions

FOCUS | Simplify expressions with radicals and rational exponents

[RECALL]

Remember that the principal square root is positive.

In this lesson, you will use your knowledge about principal square roots to simplify radical expressions. Square roots, such as $\sqrt{9}$, can also be written with rational **exponents**. For example, $\sqrt{9} = 9^{\frac{1}{2}} = 3$.

Since $(-2)^3 = -8$, you can say that -2 is the "cube root" of -8, or $\sqrt[3]{-8} = -2$. This can be also written with a rational exponent $(-8)^{\frac{1}{3}} = -2$. The **cube roots** of several common cubes are shown below.

DEFINITION
Any number raised to the third power is cubed.

$$\sqrt[3]{1} = 1^{\frac{1}{3}} = 1 \text{ since } 1^3 = 1$$
$$\sqrt[3]{8} = 8^{\frac{1}{3}} = 2 \text{ since } 2^3 = 8$$
$$\sqrt[3]{27} = 27^{\frac{1}{3}} = 3 \text{ since } 3^3 = 27$$
$$\sqrt[3]{64} = 64^{\frac{1}{3}} = 4 \text{ since } 4^3 = 64$$
$$\sqrt[3]{125} = 125^{\frac{1}{3}} = 5 \text{ since } 5^3 = 125$$

The exponent $\frac{1}{n}$ indicates the nth root. If n is even, you can only find an nth root of a positive number. For example, the 4th root of 16 is $16^{\frac{1}{4}} = \sqrt[4]{16} = 2$ since $2^4 = 16$. However, if n is odd, you can find an nth root of a positive or negative number.

For example, $(-8)^{\frac{1}{3}} = \sqrt[3]{-8} = -2$ because $(-2)^3 = -8$.

3.1 Compute Values of Radical Expressions

You can find the square of any radical expression. Carefully review the steps below to see how $\left(\sqrt[3]{-8}\right)^2 = 4$.

NOTE

Notice that the nth root is 3 (an odd number), which means you can find the cube root of −8. If the nth value was an even number, you would not be able to find the root of −8 because it is not a positive number.

$$\left(\sqrt[3]{-8}\right)^2 = (-8)^{\frac{2}{3}}$$

$$= \left((-8)^{\frac{1}{3}}\right)^2 \qquad \text{Find the cube root first.}$$

$$= (-2)^2 \qquad \text{Then square.}$$

$$= 4$$

In general, you can write a radical expression using rational exponents:

$$\left(\sqrt[n]{a}\right)^m = a^{\frac{m}{n}}$$

Rewrite each radical expression with rational exponents, and then solve.

a. $\left(\sqrt[3]{125}\right)^4$

[HINT]

To find the cube root, ask
yourself what number can be
written as a factor three times
to give the product 125?

$5 \cdot 5 \cdot 5 = 125$

$$= \left(\sqrt[3]{125}\right)^4 = (125)^{\frac{4}{3}}$$ Rewrite with rational exponents.

$$= \left(125^{\frac{1}{3}}\right)^4$$ Find the cube root.

$$= (5)^4$$ Then raise to the 4th power.

$$= \mathbf{625}$$ Simplify.

b. $\left(\sqrt[4]{81}\right)^3$

$$= \left(\sqrt[4]{81}\right)^3 = (81)^{\frac{3}{4}}$$ Rewrite with rational exponents.

$$= \left(81^{\frac{1}{4}}\right)^3$$ Find the 4th root.

$$= (3)^3$$ Then raise to the 3rd power.

$$= \mathbf{27}$$ Simplify.

c. $\left(\sqrt{49}\right)^3$

$$= \left(\sqrt{49}\right)^3 = (49)^{\frac{3}{2}}$$ Rewrite with rational exponents.

$$= \left(49^{\frac{1}{2}}\right)^3$$ Find the square root.

$$= (7)^3$$ Then raise to the 3rd power.

$$= \mathbf{343}$$ Simplify.

Try It 3.1

Rewrite each radical expression with rational exponents, and then solve.

a. $\left(\sqrt[3]{-27}\right)^2$

b. $\left(\sqrt[4]{16}\right)^5$

c. $\left(\sqrt{64}\right)^3$

3.2 Simplify Exponential Expressions

The same rules that you learned in Unit 2 about integer exponents apply for rational exponents.

Listed below are six properties of exponents when a is not equal to zero:

1. $a^0 = 1$

2. $a^{-n} = \dfrac{1}{a^n}$

3. $(ab)^n = a^n b^n$

4. $a^m a^n = a^{m+n}$

5. $\dfrac{a^m}{a^n} = a^{m-n}$

6. $(a^m)^n = a^{mn}$

EXAMPLES

Use the properties of exponents to simplify each expression. Write all answers with positive exponents.

a. $\left(x^{\frac{3}{2}}\right)^4$

$$\left(x^{\frac{3}{2}}\right)^4 = x^{\frac{3}{2} \cdot 4} \qquad \text{Use the 6}^{\text{th}}\text{ property: } (a^m)^n = a^{mn}.$$

$$= x^6$$

b. $x^{\frac{1}{2}} \cdot x^{\frac{2}{3}}$

$$x^{\frac{1}{2}} \cdot x^{\frac{2}{3}} = x^{\frac{1}{2} + \frac{2}{3}} \qquad \text{Use the 4}^{\text{th}}\text{ property: } a^m a^n = a^{m+n}.$$

$$= x^{\frac{3}{6} + \frac{4}{6}}$$

$$= x^{\frac{7}{6}}$$

c. $\dfrac{(a^{\frac{1}{3}} \cdot b^{\frac{1}{2}})^2}{a^{\frac{2}{3}} \cdot b^{\frac{4}{3}}}$

$$\dfrac{(a^{\frac{1}{3}} \cdot b^{\frac{1}{2}})^2}{a^{\frac{2}{3}} \cdot b^{\frac{4}{3}}} = \dfrac{a^{\frac{2}{3}} \cdot b}{a^{\frac{2}{3}} \cdot b^{\frac{4}{3}}} \qquad \text{Simplify the numerator.}$$

$$= a^{\frac{2}{3} - \frac{2}{3}} \cdot b^{1 - \frac{4}{3}} \qquad \text{Use the 5}^{\text{th}}\text{ property: } \tfrac{a^m}{a^n} = a^{m-n}.$$

$$= a^0 \cdot b^{-\frac{1}{3}}$$

$$= \dfrac{1}{b^{\frac{1}{3}}}$$

[RECALL]

Remember that according to the properties of exponents $a^0 = 1$.

Try It 3.2

Use the properties of exponents to simplify each expression. Write all answers with positive exponents.

a. $\left(x^{\frac{2}{3}}\right)^4$

b. $x^{\frac{4}{5}} \cdot x^{\frac{1}{3}}$

c. $\dfrac{(a^{\frac{2}{3}} \cdot b)^{\frac{1}{2}}}{ab}$

3.3 Simplify Radical Expressions

You can simplify radical expressions by using the property $\sqrt[n]{ab} = \sqrt[n]{a} \cdot \sqrt[n]{b}$.

$$\sqrt[3]{32} = \sqrt[3]{8 \cdot 4}$$ Factor out the cube, 8.

$$= \sqrt[3]{8} \cdot \sqrt[3]{4}$$

$$= 2\sqrt[3]{4}$$

This works the same way with variables.

$$\sqrt[3]{x^7} = \sqrt[3]{x^6 \cdot x}$$ Factor out the cube, x^6.

$$= \sqrt[3]{x^6} \cdot \sqrt[3]{x}$$

$$= x^2 \cdot \sqrt[3]{x}$$

> **NOTE**
>
> The cube root of x^6 is x^2 since $(x^2)^3 = x^6$.

EXAMPLES

Simplify each radical expression. Assume all variables are positive.

a. $\sqrt[3]{-24x^8}$

$$\sqrt[3]{-24x^8} = \sqrt[3]{-8x^6 \cdot 3x^2}$$ Factor out the cube, $-8x^6$.

$$= \sqrt[3]{-8x^6} \cdot \sqrt[3]{3x^2}$$ $-8x^6 = (-2)^3 (x^2)^3 = (-2x^2)^3$

$$= -2x^2 \cdot \sqrt[3]{3x^2}$$

b. $\sqrt{98x^9}$

$$\sqrt{98x^9} = \sqrt{49x^8 \cdot 2x}$$ Factor out the square, $49x^8$.

$$= \sqrt{49x^8} \cdot \sqrt{2x}$$ $49x^8 = (7x^4)^2$

$$= 7x^4 \cdot \sqrt{2x}$$

[HINT]

Find a factor of $80x^{15}$ that you can take a fourth root of: $16x^{12}$.

c. $\sqrt[4]{80x^{15}}$

$$\sqrt[4]{80x^{15}} = \sqrt[4]{16x^{12} \cdot 5x^3}$$ Factor out $16x^{12}$.

$$= \sqrt[4]{16x^{12}} \cdot \sqrt[4]{5x^3}$$ $16x^{12} = (2)^4 (x^3)^4 = (2x^3)^4$

$$= 2x^3 \cdot \sqrt[4]{5x^3}$$

Try It 3.3

Simplify each radical expression. Assume all variables are positive.

a. $\sqrt[3]{81x^4}$

b. $\sqrt{75x^7}$

c. $\sqrt[4]{81x^{13}}$

CALCULATOR TIP

Computing with Rational Exponents

You can use your graphing calculator to solve problems that have rational exponents. For example, $\left(\sqrt[3]{-125}\right)^4$ can be rewritten as $(-125)^{\frac{4}{3}}$ and then solved on your calculator as shown below.

```
(-125)^(4/3)
              625
```

Solve each absolute-value equation for x.

1. $|2x - 1| = 5$

2. $|-3x + 1| = 1$

3. $|x - 1| = -3$

For each function, determine all intercepts and the vertex. Then sketch the graph.

4. $f(x) = |x - 3| - 1$

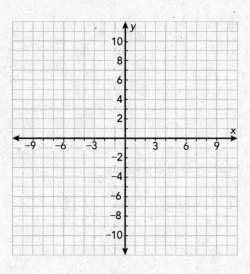

5. $f(x) = -|x - 4| + 2$

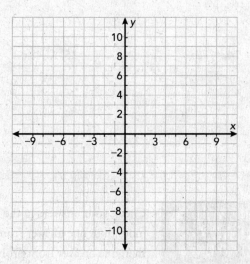

Continue on next page.

Perform the indicated operation.

6. $\dfrac{1}{2} - \dfrac{3}{x-4}$

7. $\dfrac{x}{x+2} - \dfrac{x+1}{x-4}$

8. $\dfrac{x-1}{3x-9} + \dfrac{x+1}{x^2-9}$

9. $\dfrac{x^2-2x-3}{4x} \cdot \dfrac{3x}{2x-6}$

10. $\dfrac{x^2+2x-8}{x-3} \div \dfrac{x-2}{x^2-9}$

Simplify each expression.

11. $\left(\sqrt[3]{64}\right)^2 =$

12. $x^{\frac{9}{2}} \cdot x^{\frac{2}{3}}$

13. $\dfrac{\left(a^{\frac{1}{2}}\right)^3}{a^2}$

14. $\sqrt{72x^3}$

15. $\sqrt[3]{48x^9}$

Check your answers in the *Solutions* section at the back of the book. If you missed more than one answer from problems 1 to 5, review lesson 1. If you missed more than one answer from problems 6 to 10, review lesson 2. If you missed more than one answer from problems 11 to 15, review lesson 3.

LESSON 4 Simplify Logarithmic Expressions

In this lesson, you will simplify logarithmic expressions. Logarithms are related to exponents. A logarithm is the exponent to which a specified base must be raised in order to get a certain value. Consider the exponential equation $2^4 = 16$. The base is 2, and the exponent is 4. The equivalent logarithmic equation is $\log_2 16 = 4$. Notice the placement of the base 2 and the logarithm 4. The logarithm 4 is the exponent to which 2 is raised to get 16. The table below shows exponential equations with base 2 written as logarithmic equations with base 2.

Exponential Equation	Logarithmic Equation
$2^3 = 8$	$\log_2 8 = 3$
$2^2 = 4$	$\log_2 4 = 2$
$2^1 = 2$	$\log_2 2 = 1$
$2^0 = 1$	$\log_2 1 = 0$
$2^{-1} = \dfrac{1}{2}$	$\log_2 \left(\dfrac{1}{2}\right) = -1$
$2^{-2} = \dfrac{1}{4}$	$\log_2 \left(\dfrac{1}{4}\right) = -2$

In general, you can write an exponential equation as a logarithmic equation when $b > 0$ and $b \neq 1$.

$$b^x = a \text{ is the same as } \log_b a = x$$

The table above also illustrates two important properties of logarithms. Notice that $\log_2 2 = 1$ and $\log_2 1 = 0$. This gives the following properties:

$$\log_b b = 1$$
$$\text{and}$$
$$\log_b 1 = 0$$

4.1 Compute Logarithms

You can use the fact that any logarithmic equation, $\log_b a = x$, can be written as $b^x = a$ to help you compute logarithms. For example, to compute $\log_{10} 1,000 = x$, you rewrite the equation as $10^x = 1,000$. Remember that the logarithm is just the exponent to which 10 is raised to yield 1,000. Since $10^3 = 1,000$, you know that $\log_{10} 1,000 = 3$.

Rewrite each logarithmic equation as an exponential equation, and then compute each logarithm.

a. $\log_3 81 = x$

First rewrite as an exponential equation: $3^x = 81$.

Then ask yourself what exponent would give an answer of 81.

$$3 \cdot 3 = 9 \cdot 3 = 27 \cdot 3 = 81$$

Since $3^4 = 81$, then $\log_3 81 = 4$.

b. $\log_2 \dfrac{1}{16} = x$

First rewrite as an exponential equation: $2^x = \dfrac{1}{16}$.

Then ask yourself what exponent would give an answer of $\dfrac{1}{16}$.

$$\frac{1}{2} \cdot \frac{1}{2} \cdot \frac{1}{2} \cdot \frac{1}{2} = \frac{1}{2^4} = \frac{1}{16}$$

Since $2^{-4} = \dfrac{1}{16}$, then $\log_2 \dfrac{1}{16} = -4$.

c. $\log_{10} 0.0001 = x$

Since $10^{-4} = \dfrac{1}{10^4} = \dfrac{1}{10,000} = 0.0001$, then $\log_{10} 0.0001 = -4$.

Try It 4.1

Rewrite each logarithmic equation as an exponential equation, and then compute each logarithm.

a. $\log_2 32 = x$ **b.** $\log_3 \dfrac{1}{9} = x$

c. $\log_{10} 100,000 = x$ **d.** $\log_4 \dfrac{1}{64} = x$

4.2 Apply Properties of Logarithms

You can use logarithmic equations to develop some basic properties of logarithms.

EXPLORE IT

1. Compare $\log_2(4 \cdot 8) = \log_2 32 = \underline{\quad}$ with $\log_2 4 + \log_2 8 = \underline{\quad}$.

2. Compare $\log_2\left(\dfrac{64}{16}\right) = \log_2 4 = \underline{\quad}$ with $\log_2 64 - \log_2 16 = \underline{\quad}$.

3. Compare $\log_2(4^3) = \log_2 64 = \underline{\quad}$ with $3 \log_2 4 = 6$.

If you were to write a property for each exercise above, in general, you develop the following properties of logarithms:

$$\log_b(xy) = \log_b x + \log_b y$$
$$\log_b \frac{x}{y} = \log_b x - \log_b y$$
$$\log_b x^p = p \log_b x$$

EXAMPLES

Use the properties of logarithms to express each logarithmic expression as a single logarithm. Compute the logarithm when possible.

a. $\log_4 2 + \log_4 8$

$$\log_4 2 + \log_4 8 = \log_4(2 \cdot 8)$$
$$= \log_4 16 = \mathbf{2}$$

b. $\log_{10} a + \log_{10} 2b - \log_{10} 2c$

$$(\log_{10} a + \log_{10} 2b) - \log_{10} 2c = \log_{10}(2ab) - \log_{10}(2c)$$
$$= \log_{10} \frac{2ab}{2c}$$
$$= \log_{10} \frac{ab}{c}$$

c. $2\log_{10} a - 2\log_{10} b$

$$2\log_{10} a - 2\log_{10} b = \log_{10} a^2 - \log_{10} b^2$$
$$= \log_{10} \frac{a^2}{b^2}$$

Use the properties of logarithms to express each logarithmic expression as a single logarithm. Compute the logarithm when possible.

a. $\log_4 8 + \log_4 8$

b. $\log_4 a + 2 \log_4 b - \log_4 c$

c. $2 \log_4 a + 3 \log_4 b$

4.3 Solve Problems with Common Logarithms

The base 10 logarithm is called the common logarithm. For convenience, it is written without the base, 10.

$$\log_{10} a = \log a$$

The table below shows common logarithms and their exponential equations.

Exponential Equation	Logarithmic Equation
$10^3 = 1{,}000$	$\log 1{,}000 = 3$
$10^2 = 100$	$\log 100 = 2$
$10^1 = 10$	$\log 10 = 1$
$10^0 = 1$	$\log 1 = 0$
$10^{-1} = 0.1$	$\log 0.1 = -1$
$10^{-2} = 0.01$	$\log 0.01 = -2$

NOTE

Applications from the social sciences and sciences, such as earthquakes and information retention, often involve common logarithms.

CALCULATOR TIP

The calculator computation is shown here.

```
-log(.00003)
      4.522878745
```

EXAMPLES

Solve each problem. Use the properties of logarithms or a calculator where necessary.

Scientists measure the acidity, pH, in water using the equation $pH = -\log[H^+]$. H represents the hydrogen ion concentration in moles per liter.

a. **What is the pH of a water sample with a hydrogen ion concentration of $H^+ = 0.00003$?**

Begin by substituting 0.00003 into the pH equation. Use a calculator with a log key to compute.

$$pH = -\log[0.00003] \approx 4.5$$

b. If the pH of a water sample is 6, what is the hydrogen ion concentration?

$$-\log[\text{H}^+] = \text{pH}$$

$$-\log[\text{H}^+] = 6 \qquad \text{Substitute 6 into the equation.}$$

$$\log[H^+] = -6 \qquad \text{Multiply by } -1.$$

$$\mathbf{H^+ = 10^{-6}} \qquad \text{Write an exponential equation.}$$

[RECALL]

Remember that $\log(1) = 0$ since $10^0 = 1$.

c. A testing service uses the equation $k = 90 - 10 \log(t + 1)$ to measure the amount of knowledge, k, that students retain about a subject after t months. Note that when $t = 0$:

$$k = 90 - 10 \log(t + 1)$$
$$k = 90 - 10 \log(0 + 1)$$
$$k = 90 - 10 \log(1)$$
$$k = 90 - 10 \cdot 0 = 90$$

This means that each student begins by knowing 90% of a subject. How much is retained after three years?

Since the equation calls for months, you must convert 3 years to months before solving: 3 years = 36 months.

$$k = 90 - 10 \log(t + 1)$$
$$k = 90 - 10 \log(36 + 1) \quad \text{Substitute 36 into the equation.}$$
$$k = 90 - 10 \log(37) \qquad \text{Use a calculator to solve.}$$
$$k \approx 74$$

CALCULATOR TIP

The calculator computation is:

```
90-10log(37)
        74.31798276
```

A student remembers **about 74%** of the subject after 3 years. Models like these show you why placement tests become more difficult, the more years you are out of school.

Try It 4.3

Solve each problem. Use the properties of logarithms or a calculator where necessary.

a. What is the pH of a water sample with a hydrogen ion concentration of $\text{H}^+ = 0.000042$?

b. If the pH of a water sample is 7.5, what is the hydrogen ion concentration?

A testing service uses the equation $k = 85 - 20 \log(t + 1)$ to measure the amount of knowledge, k, that a student remembers about a subject after t months.

c. How much knowledge is retained after 2 years?

d. How much knowledge is retained after 99 months?

CALCULATOR TIP

Computing Logarithms

You can use the log key on a graphing calculator to compute a logarithm in any base by using the base-changing formula: $\log_b x = \dfrac{\log x}{\log b}$.

You can see that $\log_2 \dfrac{1}{16} = \dfrac{\log \frac{1}{16}}{\log 2} = -4$, but what about $\log_2 50$? You know

$\log_2 50$ is between 4 and 5 because $\log_2 32 = 4$ and $\log_2 64 = 5$. Enter $\log_2 50$ into your calculator using the base-changing formula.

```
log(50)/log(2)
        5.64385619
```

You can see that $\log_2 50 = \dfrac{\log 50}{\log 2} \approx \textbf{5.644}$.

LESSON 5 Graph and Solve Rational Equations

In this lesson, you will graph rational functions and solve rational equations. **Rational functions** consist of the quotients of polynomials. One example is $y = \frac{2x + 3}{x - 1}$. The most basic rational function is the parent function $f(x) = \frac{1}{x}$. The table and graph of this function are shown below.

> **NOTE**
>
> *Notice that 0 is not included as an x-value in the table because $f(0) = \frac{1}{0}$ is undefined since you cannot divide by zero.*
>
> *Also note that $f\left(\frac{1}{2}\right) = \frac{1}{\frac{1}{2}} = 2$.*

x	$f(x) = \frac{1}{x}$	(x, y)
-3	$f(-3) = -\frac{1}{3}$	$\left(-3, -\frac{1}{3}\right)$
-2	$f(-2) = -\frac{1}{2}$	$\left(-2, -\frac{1}{2}\right)$
-1	$f(-1) = -\frac{1}{1} = -1$	$(-1, -1)$
1	$f(1) = \frac{1}{1} = 1$	$(1, 1)$
2	$f(2) = \frac{1}{2}$	$\left(2, \frac{1}{2}\right)$
3	$f(3) = \frac{1}{3}$	$\left(3, \frac{1}{3}\right)$

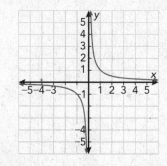

An **asymptote** is a line that a graph approaches. The y-axis, $x = 0$, is called the vertical asymptote. The x-axis, $y = 0$, is called the horizontal asymptote.

5.1 Solve Inverse-Variation Equations

Inverse-variation equations are of the form $y = \frac{k}{x}$. For the equation $y = \frac{k}{x}$, y varies inversely to x. The variable k is the **constant of variation**. As a simple example, suppose Maria is renting a beach house for the summer for \$3,000. If 10 people stay there, each person would pay $y = \frac{\$3,000}{10} = \$300$. If 20 people stay there, each person would pay $y = \frac{\$3,000}{20} = \$150$. This situation can be represented with the equation $y = \frac{3,000}{x}$.

EXAMPLES

Solve each inverse-variation problem.

a. Given that y varies inversely to x, determine k when $y = 4$ and $x = 2$.

$$y = \frac{k}{x}$$ Substitute 2 for x and 4 for y.

$$4 = \frac{k}{2}$$ Solve for k.

$$k = 2 \cdot 4 = 8$$

The constant of variation is $\boldsymbol{k = 8}$, and the equation is $y = \frac{8}{x}$.

[HINT]

The time is takes to travel varies inversely with the speed you travel.

b. **John is planning a 750-mile trip. How long will it take if he averages 60 mph?**

You can write the equation as $t = \frac{D}{r}$. The constant of variation is 750, so $t = \frac{750}{r}$.

$$t = \frac{750}{60}$$ Substitute 60 for r.

$$t = 12.5$$ Solve for t.

It will take John **12.5 hours** at an average speed of 60 mph.

What should his average speed be if he wants to make it in 10 hours?

$$t = \frac{750}{r} \quad \rightarrow \quad 10 = \frac{750}{r}$$ Substitute 10 for t.

$$10r = 750$$ Solve for r.

$$r = 75$$

John needs to average **75 mph** to make it in 10 hours.

c. **The volume, V, of a gas varies inversely to the pressure, P. Suppose the volume of air in a bicycle pump is 5 cm³ at a pressure of 15 psi (pounds per square inch). Write an inverse-variation equation, and determine what the pressure is when the volume is 2 cm³.**

$$V = \frac{k}{P} \quad \rightarrow \quad 5 = \frac{k}{15}$$ Substitute 5 for V and 15 for P.

$$k = 75$$ Solve for k.

$$V = \frac{75}{P} \quad \rightarrow \quad 2 = \frac{75}{P}$$ Substitute 2 for V, and solve for P.

$$2P = 75$$

$$P = 37.5$$

The inverse-variation equation is $V = \frac{75}{P}$. The pump has a pressure of **37.5 psi** when the volume is 2 cm³.

Try It 5.1

Solve each inverse-variation problem.

a. Given that y varies inversely with x, determine k when $y = 3$ and $x = 7$.

b. The volume, V, of a gas varies inversely with the pressure, P. If $P = 30$ when $V = 5$, write an equation of the form $V = \dfrac{k}{P}$, and then determine k.

c. Determine the volume of the gas in problem **b** if the pressure is 12 psi.

5.2 Graph Rational Functions

You can graph rational functions of the form $y = \dfrac{ax + b}{cx + d}$ by investigating transformations of the parent function $f(x) = \dfrac{1}{x}$. As with quadratics, you have horizontal and vertical shifts.

The graph at right shows that the function $y = \dfrac{1}{x - 1}$ is a graph that is shifted 1 unit to the right of the parent function. The x-axis, $y = 0$, is still the horizontal asymptote. The vertical asymptote is now $x = 1$ and occurs when the denominator of the function is zero.

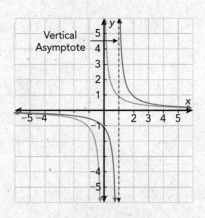

The graph at right shows that the function $y = \dfrac{1}{x - 1} + 2$ is a graph that is shifted to 1 unit to the right and 2 units up from the parent function. The horizontal asymptote is now $y = 2$, and the vertical asymptote is now $x = 1$. Also note that the y-intercept occurs when x is zero:

$$y = \frac{1}{0 - 1} + 2 = 1$$

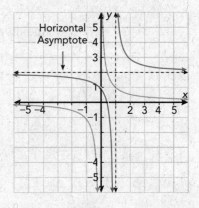

The equation can also be written as shown to the right. Note that the horizontal asymptote is $y = \frac{2}{1} = 2$, the quotient of the leading coefficients. In general, for the rational function $y = \frac{ax + b}{cx + d}$, the horizontal asymptote is $y = \frac{a}{c}$.

$$y = \frac{1}{x-1} + 2$$
$$y = \frac{1}{x-1} + 2\left(\frac{x-1}{x-1}\right)$$
$$y = \frac{1 + 2x - 2}{x - 1}$$
$$y = \frac{2x - 1}{1x - 1}$$

[RECALL]

The coefficient of 2x is 2, and the coefficient of x is 1.

To find the zero, or x-intercept, set the numerator equal to zero and solve.

$$2x - 1 = 0$$
$$x = \frac{1}{2}$$

EXAMPLES

For each rational function determine the asymptotes and intercepts. Then sketch the graph.

a. $y = \frac{x - 1}{2x - 3}$

To find the vertical asymptote, set the denominator equal to zero.

$$2x - 3 = 0$$
$$x = \frac{3}{2}$$

Sketch a vertical line at $x = \frac{3}{2}$.

The horizontal asymptote is the quotient of the coefficients: $y = \frac{1}{2}$.

Sketch a horizontal line at $y = \frac{1}{2}$.

The y-intercept is $y = \frac{0 - 1}{2(0) - 3} = \frac{1}{3}$.

Plot the point $\left(0, \frac{1}{3}\right)$.

The x-intercept is the solution of the numerator set equal to 0.

$$x - 1 = 0$$
$$x = 1$$

Plot the point $(1, 0)$.

Now sketch the graph through the points and along the asymptotes.

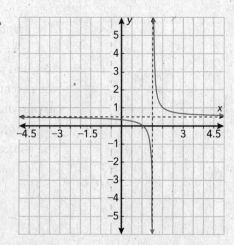

b. $y = \dfrac{4x - 8}{x + 3}$

To find the vertical asymptote, set the denominator equal to zero.

$$x + 3 = 0$$
$$\boldsymbol{x = -3}$$

Sketch a vertical line at $x = -3$.

The horizontal asymptote is the quotient of the coefficients: $\boldsymbol{y = \dfrac{4}{1} = 4}$.

Sketch a horizontal line at $y = 4$.

The y-intercept is $y = \dfrac{4(0) - 8}{0 + 3} = -\dfrac{8}{3}$.

Plot the point $\left(0, -\dfrac{8}{3}\right)$.

The x-intercept is the solution to the equation.

$$4x - 8 = 0$$
$$\boldsymbol{x = 2}$$

Plot the point $(2, 0)$.

Now sketch the graph through the points and along the asymptotes.

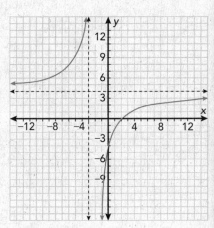

> **[HINT]**
>
> You have to estimate the y-intercept to plot it.
>
> $$y = -\dfrac{8}{3} \approx -2.3$$

■ **Try It 5.2**

For each rational function determine the asymptotes and intercepts. Then sketch the graph.

a. $y = \dfrac{x - 3}{x + 4}$

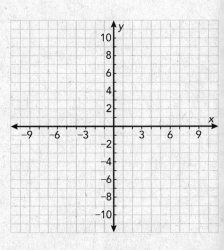

b. $y = \dfrac{2x - 6}{x - 2}$

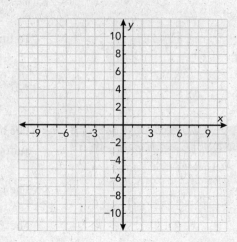

5.3 Solve Rational Equations

You can solve rational equations in much the same way as you solve simple equations with fractions—by multiplying both sides by the least common denominator.

$$\frac{x}{12} = \frac{2}{9}$$

$$\overset{3}{\cancel{36}} \cdot \frac{x}{\cancel{12}} = \overset{4}{\cancel{36}} \cdot \frac{2}{\cancel{9}}$$

$$3x = 8$$

$$x = \frac{8}{3}$$

<u>EXAMPLES</u>

Solve each rational equation.

a. $\dfrac{x + 1}{x - 4} = \dfrac{5x - 1}{x - 1}$

$$\frac{x + 1}{x - 4} = \frac{5x - 1}{x - 1}$$
Begin by multiplying both sides by $(x - 4)(x - 1)$.

$$\frac{(x - 4)(x - 1)}{1} \cdot \frac{x + 1}{x - 4} = \frac{(x - 4)(x - 1)}{1} \cdot \frac{5x - 1}{x - 1}$$

$$\frac{(\cancel{x - 4})(x - 1)}{1} \cdot \frac{x + 1}{\cancel{x - 4}} = \frac{(x - 4)(\cancel{x - 1})}{1} \cdot \frac{5x - 1}{\cancel{x - 1}}$$
Divide out common factors.

$$(x - 1)(x + 1) = (x - 4)(5x - 1)$$

$$x^2 - 1 = 5x^2 - 21x + 4$$
Multiply and combine like terms.

$$0 = 4x^2 - 21x + 5$$

$$0 = (4x - 1)(x - 5)$$
Solve.

$$x = \frac{1}{4} \text{ or } x = 5$$

Check the solutions by substituting them into the original equation. Checking is important because you sometimes get a solution from the quadratic equation that isn't really a solution. In this case, both solutions are correct.

$$\frac{x+1}{x-4} = \frac{5x-1}{x-1}$$

$$\frac{5+1}{5-4} \overset{?}{=} \frac{5(5)-1}{5-1}$$

$$\frac{6}{1} \overset{?}{=} \frac{24}{4}$$

$$6 = 6$$

Check the solution $x = \frac{1}{4}$ with a calculator.

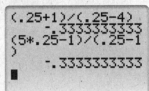

b. **Suzie's motorboat can normally average 20 mph in water without a current. Today she went 60 miles upstream and then returned downstream. The trip took 6.4 hours. What was the speed of the current?**

Recall that Distance = Rate · Time, so Time = $\frac{\text{Distance}}{\text{Rate}}$. Her rate upstream is $20 - r$, where r is the current speed. Her rate downstream is $20 + r$. You can write the equation:

$$\text{Time upstream} + \text{Time downstream} = 6.4$$

$$\frac{60}{20-r} + \frac{60}{20+r} = 6.4$$

Multiply both sides by $(20 - r)(20 + r)$.

$$\frac{(20-r)(20+r)}{1}\left(\frac{60}{20-r} + \frac{60}{20+r}\right) = \frac{(20-r)(20+r)}{1} \cdot \frac{6.4}{1}$$

$$\frac{(20-r)(20+r)}{1} \cdot \frac{60}{20-r} + \frac{(20-r)(20+r)}{1} \cdot \frac{60}{20+r} = \frac{400-r^2}{1} \cdot \frac{6.4}{1}$$

$$1{,}200 + 60r + 1{,}200 - 60r = 2{,}560 - 6.4r^2$$

$$6.4r^2 = 160$$

$$r^2 = 25$$

$$r = \pm 5$$

Since speed cannot be negative, the solution -5 does not make sense. The only solution that makes sense is $r = 5$, so the speed of the current is **5 miles per hour.**

Try It 5.3

Solve each rational equation.

a. $\dfrac{x+1}{2x-1} = \dfrac{3x+1}{4x-1}$

b. A jet can average 500 mph with no wind. It takes 10 hours for a 2,400-mile round-trip flight. The first 1,200 miles is flown against the wind. The return flight is in the same direction as the wind. What is the wind speed?

CALCULATOR TIP

Checking Solutions to Rational Equations

During the lesson, you found that the solutions to the equation $\frac{x+1}{x-4} = \frac{5x-1}{x-1}$ were $\frac{1}{4}$ and 5. You can use your graphing calculator to check these solutions by building a graph and then tracing the solutions. Enter the left side of the equation as Y1 and the right side as Y2. Then graph using the window shown below.

```
Plot1 Plot2 Plot3
\Y1◻(X+1)/(X-4)
\Y2◻(5X-1)/(X-1)

\Y3=
\Y4=
\Y5=
\Y6=
```

```
WINDOW
Xmin=-9.4
Xmax=9.4
Xscl=1
Ymin=-4.2
Ymax=8.2
Yscl=1
Xres=■
```

Then in Trace mode, input each solution while you trace each graph.

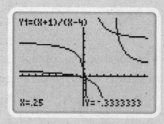

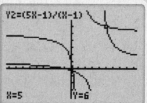

Since both solutions lie on the graph, you know that the solutions are correct.

LESSON 6 Graph and Solve Radical Equations

FOCUS | Graph and solve radical equations and their applications

[RECALL]

Remember that the domain is the set of input values (*x*) and the range is the set of output values (*y*).

In this lesson, you will graph radical functions and solve radical equations. **Radical functions** will have a variable under a square root sign. One example is $y = \sqrt{x - 1}$. The most basic radical function is the parent square root function $f(x) = \sqrt{x}$. It is only defined for the domain values $x \geq 0$ because the principal square root is never negative. The table and graph for $f(x) = \sqrt{x}$ are shown below. Note that the range contains *y*-values when $y \geq 0$.

x	$f(x) = \sqrt{x}$	(x, y)
0	$f(x) = \sqrt{0} = 0$	$(0, 0)$
1	$f(1) = \sqrt{1} = 1$	$(1, 1)$
2	$f(2) = \sqrt{2} \approx 1.414$	$(2, \sqrt{2})$
3	$f(3) = \sqrt{3} \approx 1.732$	$(3, \sqrt{3})$
4	$f(4) = \sqrt{4} = 2$	$(4, 2)$
9	$f(9) = \sqrt{9} = 3$	$(9, 3)$

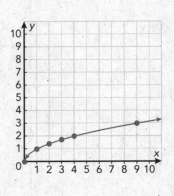

Two simple transformations are shown below. The light blue line represents the parent function, and the dark blue line represents the reflection.

$y = -\sqrt{x}$, a reflection across the *x*-axis

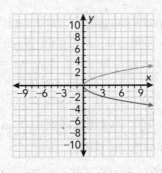

The range is now $y \leq 0$.

$y = \sqrt{-x}$, a reflection across the *y*-axis

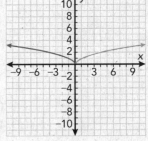

The domain is now $x \leq 0$.

[TIP]

When you set $-x \geq 0$, you must multiply both sides of the inequality by a negative number since the inequality is reversed. To find the domain of $y = \sqrt{-x}$, you can solve the inequality by multiplying both sides by -1.

$$-x \geq 0$$
$$x \leq 0$$

6.1 Graph Radical Functions

You can graph radical functions by investigating transformations of the parent function, $f(x) = \sqrt{x}$. As with quadratics, you have horizontal and vertical shifts.

The graph shows that the function $y = \sqrt{x-1}$ is shifted 1 unit to the right of the parent function. The domain changes the x-values since $x \geq 1$, but the range still contains the same y-values since $y \geq 0$. To compute the domain, set the expression under the radical to be greater than or equal to zero.

$$x - 1 \geq 0$$
$$x \geq 1$$

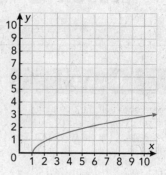

The graph shows that $y = \sqrt{x-1} - 2$ is shifted 1 unit to the right and -2 unit down from the parent function. The domain still contains x-values of $x \geq 1$, and the range still contains y-values of $y \geq -2$. Note that there is a zero at the x-intercept, $x = 5$.

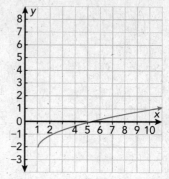

$$\sqrt{x-1} - 2 = 0$$
$$\sqrt{x-1} = 2 \qquad \text{Square both sides.}$$
$$x - 1 = 4$$
$$x = 5$$

EXAMPLES

For each radical function, determine the domain and range, any intercepts, and sketch the graph.

a. $y = -\sqrt{x+3} + 4$

First, the negative sign tells you that the function is reflected over the x-axis. By reading the equation, you also know that the graph will be shifted left -3 units and up 4 units. To find the domain, solve:
$$x + 3 \geq 0$$
$$x \geq -3$$

The range is $y \leq 4$ because of the vertical shift of 4, so the first point you plot will be $(-3, 4)$ to represent the domain and range.

The y-intercept is $y = -\sqrt{0+3} + 4 = 4 - \sqrt{3} \approx 2.27$, so the second point you will plot will be at $(0, 2.27)$. Remember the y-intercept is always on the vertical line $x = 0$.

To find the x-intercept, solve:
$$-\sqrt{x+3} + 4 = 0$$
$$-\sqrt{x+3} = -4$$
$$x + 3 = 16$$
$$x = 13$$

Remember the x-intercept is always on the horizontal line $y = 0$, so the third point you plot is at $(13, 0)$. Then connect the points.

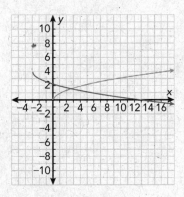

b. $y = \sqrt{4 - x} - 3$

First, the negative x tells you that the function is reflected over the y-axis. The graph is then shifted right 4 units and down -3 units. To find the domain, solve:

$$4 - x \geq 0$$
$$-x \geq -4$$
$$x \leq 4$$

The range is $y \geq -3$.

The y-intercept is:

$$y = \sqrt{4 - 0} + -3 = 2 - 3 = -1$$

To find the x-intercept, solve:

$$\sqrt{4 - x} - 3 = 0$$
$$\sqrt{4 - x} = 3$$
$$4 - x = 9$$
$$x = -5$$

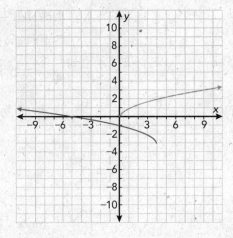

Try It 6.1

For each radical function determine the domain and range, any intercepts, and sketch the graph.

a. $y = -\sqrt{x - 2} + 1$

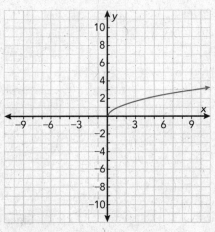

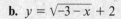

b. $y = \sqrt{-3 - x} + 2$

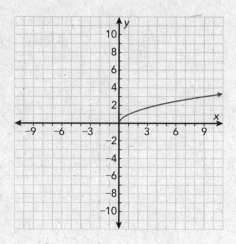

[TIP]

There is no x-intercept because the principal square root cannot be negative.

$\sqrt{-3 - x} + 2 \neq 0$

$\sqrt{-3 - x} \neq -2$

6.2 Solve Radical Equations

When you solve radical equations, it is important to check solutions. Sometimes you get an "extraneous solution," which means it does not satisfy the original equation.

EXAMPLES

Solve each radical equation.

a. $\sqrt{2x - 7} = 4$

Begin by squaring both sides.

$$\sqrt{2x - 7} = 4$$
$$2x - 7 = 16$$
$$2x = 23$$
$$\mathbf{x = 11.5}$$

Check by substituting 11.5 for x.

$$\sqrt{2x - 7} = 4$$
$$\sqrt{2(11.5) - 7} \stackrel{?}{=} 4$$
$$\sqrt{23 - 7} \stackrel{?}{=} 4$$
$$\sqrt{16} = 4$$

Since $\sqrt{16} = 4$ is true, your solution is correct.

b. $x = \sqrt{2 - x}$

$$x = \sqrt{2 - x} \qquad \text{Square both sides.}$$
$$x^2 = 2 - x$$
$$x^2 + x - 2 = 0 \qquad \text{Collect all terms on the left.}$$
$$(x - 1)(x + 2) = 0 \qquad \text{Solve by factoring.}$$
$$x = 1 \text{ or } x = -2$$

Check by substituting the solutions for x.

$$\sqrt{2 - x} = x \qquad\qquad\qquad \sqrt{2 - x} = x$$
$$\sqrt{2 - 1} \stackrel{?}{=} 1 \qquad\qquad \sqrt{2 - (-2)} \stackrel{?}{=} -2$$
$$\sqrt{1} = 1 \qquad\qquad\qquad \sqrt{4} \neq -2$$

Since only $\sqrt{1} = 1$, the only solution is $\mathbf{x = 1}$.

■ **Try It 6.2**

Solve each radical equation.

a. $\sqrt{3x + 5} = 2$

b. $\sqrt{x + 6} = x$

6.3 Solve Applications

There are many real-world applications that involve radical equations or equations with rational exponents. In astronomy, one astronomical unit (au) is the distance from Earth to the sun. Astronomers use the equation $P^2 = a^3$, where P is the orbit time of a planet in Earth years and a is the number of astronomical units.

<u>EXAMPLES</u>

Solve each application.

a. **The time it takes Jupiter to orbit the sun is approximately $P = 11.86$ Earth years. Find Jupiter's distance from the sun in astronomical units.**

$$a^3 = P^2$$
$$a^3 = (11.86)^2 \qquad \text{Substitute 11.86 for } P.$$
$$a = \sqrt[3]{(11.86)^2} = (11.86)^{\frac{2}{3}} \qquad \text{Find the cube root of both sides.}$$
$$a = (11.86)^{\frac{2}{3}} \approx 5.2 \text{ au} \qquad \text{Use a calculator to solve.}$$

Jupiter is about **5.2 astronomical units** from the sun.

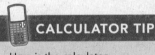

CALCULATOR TIP

Here is the calculator computation.

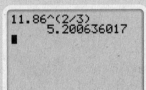

```
11.86^(2/3)
        5.200636017
■
```

b. **A department of wildlife scientist predicts the elk population, y, in a park will grow according to the model $y = 2{,}500\sqrt{0.5x + 1}$, where x is time in years. When will the population reach 5,000?**

Begin by writing the equation $2{,}500\sqrt{0.5x + 1} = 5{,}000$.

$$2{,}500\sqrt{0.5x + 1} = 5{,}000$$
$$\sqrt{0.5x + 1} = 2 \qquad \text{Divide by 2,500.}$$
$$0.5x + 1 = 4 \qquad \text{Square both sides.}$$
$$0.5x = 3 \qquad \text{Solve.}$$
$$x = 6$$

The population will reach 5,000 in **6 years**.

Try It 6.3

Solve each application.

a. Mercury is 0.39 au from the sun. How many Earth years does it take Mercury to orbit the sun?

b. A city planner proposes to control population expansion according to the model $y = 15{,}000\sqrt{0.2x + 1}$, where x is time in years. How long will it be before a population of 30,000 is possible?

CALCULATOR TIP

Evaluating Functions

You can evaluate the function $y = 2{,}500\sqrt{0.5x + 1}$ for 5,000 using the table feature of your graphing calculator.

You can see from the table that when $y = 5{,}000$, then **x = 6**.

Solve each equation.

1. $|x + 5| = 1$ **2.** $|2x - 4| = 4$ **3.** $|x - 4| = -1$

Determine all intercepts, the vertex, and then sketch the graph for problems 4 and 5.

4. $f(x) = |x - 1| + 3$

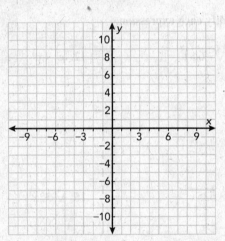

5. $f(x) = -|x - 1| + 4$

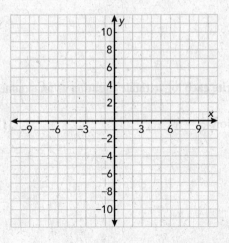

Continue on next page.

Find a common denominator, and add or subtract for problems 6–8.

6. $\dfrac{1}{2} + \dfrac{4}{x+3}$

7. $\dfrac{x+1}{x-3} - \dfrac{x}{x^2-9}$

8. $\dfrac{x+3}{x^2-1} - \dfrac{2x}{x^2+x-2}$

Divide out common factors. Then multiply or divide.

9. $\dfrac{x^2-4}{x} \cdot \dfrac{3x}{2x-4}$

10. $\dfrac{x^2+2x+1}{x-3} \div \dfrac{x+1}{x^2-9}$

Simplify each expression.

11. $\left(\sqrt[3]{-64}\right)^2 =$

12. $x^{\frac{2}{3}} \cdot x^{\frac{1}{2}}$

13. $\dfrac{(a^2 \cdot b)^{\frac{1}{2}}}{a^3 b}$

14. $\sqrt[3]{625x^7}$

15. $\sqrt[4]{32x^{11}}$

Rewrite each logarithmic equation as an exponential equation, and then compute each logarithm.

16. $\log_2 \dfrac{1}{8} = x$

17. $\log 1{,}000 = x$

Use the properties of logarithms to express each logarithm expressions as a single logarithm.

18. $3 \log a + 4 \log b - \log c$

19. $2 \log_4 a - \log_4 b$

20. A testing service uses the equation $k = 95 - 15 \log(t + 1)$ to measure the amount of knowledge, k, that students remember about a subject after t months. How much knowledge does a student remember after 2 years?

21. Given that y varies inversely with x, determine k when $y = 2.5$ and $x = 10$.

For problems 22 and 23, determine the asymptotes and intercepts. Then sketch the graph.

22. $y = \dfrac{x - 1}{x}$

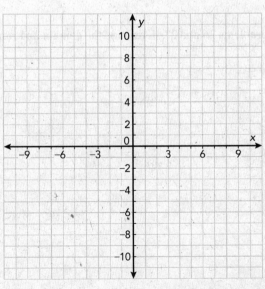

Continue on next page.

23. $y = \dfrac{2x-4}{x+1}$

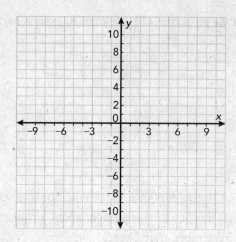

Solve each rational equation.

24. $\dfrac{x-2}{2x-1} = \dfrac{x+4}{3x+3}$

25. Rashawn can row his boat at a rate of 5 mph in water without a current. He travels 12 miles upstream and then returns downstream. The trip takes 5 hours. What is the speed of the current?

For problems 26 and 27, determine the domain and range, any intercepts, and then sketch the graph.

26. $y = \sqrt{x-2} - 1$

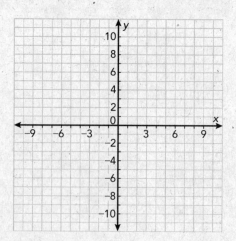

27. $y = -\sqrt{x-2} + 4$

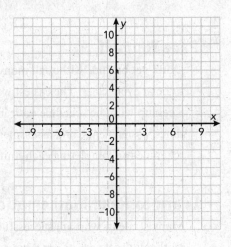

Solve each radical equation.

28. $\sqrt{x-1} = 4$

29. $\sqrt{2x-1} = x$

30. A biologist predicts the fish population, y, in a lake will grow according to the model $y = 500\sqrt{0.25x + 1}$, where x is time in years. When will the population reach 1,000?

- Check your answers in the Solutions section at the back of the book. Reading the solution for each problem will help you understand why the correct answers are right and will allow you to see each step of the solutions.
- On the chart below, circle the problem numbers that you did not solve correctly. If you answered more than one problem per lesson incorrectly, you should review that lesson before moving to the next unit.

Performance Analysis Chart

LESSON	PROBLEM NUMBER
1	1, 2, 3, 4, 5
2	6, 7, 8, 9, 10
3	11, 12, 13, 14, 15
4	16, 17, 18, 19, 20
5	21, 22, 23, 24, 25
6	26, 27, 28, 29, 30

Student Tips for Success

- ## Pace Yourself

  Don't get behind. Although many instructors don't keep track of your attendance, you need to be at every class. The easiest way to fall behind is to skip a class or to not complete a lesson. Keep up with the schedule your instructor provides. Use a calendar to keep track of all class times, assignments, and assessments. If you are working independently, create a personal schedule for completing each unit—and stick to it!

- ## Learn to Read Mathematics

  Many students who are successful in college-level mathematics learn to actually read mathematics. Learn the meanings of all symbols, and translate those symbols into words. Thinking in terms of words instead of symbols and digits will make the meanings of expressions easier to understand and more accessible.

- ## Seek Assistance

  If your instructor has regular office hours, take advantage of them. Visit you instructor and ask very specific questions about the problems you are working on. Remember that your instructors want you to be successful. Most campuses also have math tutors available for free. Tutors are prepared to give you one-on-one assistance.

- ## Ask Questions

  Don't wait until the day an assignment is due or the day before an assessment to ask for help. Whether you are in a traditional classroom setting or not, ask questions. Chances are that other students have the same question. Asking questions can help to clarify your thinking. Students who ask questions develop deeper mathematical understanding than students who don't—and there's no such thing as a bad question.

- ## Take Notes as You Read

  Math is not a spectator sport. Before each class, read each lesson carefully and take notes. Read each lesson once before class to familiarize yourself with the new vocabulary and general concept of the lesson. Then read each lesson a second time to highlight important notes in the book and work out the examples in the text before you complete the *Try It* section. Remember that this is your book—mark it up! If you do this before attending class, you will better understand what your instructor is doing and know what questions to ask during class. Whether you are working independently or with an instructor, be attentive and take detailed notes of the definitions, rules, and examples.

• Collaborate With Your Peers

Research has shown that if you work on mathematics in a study group you will experience greater success. It is important that you understand and not copy others' work. Study with other students and discuss solution methods until each student understands. If you are able to explain mathematics to others, you will develop a deeper understanding for yourself.

• Don't Just Memorize

While it is important to remember formulas, properties, and definitions, memorization only provides an artificial knowledge of the concepts. For each algebraic process, you must understand the purpose of each step and the order in which they occur. You must also be able to identify what type of problems can be solved using each process and why. This deeper understanding will help you solve progressively more difficult problems.

• Prepare for Assessments

The best way to prepare for assessments is to go back and reconstruct your notes and examples. Write down everything that you remember on notecards or in a different notebook, and then go back and use your notes from class and your readings to fill in the blanks. This will help you identify what you need to review again and will tie the big ideas together.

• Manage Your Time

Spending three to four hours in class a day may not seem like much, but remember that your time out of class is not necessarily "free time." You are expected to do most of your classwork out of class. Expect to spend one to two hours studying outside of class for every hour that you spend in class. If you are studying independently, be sure to set aside enough time to preview each lesson, complete the lesson, and then review the lesson.

• Enjoy Mathematics!

Learn to enjoy working with mathematics. Problem solving is a complex process, and part of the joy of mathematics is the satisfaction of solving a problem. Don't be afraid to get started or to try different methods. Mathematicians make many mistakes before they reach the solutions to difficult problems—you are not alone.

Solutions

UNIT 1
Lesson 1
Try It 1.1
a. $16 = 2 \cdot 2 \cdot 2 \cdot 2$
b. $20 = 2 \cdot 2 \cdot 5$
c. $32 = 2 \cdot 2 \cdot 2 \cdot 2 \cdot 2$
d. $100 = 2 \cdot 2 \cdot 5 \cdot 5$

Try It 1.2
a. $14 = 2 \cdot 7$
$16 = 2 \cdot 2 \cdot 2 \cdot 2$
GCF = 2
b. $30 = 2 \cdot 3 \cdot 5$
$40 = 2 \cdot 2 \cdot 2 \cdot 5$
GCF $= 2 \cdot 5 = 10$
c. $100 = 2 \cdot 2 \cdot 5 \cdot 5$
$75 = 3 \cdot 5 \cdot 5$
GCF $= 5 \cdot 5 = 25$
d. $8 = 2 \cdot 2 \cdot 2$
$24 = 2 \cdot 2 \cdot 2 \cdot 3$
$32 = 2 \cdot 2 \cdot 2 \cdot 2 \cdot 2$
GCF $= 2 \cdot 2 \cdot 2 = 8$

Try It 1.3
a. $4 = 2 \cdot 2$
$6 = 2 \cdot 3$
LCM $= 2 \cdot 2 \cdot 3 = 12$
b. $30 = 2 \cdot 3 \cdot 5 = 15 \cdot 2$
$15 = 3 \cdot 5 = 15$
LCM $= 15 \cdot 2 = 30$
c. $8 = 2 \cdot 2 \cdot 2 = 4 \cdot 2$
$12 = 2 \cdot 2 \cdot 3 = 4 \cdot 3$
LCM $= 4 \cdot 3 \cdot 2 = 24$
d. $24 = 2 \cdot 2 \cdot 2 \cdot 3 = 8 \cdot 3$
$32 = 2 \cdot 2 \cdot 2 \cdot 2 \cdot 2 = 8 \cdot 4$
LCM $= 8 \cdot 4 \cdot 3 = 96$

Lesson 2
Try It 2.1
a. $\frac{1}{4} = \frac{1 \cdot 3}{4 \cdot 3} = \frac{3}{12}$
$\frac{1}{6} = \frac{1 \cdot 2}{6 \cdot 2} = \frac{2}{12}$
Since $\frac{3}{12} > \frac{2}{12}, \frac{1}{4} > \frac{1}{6}$.
b. $\frac{1}{2} = \frac{1 \cdot 5}{2 \cdot 5} = \frac{5}{10}$
Since $\frac{7}{10} > \frac{5}{10}, \frac{7}{10} > \frac{1}{2}$.
c. $\frac{5}{12} = \frac{5 \cdot 3}{12 \cdot 3} = \frac{15}{36}$
$\frac{7}{18} = \frac{7 \cdot 2}{18 \cdot 2} = \frac{14}{36}$
Since $\frac{15}{36} > \frac{14}{36}, \frac{5}{12} > \frac{7}{18}$.

Try It 2.2
a. $50\% = \frac{50}{100} = 0.50$
$= \frac{50}{100} = \frac{1}{2}$
b. $6\% = \frac{6}{100} = 0.06$
$= \frac{6 \div 2}{100 \div 2} = \frac{3}{50}$
c. $62.5\% = \frac{62.5}{100} = \frac{625}{1,000} = 0.625$
$= \frac{625 \div 125}{1,000 \div 125} = \frac{5}{8}$

Lesson 3
Try It 2.3
a. $\frac{2}{5} = \frac{2 \cdot 20}{5 \cdot 20} = \frac{40}{100} = 0.40 = 40\%$
b. $\frac{7}{8} = \frac{7 \cdot 125}{8 \cdot 125} = \frac{875}{1,000} = 0.875 = 87.5\%$
c. $\frac{2}{3} = 0.\overline{6} = 66\frac{2}{3}\%$

Lesson 3
Try It 3.1
a. $\frac{7}{8} + \frac{5}{8} = \frac{12}{8} = 1\frac{4}{8} = 1\frac{1}{2}$
Check: $0.875 + 0.625 = 1.5$
b. $\frac{3}{4} + \frac{1}{3} = \frac{3 \cdot 3}{4 \cdot 3} + \frac{1 \cdot 4}{3 \cdot 4} = \frac{9 + 4}{12}$
$= \frac{13}{12} = 1\frac{1}{12}$
Check: $0.75 + 0.\overline{3} = 1.08\overline{3}$
c. $2\frac{1}{3} + 1\frac{5}{6} = \frac{7}{3} + \frac{11}{6} = \frac{14}{6} + \frac{11}{6}$
$= \frac{25}{6} = 4\frac{1}{6}$
Check: $2.\overline{3} + 1.8\overline{3} = 4.1\overline{6}$

Try It 3.2
a. $\frac{7}{8} - \frac{5}{8} = \frac{2 \div 2}{8 \div 2} = \frac{1}{4}$
Check: $0.875 - 0.625 = 0.25$
b. $\frac{3}{4} - \frac{1}{3} = \frac{3 \cdot 3}{4 \cdot 3} - \frac{1 \cdot 4}{3 \cdot 4} = \frac{9 - 4}{12} = \frac{5}{12}$
Check: $0.75 - 0.\overline{3} = 0.41\overline{6}$
c. $2\frac{1}{3} - 1\frac{5}{6} = \frac{7}{3} - \frac{11}{6} = \frac{14}{6} - \frac{11}{6}$
$= \frac{3}{6} = \frac{1}{2}$
Check: $2.\overline{3} - 1.8\overline{3} = 0.5$

Unit 1 Checkpoint
1. $60 = 2 \cdot 2 \cdot 3 \cdot 5$
2. $24 = 2 \cdot 2 \cdot 2 \cdot 3$
$36 = 2 \cdot 2 \cdot 3 \cdot 3$
$48 = 2 \cdot 2 \cdot 2 \cdot 2 \cdot 3$
GCF $= 2 \cdot 2 \cdot 3 = 12$
3. $15 = 3 \cdot 5$
$20 = 2 \cdot 2 \cdot 5$
LCM $= 5 \cdot 2 \cdot 2 \cdot 3 = 60$
4. $\frac{9}{16} = \frac{9 \cdot 3}{16 \cdot 3} = \frac{27}{48}$
$\frac{7}{12} = \frac{7 \cdot 4}{12 \cdot 4} = \frac{28}{48}$
Since $\frac{28}{48} > \frac{27}{48}, \frac{7}{12} > \frac{9}{16}$.
5. $\frac{3}{5} = \frac{3 \cdot 2}{5 \cdot 2} = \frac{6}{10}$
Since $\frac{7}{10} > \frac{6}{10}, \frac{7}{10} > \frac{3}{5}$.
6. $80\% = 0.80 = \frac{80}{100} = \frac{8}{10} = \frac{4}{5}$
7. $5\% = 0.05 = \frac{5}{100} = \frac{1}{20}$
8. $\frac{4}{5} = \frac{80}{100} = 0.80 = 80\%$
9. $\frac{5}{8} = \frac{625}{1,000} = 0.625 = 62.5\%$
10. $\frac{5}{9} = 0.\overline{5} = 55.\overline{5}\% = 55\frac{5}{9}\%$
11. $\frac{3}{4} + \frac{3}{4} = \frac{6}{4} = \frac{3}{2} = 1\frac{1}{2}$
Check: $0.75 + 0.75 = 1.5$

12. $\frac{5}{9} + \frac{1}{2} = \frac{10}{18} + \frac{9}{18} = \frac{19}{18} = 1\frac{1}{18}$
Check: $0.\overline{5} + 0.5 = 1.0\overline{5}$
13. $1\frac{3}{4} + 2\frac{5}{16} = \frac{7}{4} + \frac{37}{16}$
$= \frac{28}{16} + \frac{37}{16} = \frac{65}{16} = 4\frac{1}{16}$
Check: $1.75 + 2.3125 = 4.0625$
14. $\frac{3}{5} - \frac{1}{2} = \frac{6}{10} - \frac{5}{10} = \frac{1}{10}$
Check: $0.6 - 0.5 = 0.1$
15. $2\frac{1}{2} - 1\frac{3}{4} = \frac{5}{2} - \frac{7}{4} = \frac{10}{4} - \frac{7}{4} = \frac{3}{4}$
Check: $2.5 - 1.75 = 0.75$

Lesson 4
Try It 4.1
a. 25% of $18 = \frac{1}{\cancel{4}_2} \cdot \frac{\cancel{18}^9}{1} = \frac{9}{2} = 4\frac{1}{2}$
$= 0.25(18) = 4.5$
b. 60% of $25 = \frac{3}{\cancel{5}} \cdot \frac{\cancel{25}^5}{1} = 15$
$= 0.60(25) = 15$
c. 10% of $120 = \frac{1}{\cancel{10}} \cdot \frac{\cancel{120}^{12}}{1} = 12$
$= 0.10(120) = 12$

Try It 4.2
a. $\frac{3}{4} \cdot \frac{1}{3} = \frac{3}{12} = \frac{1}{4}$
b. $\frac{2}{3} \cdot 1\frac{3}{4} = \frac{2}{3} \cdot \frac{7}{\cancel{4}_2} = \frac{7}{6} = 1\frac{1}{6}$
c. $1\frac{3}{4} \cdot 2 = \frac{7}{\cancel{4}} \cdot \frac{\cancel{2}}{1} = \frac{7}{2}$
$= \frac{7}{2} \cdot 640 = \frac{7}{\cancel{2}} \cdot \frac{\cancel{640}^{320}}{1} = 2,240$ acres

Try It 4.3
a. $1\frac{3}{4} \div \frac{2}{5} = \frac{7}{4} \cdot \frac{5}{2} = \frac{35}{8}$
b. $2\frac{2}{3} \div \frac{4}{9} = \frac{\cancel{8}}{\cancel{3}} \cdot \frac{\cancel{9}}{\cancel{4}} = 6$
c. $8 \div \frac{1}{3} = \frac{8}{1} \cdot \frac{3}{1} = 24$

Lesson 5
Try It 5.1
a. $0.25d = 0.25(\$15) = \$3.75$
b. $x + 8 = \$39.95 + 8 = \$47.95$
c. $\frac{d}{7} = \frac{364}{7} = 52$

Try It 5.2
a. $x + 10 + 7x - 1 = 8x + 9$
Check: $8(10) + 9 = 89$
$10 + 10 + 7(10) - 1 = 89$
b. $\frac{5}{2}x - \frac{3}{4}x = \frac{10}{4}x - \frac{3}{4}x = \frac{7}{4}x$
Check:
$\frac{5}{2}(10) - \frac{3}{4}(10) = 25 - \frac{15}{2} = 17.5$
$\frac{7}{4}(10) = 17.5$

c. $3x - 3 - 2x = x - 3$
Check:
$3(10) - 3 - 2(10) = 7$
$(10) - 3 = 7$

Lesson 6
Try It 6.1
a. $x + 4 - 4 = 16 - 4$
$x = 12$
b. $x - 6.75 + 6.75 = 1.25 + 6.75$
$x = 8$
c. $x - \frac{1}{2} + \frac{1}{2} = \frac{2}{3} + \frac{1}{2}$
$x = \frac{4}{6} + \frac{3}{6} = \frac{7}{6} = 1\frac{1}{6}$

Try It 6.2
a. $\frac{4x}{4} = \frac{15}{4}, x = \frac{15}{4}$
b. $\left(\frac{5}{4}\right) \cdot \frac{4}{5}x = \left(\frac{5}{4}\right) \cdot 12$
$x = \frac{60}{4} = 15$
c. To find the hourly rate, multiply the overtime rate by the reciprocal of $1.5 = \frac{3}{2}$ or $\frac{2}{3}$.
$13.5\left(\frac{2}{3}\right) = \$9$

Try It 6.3
a. $3x - 1 + 1 = 11 + 1$
$\frac{3x}{3} = \frac{12}{3}$
$x = 4$
b. $\frac{1}{2}x + 2 - 2 = 5 - 2$
$\left(\frac{2}{1}\right) \cdot \frac{1}{2}x = \left(\frac{2}{1}\right) \cdot 3$
$x = 6$
c. $1.5x + 10 - 10 = 28.75 - 10$
$\frac{1.5x}{1.5} = \frac{18.75}{1.5}$
$x = 12.5$ lbs

Unit 1 Self-Evaluation
1. $80 = 2 \cdot 2 \cdot 2 \cdot 2 \cdot 5$
2. GCF=10
3. LMC= 48
4. $\frac{6}{16} = \frac{3}{8}$
5. $70\% = 0.70 = \frac{70}{100} = \frac{7}{10}$
6. $15\% = 0.15 = \frac{15}{100} = \frac{3}{20}$
7. $\frac{3}{5} = 0.60 = 60\%$
8. $\frac{3}{8} = \frac{375}{1,000} = 0.375 = 37.5\%$
9. $\frac{1}{6} = 0.1\overline{6} = 16.\overline{6}\% = 16\frac{2}{3}\%$
10. $\frac{8}{9} + \frac{7}{9} = \frac{15}{9} = 1\frac{6}{9} = 1\frac{2}{3}$
    Check: $0.\overline{8} + 0.\overline{7} = 1.\overline{6}$
11. $\frac{3}{4} + \frac{2}{3} = \frac{9+8}{12} = \frac{17}{12} = 1\frac{5}{12}$
    Check: $0.75 + 0.\overline{6} = 1.41\overline{6}$
12. $3\frac{1}{4} + 2\frac{3}{8} = \frac{13}{4} + \frac{19}{8}$
    $= \frac{26 + 19}{8} = \frac{45}{8} = 5\frac{5}{8}$
    Check: $3.25 + 2.375 = 5.625$

13. $\frac{5}{9} - \frac{2}{9} = \frac{3}{9} = \frac{1}{3}$
    Check: $0.\overline{5} - 0.\overline{2} = 0.\overline{3}$
14. $\frac{7}{9} - \frac{1}{2} = \frac{14 - 9}{18} = \frac{5}{18}$
    Check: $0.\overline{7} - 0.5 = 0.2\overline{7}$
15. $4\frac{1}{5} - 1\frac{7}{10} = \frac{21}{5} - \frac{17}{10}$
    $= \frac{42 - 17}{10} = \frac{25}{10} = \frac{5}{2} = 2.5$
    Check: $4.2 - 1.7 = 2.5$
16. $0.4(120) = 48$
17. $\frac{5}{6} \cdot \frac{3}{10} = \frac{15}{60} = \frac{1}{4}$
18. $1\frac{2}{3} \cdot 1\frac{4}{5} = \frac{5}{3} \cdot \frac{9}{5} = \frac{45}{15} = 3$
19. $3\frac{3}{5} \div \frac{3}{10} = \frac{18}{5} \cdot \frac{10}{3} = \frac{180}{15} = 12$
20. $9 \div \frac{3}{4} = \frac{9}{1} \cdot \frac{4}{3} = \frac{36}{3} = 12$ pieces
21. $0.15(15) = \$2.25$
22. $\$135 - \$25 = \$110$
23. $6x + 5 + x - 1 = 7x + 4$
24. $\frac{1}{2}x - \frac{1}{4}x = \frac{1}{4}x$
25. $x - \frac{1}{2} + \frac{1}{2} = \frac{5}{6} + \frac{1}{2}$
    $x = \frac{5 + 3}{6} = \frac{8}{6} = 1\frac{2}{6} = 1\frac{1}{3}$
26. $\left(\frac{3}{1}\right) \cdot \frac{1}{3}x = \left(\frac{3}{1}\right) \cdot 12$
    $x = 36$
27. $3x + 4 - 4 = 25 - 4$
    $\frac{3x}{3} = \frac{21}{3}$
    $x = 7$
28. $\frac{3}{4}x - 1 + 1 = 5 + 1$
    $\left(\frac{4}{3}\right) \cdot \frac{3}{4}x = \left(\frac{4}{3}\right) \cdot 6$
    $x = \frac{24}{3} = 8$
29. $\frac{\$402}{\$12} = 33.5$ hours
30. $12.5x + 10 - 10 = 97.5 - 10$
    $\frac{12.5x}{12.5} = \frac{87.5}{12.5}$
    $x = 7$

UNIT 2
Lesson 1
Try It 1.1
a. 52
b. -60
c. -34
Try It 1.2
a. 45
b. -39
c. -350
Try It 1.3
a. -39
b. 120
c. -75
Try It 1.4
a.
$10\left(\frac{-3}{2} + \frac{4}{5}\right) = 10\left(\frac{-15}{10} + \frac{8}{10}\right)$
$= 10\left(\frac{-7}{10}\right) = -7$

b. $10\left(\frac{-3}{2} + \frac{4}{5}\right) = \left(\frac{-30}{2} + \frac{40}{5}\right)$
$= -15 + 8 = -7$
c. $-0.75\left(\frac{-20}{3}\right) = -\frac{3}{4}\left(\frac{-20}{3}\right)$
$= \frac{20}{4} = 5$

Lesson 2
Try It 2.1
a.

Gadgets: x	Revenue (\$): $30x$	Cost (\$): $1500 + 20x$
0	0	1,500
50	1,500	2,500
100	3,000	3,500
150	4,500	4,500
200	6,000	5,500

b.

Videos: x	Rental A: $10 + 2.5x$	Rental B: $12.5 + 2x$
5	22.5	22.5
10	35	32.5
15	47.5	42.5
20	60	52.5
25	72.5	62.5
30	85	72.5

Try It 2.2
a. $30x = 1,500 + 20x$
$30x - 20x = 1,500 + 20x - 20x$
$10x = 1,500$
$\frac{10}{10}x = \frac{1,500}{10}$
$x = 150$
b. $10 + 2.5x = 12.5 + 2x$
$10 - 10 + 2.5x = 12.5 - 10 + 2x$
$2.5x - 2x = 2.5 + 2x - 2x$
$\frac{.5}{.5}x = \frac{2.5}{.5}$
$x = 5$

Try It 2.3
a. $-\frac{1}{2}x + 7 = 9$
$-\frac{1}{2}x + 7 - 7 = 9 - 7$
$-2\left(-\frac{1}{2}\right)x = -2(2)$
$x = -4$
b. $4(2x - 5) = 5 - (2x - 1)$
$8x - 20 = 5 - 2x + 1$
$8x - 20 = 6 - 2x$
$8x + 2x - 20 = 6 - 2x + 2x$
$10x - 20 + 20 = 6 + 20$
$10x = 26$
$x = \frac{26}{10} = 2.6$

c. $\frac{2}{3}(2x - 3) = -(x + 4)$

$\frac{4}{3}x - 2 = -x - 4$

$\frac{4}{3}x - 2 + 2 = -x - 4 + 2$

$\frac{4}{3}x + x = -x + x - 2$

$\frac{4}{3}x + \frac{3}{3}x = -2$

$\left(\frac{3}{7}\right)\frac{7}{3}x = \frac{3}{7}(-2)$

$x = -\frac{6}{7}$

Lesson 3

Try It 3.1

a.

$30x - (1{,}500 + 20x) > 3{,}000$

$10x - 1{,}500 > 3{,}000$

$10x - 1{,}500 + 1{,}500 > 3{,}000 + 1{,}500$

$\frac{10x}{10} > \frac{4{,}500}{10}$

$x > 450$

b.

$10 + 2.5x > 12.5 + 2x$

$10 + 2.5x - 2x > 12.5 + 2x - 2x$

$10 - 10 + .5x > 12.5 - 10$

$\frac{.5x}{.5} > \frac{2.5}{.5}$

$x > 5$

Try It 3.2

a. $4{,}000 < 30x - (1{,}500 + 20x) < 6{,}000$

$4{,}000 < 10x - 1{,}500 < 6{,}000$

$4{,}000 < 10x - 1{,}500 < 6{,}000$

$+1{,}500 \qquad +1{,}500 + 1{,}500$

$\frac{5{,}500}{10} < \frac{10x}{10} < \frac{7{,}500}{10}$

$550 < x < 750$

b.

$20 \leq 10 + 2.5x \leq 50$

$20 - 10 \leq 10 - 10 + 2.5x \leq 50 - 10$

$\frac{10}{2.5} \leq \frac{2.5x}{2.5} \leq \frac{40}{2.5}$

$4 \leq x \leq 16$

Try It 3.3

a.

$-\frac{1}{2}x + 5 > 9$

$-\frac{1}{2}x + 5 - 5 > 9 - 5$

$(-2)\left(-\frac{1}{2}x\right) < (-2)4$

$x < -8$

b.

$2x - 5 \geq 5 - (2x - 1)$

$2x - 5 \geq 5 - 2x + 1$

$2x - 5 + 5 \geq 6 + 5 - 2x$

$2x + 2x \geq 11 - 2x + 2x$

$\frac{4x}{4} \geq \frac{11}{4}$

$x \geq \frac{11}{4}$

c.

$-1 \leq -2x - 3 < 4$

$-1 + 3 \leq -2x - 3 + 3 < 4 + 3$

$\frac{2}{-2} \geq \frac{-2x}{-2} > \frac{7}{-2}$

$-1 \geq x > -\frac{7}{2}$

or

$-\frac{7}{2} < x \leq -1$

Unit 2 Checkpoint

1. -6

2. 6.25

3. $-\frac{13}{10} = -1.3$

4. -7

5. $258.67 - 152.25 = 106.42$
$106.42 - 48.67 = 57.75$
$57.75 - 112 = -54.25$
(Add $-$ \$25 charge.)
$-54.25 - 25 = -79.25$

6. $2\left(\left(\frac{1}{2}\right) - 5\right) = 1 - 10 = -9$

7. $4\left(\frac{1}{2}\right) - \left(\left(\frac{1}{2}\right) + 2\right) = 2 - \frac{5}{2} = -\frac{1}{2}$

8.

Gadgets: x	Revenue (\$): $30x$	Cost (\$): $1500 + 20x$
0	0	160
50	500	535
100	1,000	910
150	1,500	1,285
200	2,000	1,660

9.

Hour: x	Rental A: $2.5x + 5$	Cost: $2x + 8$
0	5	8
1	7.5	10
2	10	12
3	12.5	14
4	15	16
5	17.5	18

To find the break-even point:
$2.5x + 5 = 2x + 8$
$2.5x + 5 - 5 = 2x + 8 - 5$
$2.5x - 2x = 2x - 2x + 3$
$0.5x = 3$
$(2)\frac{1}{2}x = (2)3$
$x = 6$

10.

$x - 5(x + 1) = 4(x - 1) + 2$
$x - 5x - 5 = 4x - 4 + 2$
$-4x - 5 = 4x - 2$
$-4x = 4x + 3$
$-8x = 3$
$x = -\frac{3}{8}$

11. For example:

$2(8) - 10 < 7$

$6 < 7$

Other possible values: 4, -2, 0

12. For example:

$-4(-2) - ((-2) + 2) > 3$

$8 > 3$

Other possible values: $-4, -10, -20$

13.

$10x - 7.5x > 100 + 7.5x - 7.5x$

$\frac{2.5x}{2.5} > \frac{100}{2.5}$

$x > 40$

To find when the profit is between \$500 and \$1,000

$500 + 100 < 2.5x - 100 + 100 < 1{,}000 + 100$

$\frac{600}{2.5} < \frac{2.5x}{2.5} < \frac{1{,}100}{2.5}$

$240 < x < 440$

14.

$-\frac{2}{3}x - 2 + 2 \leq -4 + 2$

$\left(-\frac{3}{2}\right)\left(-\frac{2}{3}x\right) \geq -2\left(-\frac{3}{2}\right)$

$x \geq 3$

15.

$4 - 4 < -\frac{1}{2}x + 4 - 4 < 10 - 4$

$0(-2) > (-2)\left(-\frac{1}{2}x\right) > 6 (-2)$

$0 > x > -12$

or

$-12 < x < 0$

Lesson 4

Try It 4.1

a. Find the break-even point:
$R(x) = C(x)$
$15x = 7.5x + 120$
$7.5x = 120$
$x = 16$

To evaluate for $x = 16$:
$R(16) = 15(16) = 240$
$C(16) = 7.5(16) + 120 = 240$
The break-even point is at (16, 240).

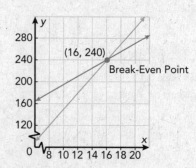

b.
$$P(x) = R(x) - C(x)$$
$$= 15x - (7.5x + 120)$$
$$= 7.5x - 120$$
Constant function: $y = 300$
Determine when the profit is $300.
Solve for x:
$$300 + 120 = 7.5x - 120 + 120$$
$$\frac{420}{7.5} = \frac{7.5x}{7.5}$$
$$x = 56$$

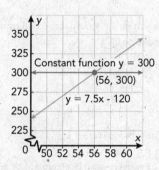

The profit is $300 when $x = 56$.

c. $G(x) = 42{,}000 - 50x$
Find when the tank will have 20,000 gallons. Solve for x:
$$20{,}000 - 42{,}000 = 42{,}000 - 42{,}000 - 50x$$
$$\frac{-22{,}000}{-50} = \frac{-50x}{-50}$$
$$x = 440$$

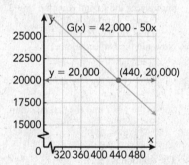

The tank will have 20,000 gallons after 440 minutes or 7 hrs and 20 min.

Explore It 4.2
1. The initial cost is $5, or the y-intercept is (0, 5).
2. The hourly rate is $2 per hour, or the rate of change is 2.
3. $y = 2x + 5$ is the function based on the x and y values on the graph.

Try It 4.2
a. The y-intercept is (0, 2).
Use the point (1, 5) to find the value of m, or the slope.
Solve for m:
$$5 = m(1) + 2$$
$$m = 3$$
The function for the given graph is $f(x) = 3x + 2$.

b. The y-intercept is (0, −1).
Use the point (4, 1) to find the value of m, or the slope.
Solve for m:
$$1 = m(4) - 1$$
$$2 = 4m$$
$$m = \frac{1}{2} \text{ or } 0.5$$
The function for the given graph is $f(x) = \frac{1}{2}x - 1$.

c. The y-intercept is (0, 24).
Use the point (4, 12) to find the value of m, or the slope.
Solve for m:
$$12 = m(4) + 24$$
$$-12 = 4m$$
$$m = -3$$
The function for the given graph is $f(x) = -3x + 24$.

Lesson 5

Explore It 5.1
1. The increase in cost is 100. This is the change in the y-variable.
2. The increase in units is 40. This is the change in the x-variable.
3. The cost/unit is $\frac{100}{40} = 2.5$. This is value of the rate of change or the slope.
4. Find the y-intercept.
$$60 = 2.5(20) + b$$
$$b = 10$$
5. $y = 2.5x + 10$

Try It 5.1
a. Determine the slope, m.
$$m = \frac{\Delta y}{\Delta x} = \frac{145 - 100}{8 - 5} = 15$$
Determine the y-intercept, b.
$$100 = 15(5) + b$$
$$b = 25$$
The linear equation is $y = 15x + 25$.

b. Determine the slope, m.
$$m = \frac{\Delta y}{\Delta x} = \frac{600 - (-200)}{200 - 100} = 8$$
Determine the y-intercept, b.
$$600 = 8(200) + b$$
$$b = -1{,}000$$
The linear equation is $y = 8x - 1{,}000$.

Try It 5.2
a. Determine the slope, m.
$$m = \frac{\Delta y}{\Delta x} = \frac{-4 - 2}{3 - (-3)} = \frac{-6}{6} = -1$$

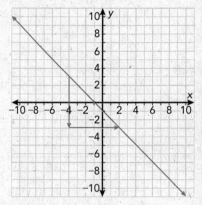

Determine the y-intercept, b.
$$2 = (-1)(-3) + b$$
$$2 = 3 + b$$
$$b = -1$$
The linear equation in slope-intercept form is $y = -x - 1$.
The linear equation in standard form is shown below.
$$y + x = -x - 1 + x$$
$$x + y = -1$$

b. Determine the slope, m.
$$m = \frac{\Delta y}{\Delta x} = \frac{-5 - 4}{3 - (-1)} = -\frac{9}{4}$$
Determine the y-intercept, b.
$$4 = -\frac{9}{4}(-1) + b$$
$$4 - \frac{9}{4} = \frac{9}{4} - \frac{9}{4} + b$$
$$\frac{16}{4} - \frac{9}{4} = b$$
$$b = \frac{7}{4}$$
The linear equation in slope-intercept form is $y = -\frac{9}{4}x + \frac{7}{4}$.

The linear equation in standard form is shown below.
$$4y = 4\left(-\frac{9}{4}x + \frac{7}{4}\right)$$
$$4y = -9x + 7$$
$$9x + 4y = 7$$

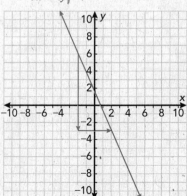

Try It 5.3

a. The slope of the parallel line is $m = \frac{1}{2}$. Find the value for b.

$$2 = \frac{1}{2}(-4) + b$$

$$2 = -2 + b$$

$$b = 4$$

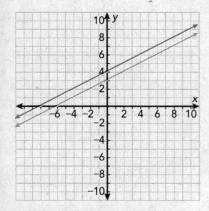

The equation for the parallel line is $y = \frac{1}{2}x + 4$.

b. The slope of the perpendicular line is $m = -\frac{1}{3}$. Find the value for b.

$$5 = -\frac{1}{3}(3) + b$$

$$5 = -1 + b$$

$$b = 6$$

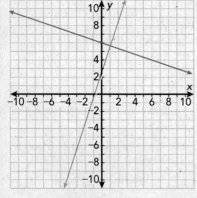

The equation for the perpendicular line is $y = -\frac{1}{3}x + 6$.

Lesson 6

Try It 6.1

a.

$$y = 2x + 7$$

$$y = -\frac{1}{2}x - \frac{1}{2}$$

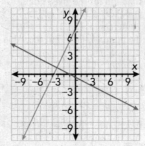

The solution is $(-3, 1)$.

b.

$$y = \frac{1}{2}x + 2$$

$$y = \frac{1}{2}x - 2$$

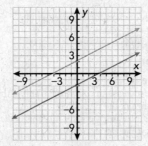

There is no solution, the lines are parallel.

Try It 6.2

a. Solve the first equation for y.

$$-x + y = 3$$

$$y = x + 3$$

Substitute $x + 3$ in for y in the second equation and solve for x.

$$2x - (x + 3) = -4$$

$$2x - x - 3 = -4$$

$$x - 3 = -4$$

$$x = -1$$

Substitute $x = -1$ into the first equation and solve for y.

$$-(-1) + y = 3$$

$$1 + y = 3$$

$$y = 2$$

The solution is $(-1, 2)$.

b. Solve the first equation for y.

$$6x - 2y = 1$$

$$-2y = -6x + 1$$

$$y = 3x - \frac{1}{2}$$

Substitute $3x - \frac{1}{2}$ in for y in the second equation and solve for x.

$$-2x + 3\left(3x - \frac{1}{2}\right) = 2$$

$$-2x + 9x - \frac{3}{2} = 2$$

$$7x = \frac{7}{2}$$

$$x = \frac{1}{2}$$

Substitute $x = \frac{1}{2}$ into the second equation and solve for y.

$$-2\left(\frac{1}{2}\right) + 3y = 2$$

$$-1 + 3y = 2$$

$$3y = 3$$

$$y = 1$$

The solution is $\left(\frac{1}{2}, 1\right)$.

Try It 6.3

a. The variable y can be eliminated by adding the two equations as they are.

$$\begin{aligned} x + y &= 5 \\ + \quad x - y &= -1 \\ \hline 2x &= 4 \\ x &= 2 \end{aligned}$$

Substitute $x = 2$ into the first equation.

$$(2) + y = 5$$

$$y = 3$$

The solution is $(2, 3)$.

b. The variable x can be eliminated by multiplying the second equation by -2.

$$2x - y = 2$$

$$-2(x - 3y) = -2(-4)$$

Now add the two equations.

$$\begin{aligned} 2x - y &= 2 \\ -2x + 6y &= 8 \\ \hline 5y &= 10 \\ y &= 2 \end{aligned}$$

Substitute $y = 2$ into the first equation.

$$2x - (2) = 2$$

$$2x = 4$$

$$x = 2$$

The solution is $(2, 2)$.

c. Write two equations for the situation.

$$4x + 20y = 600$$

$$2x + 11y = 320$$

Multiply the second equation by -2.

$$4x + 20y = 600$$

$$-2(2x + 11y) = -2(320)$$

Now add the two equations.

$$\begin{aligned} 4x + 20y &= 600 \\ -4x - 22y &= -640 \\ \hline -2y &= -40 \\ y &= 20 \end{aligned}$$

Substitute $y = 20$ into the second equation.

$$2x + 11(20) = 320$$

$$2x + 220 = 320$$

$$2x = 100$$

$$x = 50$$

The solution is $(50, 20)$.

Unit 2 Self-Evaluation

1. -6

2. 6

3.
$$-4\left(-\frac{1}{2}+\frac{3}{4}\right)=$$
$$= 2 - 3$$
$$= -1$$

4.
$$-0.25\left(-\frac{20}{7}\right)=$$
$$= -\frac{1}{4}\left(-\frac{20}{7}\right)$$
$$= \frac{5}{7}$$

5.
$$4(x-1)=-1$$
$$4x-4=-1$$
$$4x=3$$
$$x=\frac{3}{4}$$

6.
$$-\frac{1}{2}(2x-4)=6$$
$$-x+2=6$$
$$x=-4$$

7.
$$2x-(x-3)=3(x-3)-1$$
$$2x-x+3=3x-9-1$$
$$x+3=3x-10$$
$$-2x=-13$$
$$x=\frac{13}{2}=6.5$$

8.
$$-\frac{2}{3}(3x-5)=-(x-3)$$
$$-2x+\frac{10}{3}=-x+3$$
$$-x=-\frac{1}{3}$$
$$x=\frac{1}{3}$$

9.
$$-2x+1\ge-3$$
$$-2x\ge-4$$
$$x\le2$$

10.
$$\frac{3}{4}(2x-8)\le-3$$
$$\frac{3}{2}x-6\le-3$$
$$\frac{3}{2}x\le3$$
$$x\le2$$

11.
$$-3<-x-1<4$$
$$-2<-x<5$$
$$2>x>-5$$
$$-5<x<2$$

12.
$$3<\frac{1}{2}x-4<5$$
$$7<\frac{1}{2}x<9$$
$$14<x<18$$

13. To begin, you know that the y-intercept of the given linear function is $-1{,}000$, or $b=-1{,}000$. You can also find another point, $(40, 0)$, which shows that you have broken even when you have sold 40 units. Use this information to solve for m, the slope.
$$y=mx+b$$
$$0=40m-1{,}000$$
$$-40m=-1{,}000$$
$$m=25$$
The linear equation for this graph is $y=25x-1{,}000$.

14. To begin, you know that the y-intercept of the given linear function is 8, or $b=8$. You can also find another point, namely $(2, 5)$. You can use this information to solve for m, the slope.
$$y=mx+b$$
$$5=2m+8$$
$$m=-\frac{3}{2}$$
The linear equation for this graph is $y=-\frac{3}{2}x+8$.

15. To begin, you know that the y-intercept of the given linear function is -5, or $b=-5$. You can also find another point, namely $(1, -3)$. You can use this information to solve for m, the slope.
$$y=mx+b$$
$$-3=m-5$$
$$m=2$$
The linear equation for this graph is $y=2x-5$.

16. To begin, you know that the y-intercept of the given linear function is 2, or $b=2$. You can also find another point, namely $(3, 0)$. You can use this information to solve for m, the slope.
$$y=mx+b$$
$$0=3m+2$$
$$m=-\frac{2}{3}$$
The linear equation for this graph is $y=-\frac{2}{3}x+2$.

17. To begin, find the slope of the line between the two given points.
$$m=\frac{4-0}{1-(-3)}$$
$$=\frac{4}{4}=1$$
Now use slope-intercept form of a linear equation along with one of the given points to solve for b.
$$y=x+b$$
$$0=-3+b$$
$$b=3$$
The linear equation in slope intercept form is $y=x+3$.
The linear equation in standard form is $x-y=-3$.

18. To begin, find the slope of the line between the two given points.
$$m=\frac{-2-(-5)}{3-1}$$
$$=\frac{3}{2}$$
Now use slope-intercept form of a linear equation along with one of the given points to solve for b.
$$y=\frac{3}{2}x+b$$
$$-5=\frac{3}{2}(1)+b$$
$$-10=3+2b$$
$$2b=-13$$
$$b=-\frac{13}{2}$$
The linear equation in slope-intercept form is $y=\frac{3}{2}x-\frac{13}{2}$.
To find the linear equation in standard form, first multiply the equation by 2.
$$2y=3x-13$$
The linear equation in standard form is $3x-2y=13$.

19. To begin, find the slope of the line between the two given points.
$$m=\frac{2-(-1)}{2-(-4)}$$
$$=\frac{3}{6}=\frac{1}{2}$$
Now use slope-intercept form of a linear equation along with one of the given points to solve for b.
$$y=\frac{1}{2}x+b$$
$$2=\frac{1}{2}(2)+b$$
$$b=1$$
The linear equation in slope-intercept form is $y=\frac{1}{2}x+1$.
To find the linear equation in standard form, first multiply the equation by 2.
$$2y=x+2$$
The linear equation in standard form is $x-2y=-2$.

20. The variable y can be eliminated by adding the two equations as they are.
$$\begin{array}{r}x-y=1\\2x+y=-5\\\hline3x=-4\end{array}$$
$$x=-\frac{4}{3}$$
Substitute $x=-\frac{4}{3}$ into the first equation.
$$\left(-\frac{4}{3}\right)-y=1$$
$$-y=\frac{3}{3}+\frac{4}{3}$$
$$y=-\frac{7}{3}$$
The solution is $\left(-\frac{4}{3},-\frac{7}{3}\right)$.

21. Solve the first equation for x.
$$x - 2y = -5$$
$$x = 2y - 5$$
Substitute $2y - 5$ in for x in the second equation and solve for y.
$$3(2y - 5) + y = -1$$
$$6y - 15 + y = -1$$
$$7y = 14$$
$$y = 2$$
Substitute $y = 2$ into the first equation and solve for x.
$$x - 2(2) = -5$$
$$x - 4 = -5$$
$$x = -1$$
The solution is $(-1, 2)$.

22. The variable x can be eliminated by multiplying the first equation by 3.
$$3(x - 3y) = 3(4)$$
$$-3x + 2y = 7$$
Now add the two equations.
$$3x - 9y = 12$$
$$\underline{-3x + 2y = 7}$$
$$-7y = 19$$
$$y = -\frac{19}{7} \approx -2.71$$
Substitute $y = -\frac{19}{7}$ into the first equation.
$$x - 3\left(-\frac{19}{7}\right) = 4$$
$$x + \frac{57}{7} = 4$$
$$x = \frac{28}{7} - \frac{57}{7}$$
$$x = -\frac{29}{7} \approx -4.14$$
The solution is $\left(-\frac{29}{7}, -\frac{19}{7}\right)$.

23. The variable y can be eliminated by multiplying the first equation by 2.
$$2(5x - 2y) = 2(-2)$$
$$3x + 4y = 4$$
Now add the two equations.
$$10x - 4y = -4$$
$$\underline{+ 3x + 4y = 4}$$
$$13x = 0$$
$$x = 0$$
Substitute $x = 0$ into the first equation.
$$5(0) - 2y = -2$$
$$-2y = -2$$
$$y = 1$$
The solution is $(0, 1)$.

24. $21° - 27° = -6°$

25.
$$50 + 25x = 100 + 20x$$
$$5x = 50$$
$$x = 10$$

26. Determine when the revenue is greater than the cost.
$$R(x) > C(x)$$
$$10x > 100 + 7.5x$$
$$2.5x > 100$$
$$x > 40$$
Write a profit function.
$$P(x) = R(x) - C(x)$$
$$= 10x - (100 + 7.5x)$$
$$P(x) = 2.5x - 100$$
Find when the profit is between 500 and 1,000.
$$500 < 2.5x - 100 < 1,000$$
$$600 < 2.5x < 1,100$$
$$240 < x < 440$$

27. Find the break-even point:
$$R(x) = C(x)$$
$$7.5x = 5x + 60$$
$$2.5x = 60$$
$$x = 24$$
Evaluate for $x = 24$:
$$R(24) = 7.5(24) = 180$$
$$C(24) = 5(24) + 60 = 180$$
The break-even point is at $(24, 180)$.

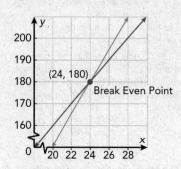

28. Use the two points to find the slope of the profit equation.
$$m = \frac{2,000 - (-200)}{1,000 - 40}$$
$$= \frac{2,200}{960} = \frac{55}{24} \approx 2.29$$
Use the value for m and one of the given points to solve for b.
$$y = mx + b$$
$$2,000 = \frac{55}{24}(1,000) + b$$
$$b = -\frac{875}{3} = -291.\overline{66}$$
The profit equation for the two given points is
$$P(x) = \frac{55}{24}x - \frac{875}{3} \text{ or}$$
$$P(x) = 2.29x - 291.67$$

29. The slope of the line perpendicular will be $m = -\frac{1}{2}$. Use the given point and this slope value to solve for the y-intercept.
$$y = mx + b$$
$$2 = -\frac{1}{2}(-1) + b$$
$$2 = \frac{1}{2} + b$$
$$b = \frac{3}{2}$$
The equation for the perpendicular line is $y = -\frac{1}{2}x + \frac{3}{2}$.

30. Write two equations for the situation.
$$5x + 8y = 1,200$$
$$3x + 6y = 800$$
The variable x can be eliminated by multiplying the first equation by 3 and the second equation by -5.
$$3(5x + 8y) = 3(1,200)$$
$$-5(3x + 6y) = -5(800)$$
Now, add the two equations.
$$15x + 24y = 3,600$$
$$\underline{-15x - 30y = -4,000}$$
$$-6y = -400$$
$$y = \frac{200}{3} = 66.\overline{66}$$
Substitute $y = \frac{200}{3}$ into the first equation.
$$5x + 8\left(\frac{200}{3}\right) = 1,200$$
$$5x + \frac{1,600}{3} = 1,200$$
$$5x = 1,200 - \frac{1,600}{3}$$
$$x = \frac{400}{3} = 133.\overline{33}$$
Since you cannot have a partial boat, the solution to this problem is $(66, 133)$.

UNIT 3
Lesson 1
Try It 1.1
a.
$$R \cdot B = A$$
$$R(90) = 50$$
$$R = \frac{50}{90} = \frac{5}{9} = 0.\overline{5} \approx 56\%$$

b.
$$R \cdot B = A$$
$$R(4,096) = 544$$
$$R = \frac{544}{4,096} \approx 0.13 \approx 13\%$$

c.
$$R \cdot B = A$$
$$R(5,000) = 3,525$$
$$R = \frac{3,525}{5,000} = 0.705 = 70.5\%$$

Try It 1.2
a.
$$R \cdot B = A$$
$$(0.75)(39) = 29.25$$

b.
$$R \cdot B = A$$
$$(0.15)(212) = 31.8$$
Since you can't have only 0.8 of a teacher, you would round down to 31 teachers.

c.
$$R \cdot B = A$$
$$(0.95)(59,845) = 56,852.75$$
Since you can't have 0.75 of a homeowner, you would round to 56,852 homeowners.

Try It 1.3

a.

$$R \cdot B = A$$
$$(0.005)B = 21,500$$
$$B = \frac{21,500}{0.005} = 4,300,000$$

The total gas sales must be \$4.3 million dollars in order to fund a \$21,500 project.

b.

$$R \cdot B = A$$
$$(0.16)B = 217$$
$$B = \frac{217}{0.16} = 1,356.25$$

Lesson 2

Try It 2.1

a.

$$r = 0.0475 \qquad R = 1.0475$$
$$A = B \cdot R$$
$$A = 5,000(1.0475) = 5,237.50$$

The value of her account at the end of the year is \$5,237.50 and her account earned \$237.50.

b.

$$r = 0.20 \qquad R = 1.20$$
$$A = B \cdot R$$
$$A = 24.87(1.20) \approx \$29.84$$

The total bill is \$29.84 and the tip is \$4.97.

c.

$$r = 0.0675 \quad R = 1.0675$$
$$A = B \cdot R$$
$$A = 895(1.0675) \approx \$955.41$$

The total cost is \$955.41 and the sales tax is \$60.41.

Try It 2.2

a.

$$r = 0.20 \qquad R = 1 - 0.20 = 0.80$$
$$A = B \cdot R$$
$$A = 17,500(0.80) = 14,000$$

The car is worth \$14,000 and the decrease in value is \$3,500.

b.

$$r = 0.40 \qquad R = 0.60$$
$$A = B \cdot R$$
$$A = 189(0.60) = 113.40$$

The reduced price for the coat is \$113.40 and the discount is \$75.60.

c.

$$r = 0.08 \qquad R = 1.08$$
$$A = B \cdot R$$
$$A = 113.40(1.08) = \$122.47$$

Try It 2.3

a.

$$R = \frac{A}{B}$$
$$R = \frac{17,550}{19,500} = 0.9$$
$$r = 1.0 - 0.9 = 0.1$$

The depreciation rate is 10%.

b.

$$B = \frac{A}{R}$$
$$B = \frac{82.50}{0.60} = \$137.50$$

---

c.

$$B = \frac{A}{R}$$
$$B = \frac{100}{1.219} \approx \$82.03$$

Lesson 3

Explore It 3.1

1. 1
2. 0.5
3. 0.25
4. 0.0625
5.

$$(2 \cdot 3)^4 = (6)^4 = 1,296$$
$$2^4 \cdot 3^4 = 16 \cdot 81 = 1,296$$

Try It 3.1

a. $(-2)^4 = (-2)(-2)(-2)(-2) = 16$
b. $-5^2 = -(5)^2 = -25$
c. $10^{-3} = \frac{1}{10^3} = \left(\frac{1}{10}\right)\left(\frac{1}{10}\right)\left(\frac{1}{10}\right) = \frac{1}{1,000}$
d. $10^3 = (10)(10)(10) = 1,000$
e. $\left(\frac{1}{3}\right)^4 = \left(\frac{1}{3}\right)\left(\frac{1}{3}\right)\left(\frac{1}{3}\right)\left(\frac{1}{3}\right) = \frac{1}{81}$
f. $\left(\frac{4}{3}\right)^{-2} = \left(\frac{3}{4}\right)^2 = \left(\frac{3}{4}\right)\left(\frac{3}{4}\right) = \frac{9}{16}$

Explore It 3.2

1.

$$2^2 \cdot 2^4 = 2^6$$
$$2^1 \cdot 2^6 = 2^7$$
$$2^3 \cdot 2^8 = 2^{11}$$

2.

$$\frac{2^5}{2^2} = 2^3$$
$$\frac{2^7}{2^6} = 2^1$$
$$\frac{2^8}{2^3} = 2^5$$

3.

$$\left(2^2\right)^3 = 2^6$$
$$\left(2^3\right)^4 = 2^{12}$$

Try It 3.2

a. $x^3 x^{-4} = x^{-1} = \frac{1}{x}$
b. $10^5 \cdot 10^7 = 10^{5+7} = 10^{12}$
c. $\frac{(-2)^4}{-2} = (-2)^3$
d. $\frac{x^7}{x^{-5}} = x^{7-(-5)} = x^{12}$
e. $(x^{-3})^2 = x^{-6} = \frac{1}{x^6}$
f. $(a^4 b^2)^3 = a^{4 \cdot 3} b^{2 \cdot 3} = a^{12} b^6$
g. $\frac{a^{-1} b^3}{a^2 b^2} = \frac{b}{a^3}$

Unit 3 Checkpoint

1. $\frac{21}{42} = 0.5 = 50\%$

2. $\frac{120}{(2/3)} = 180$

3. $\$35.62(1.15) \approx \$40.96$

   The tip is \$5.34.

---

4. $\frac{2,580}{21,500} = 0.12 = 12\%$
5. $\frac{\$15,360}{0.85} \approx \$18,070.59$
6. Reduced Price:

   $$\$599\left(1 - \frac{1}{3}\right) = \$599\left(\frac{2}{3}\right) \approx \$399.33$$

   Discount:

   $$\$599\left(\frac{1}{3}\right) \approx \$199.67$$

7. $\$12.50(1.055) \approx \$13.18$
8. $\frac{\$2,200}{\$2,500} = 0.88$

   Discount rate:
   $$1 - 0.88 = 0.12 = 12\%$$

9. $\frac{\$15,600}{\$15,000} = 1.04$

   The rate is 4%.

10. To get the pre-tax sale price:

    $\frac{\$450}{1.08} = \$416.67.$ Then to find the

    pre-sale price: $\frac{\left(\$416\frac{2}{3}\right)}{0.80} = \$520.83.$

11. $-10^{-4} = -\frac{1}{10^4}$
12. 1
13. $(-5)^{-2} = \frac{1}{(-5)^2} = \frac{1}{25}$
14.

    $$10^5 \cdot 10^{-9} = \frac{10^5}{10^9} =$$
    $$\frac{1}{10^4} = \frac{1}{10,000} = 0.0001$$

15. $(x^5)^{-2} = x^{-10} = \frac{1}{x^{10}}$

Lesson 4

Try It 4.1

a.

x	$y = 3^x$
-2	$\frac{1}{9}$
-1	$\frac{1}{3}$
0	1
1	3
2	9
3	27

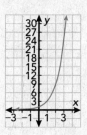

x	$y = 4 \cdot 3^x$
-2	$\frac{4}{9}$
-1	$\frac{4}{3}$
0	4
1	12
2	36
3	108

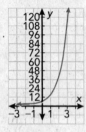

xplore It 4.2

$A = 5,000(1.06)(1.06)$
$\quad = 5,000(1.06)^2 = 5,618$

$A = 5,000(1.06)^3 = 5,955.08$

To find the value after 7 years multiply
5,000 by $(1.06)^7$.

$A = 5,000(1.06)^7 = 7,518.15$

ry It 4.2

$y = a \cdot b^x$
$y = 1,000(1.05)^2 = 1,102.50$

$y = a \cdot b^x$
$y = 5,000(1.0325)^5 \approx 5,867.06$

ry It 4.3

$y = a \cdot b^x$
$y = 16,450(1.035)^{10} \approx 23,204$

$y = a \cdot b^x$
$y = 140,000(1.05)^1 = 147,000$
$y = 140,000(1.05)^2 = 154,350$
$y = 140,000(1.05)^3 = 162,067.50$

Lesson 5

Try It 5.1

a.

x	$y = 3^{-x}$
-2	$y = 3^{-(-2)} = 9$
-1	$y = 3^{-(-1)} = 3$
0	$y = 3^{-(0)} = 1$
1	$y = 3^{-(1)} = \frac{1}{3} = 0.\overline{33}$
2	$y = 3^{-(2)} = \frac{1}{9} = 0.\overline{11}$
3	$y = 3^{-(3)} = \frac{1}{27} = 0.\overline{037}$

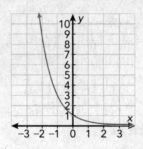

b.

x	$y = 20 \cdot 2^{-x}$
-2	$y = 20 \cdot 2^{-(-2)} = 80$
-1	$y = 20 \cdot 2^{-(-1)} = 40$
0	$y = 20 \cdot 2^{-(0)} = 20$
1	$y = 20 \cdot 2^{-1} = 20\left(\frac{1}{2}\right) = 10$
2	$y = 20 \cdot 2^{-2} = 20\left(\frac{1}{4}\right) = 5$
3	$y = 20 \cdot 2^{-3} = 20\left(\frac{1}{8}\right) = 2.5$

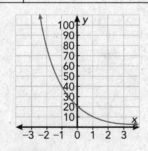

Explore It 5.2

1. $y = 300(0.9)^1 = 270$
2. $y = 300(0.9)^2 = 243$
3. $y = 300(0.9)^3 \approx 219$

Try It 5.2

a. $y = 1,200(0.88)^5 \approx 633$

b.

x	$y = 79,000(0.90)^x$
0	$y = 79,000(0.90)^0 = 79,000$
1	$y = 79,000(0.90)^1 = 71,100$
2	$y = 79,000(0.90)^2 = 63,990$
3	$y = 79,000(0.90)^3 = 57,591$

Lesson 6

Try It 6.1

a.

$a = 125,300$

$b = \frac{132,931}{129,059} \approx 1.03$

$y = 125,300(1.03)^x$
$y = 125,300(1.03)^3 \approx 136,918.69$
$y = 125,300(1.03)^4 \approx 141,026.25$

The population will be at least 140,000
in year 4.

b.

$a = 5,000$

$b = \frac{5,618}{5,300} = 1.06$

$y = 5,000(1.06)^x$
$y = 5,000(1.06)^3 = 5,955.08$
$y = 5,000(1.06)^6 \approx 7,092.60$

The investment will be at least $7,000
in year 6.

c.

$b = \frac{5,203}{4,730} = 1.10$

$a = \frac{4,300}{1.10} \approx 3,909$

$y = 3,909(1.10)^x$
$y = 3,909(1.10)^7 \approx 7,617$

Try It 6.2

a.

$a = 40,000$

$b = \frac{14,400}{24,000} = 0.6$

$y = 40,000(0.6)^x$
$y = 40,000(0.6)^3 = 8,640$
$y = 40,000(0.6)^4 = 5,184$
$y = 40,000(0.6)^5 = 3,110.40$
$y = 40,000(0.6)^6 = 1,866.24$

The equipment will be less than $2,000
in the 6th year.

b.

$b = \frac{171,475}{180,500} = 0.95$

$a = \frac{190,000}{0.95} = 200,000$

$y = 200,000(0.95)^x$
$y = 200,000(0.95)^4 \approx 162,901$
$y = 200,000(0.95)^7 \approx 139,667$

The population will drop below 140,000
in the 7th year.

Unit 3 Self-Evaluation

1. $\frac{15}{75} = 0.2 = 20\%$

2. $\frac{27}{0.30} = 90$

3. $\$29.68(0.20) \approx \$5.93$

4. $\frac{\$28,400}{\$31,500} \approx 0.902$

The discounted rate would then be

$$1 - 0.902 = 0.098 = 9.8\%$$

5. $\frac{\$25,300}{0.82} \approx \$30,853.65$

6. $\$14.50(1.035) \approx \$15.00$

7. $\frac{\$30,600}{\$30,000} = 1.02$; The percent increase is 2%.

8. $\frac{2,400}{2,500} = 0.96$; The discount rate is 4%.

9. $\$1,250(1.075) = \$1,343.75$

10. $\frac{\$300}{1.06} \approx \$283.02$

$\frac{\$283.02}{0.7} = \$404.31$

11. $x^{-3}x^3 = \frac{x^3}{x^3} = x^0 = 1$

12. $(x^{-3})^{-2} = x^6$

13. $\frac{x^{-6}}{x^7} = \frac{1}{x^7 \cdot x^6} = \frac{1}{x^{13}}$

14. $\frac{a^{-4}b^3}{a^2b^3} = \frac{1}{a^6}$

15. $\frac{(3a^{-1})^2 b^{-2}}{a^{-3}(2b)^2} = \frac{9a^{-2}b^{-2}}{8a^{-3}b^3}$

$= \frac{9ab^{-5}}{8} = \frac{9a}{8b^5}$

16.

x	$y = 3 \cdot 2^x$
-2	3/4
-1	3/2
0	3
1	6
2	12
3	24

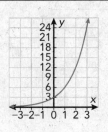

17.

x	$y = 2 \cdot 3^x$
-2	2/9
-1	2/3
0	2
1	6
2	18
3	54

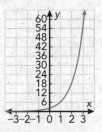

18. $\$1,000(1.035)^5 \approx \$1,187.68$

19. $\$10,000(1.06)^2 = \$11,236$

20. $\$325,000(1.05)^1 = \$341,250$
$\$325,000(1.05)^2 = \$358,312.50$
$\$325,000(1.05)^3 \approx \$376,228.12$

21. $1,220(1.075)^{10} \approx 2,514$

22. $\$500(1.05)^{10} \approx \$814.44$

23. $200,000(0.955)^{10} \approx 126,201$

24. $1,500 \, 0.935^5 \approx 1,071$

25. $\$37,000(0.88)^3 \approx \$25,214.46$

26. $\$220,000(0.94)^4 \approx \$171,764.77$

27. $\$3,000(0.50)^3 = \$375$

28.
$a = 15,000$
$b = \frac{15,825}{15,000} = 1.055$
$y = 15,000(1.055)^x$
The account grows to at least $20,000 in the 6th year.

29.
$b = \frac{3,025}{2,750} = 1.1$
$2,750 = a(1.1)^1$
$a = \frac{2,750}{1.1} = 2,500$
$y = 2,500(1.1)^x$
The population will be at least 4,000 in the 5th year.

30.
$b = \frac{14,800}{18,500} = (0.8)$
$18,500 = a(0.8)^1$
$a = \frac{18,500}{0.8} = 23,125$
$y = 23,125 (0.8)^x$
The account falls below $4,000 in the 8th year.

UNIT 4
Lesson 1
Try It 1.1
a.
$(-5x) \cdot (-4x^2) = (-5 \cdot -4)(x \cdot x^2)$
$= 20x^3$

b. $2x(3x^2 - x + 5) = 6x^3 - 2x^2 + 10x$

c. $(-3x + 2)(-4x) = 12x^2 - 8x$

Try It 1.2
a.
$(x + 1)(x + 6) = x(x + 6) + 1(x + 6)$
$= x^2 + 6x + x + 6$
$= x^2 + 7x + 6$

b.
$(x - 2)(x + 7) = x(x + 7) - 2(x + 7)$
$= x^2 + 7x - 2x - 14$
$= x^2 + 5x - 14$

c.
$(4x - 2)(x - 5) = 4x(x - 5) - 2(x - 5)$
$= 4x^2 - 20x - 2x + 10$
$= 4x^2 - 22x + 10$

Try It 1.3
a.
$(x + 6)^2 = (x + 6)(x + 6)$
$= x(x + 6) + 6(x + 6)$
$= x^2 + 6x + 6x + 36$
$= x^2 + 12x + 36$

b.
$(4x - 3)^2 = (4x - 3)(4x - 3)$
$= 4x(4x - 3) - 3(4x - 3)$
$= 16x^2 - 12x - 12x + 9$
$= 16x^2 - 24x + 9$

c.
$(x - 3)(x + 3) = x(x + 3) - 3(x + 3)$
$= x^2 + 3x - 3x - 9$
$= x^2 - 9$

d.
$(2x - 5)(2x + 5) = 2x(2x + 5) - 5(2x + 5)$
$= 4x^2 + 10x - 10x - 25$
$= 4x^2 - 25$

Lesson 2
Try It 2.1
a. $15x^2 - 20x = 5x(3x - 4)$
b. $6x^3 - 9x^2 - 3x = 3x(2x^2 - 3x - 1)$
c. $-16x^3 - 24x^2 = -8x^2(2x + 3)$

Try It 2.2
a.
$x^2 + 2x + 1 = x^2 + x + x + 1$
$= x(x + 1) + 1(x + 1)$
$= (x + 1)(x + 1) = (x + 1)^2$

b.
$x^2 - 2x - 8 = x^2 + 2x - 4x - 8$
$= x(x + 2) - 4(x + 2)$
$= (x + 2)(x - 4)$

c.
$3x^2 - 15x + 18 = 3(x^2 - 5x + 6)$
$= 3(x^2 - 2x - 3x + 6)$
$= 3(x(x - 2) - 3(x - 2))$
$= 3 (x - 3)(x - 2)$

d.
$x^2 - 100 = x^2 + 10x - 10x - 100$
$= x(x + 10) - 10(x + 10)$
$= (x + 10)(x - 10)$

Try It 2.3
a. $2x^2 + 7x + 6 = 2x^2 + 4x + 3x + 6$
$= 2x(x + 2) + 3(x + 2)$
$= (x + 2)(2x + 3)$

b. $4x^2 - 10x - 3$

Since no two factors of -12 have a sum of -10, this polynomial cannot be factored.

c. $4x^2 + 3x - 10 = 4x^2 + 8x - 5x - 10$
$= 4x(x + 2) - 5(x + 2)$
$= (x + 2)(4x - 5)$

Lesson 3

Try It 3.1

a $\sqrt{169} = 13$

b $\sqrt{900} = 30$

c. $\sqrt{57} \approx 7.5$ because $7^2 = 49$ and $8^2 = 64$.

d. $\sqrt{212} \approx 14.5$ because $14^2 = 196$ and $15^2 = 225$.

Try It 3.2

a. $\sqrt{32} = \sqrt{16 \cdot 2} = \sqrt{16} \cdot \sqrt{2} = 4\sqrt{2}$

b. $\sqrt{125} = \sqrt{25 \cdot 5} = \sqrt{25} \cdot \sqrt{5} = 5\sqrt{5}$

c. $\dfrac{6}{\sqrt{5}} = \dfrac{6}{\sqrt{5}} \cdot \dfrac{\sqrt{5}}{\sqrt{5}} = \dfrac{6\sqrt{5}}{5}$

Try It 3.3

a.
$$a^2 + b^2 = c^2$$
$$4^2 + b^2 = 12^2$$
$$16 + b^2 = 144$$
$$b^2 = 144 - 16$$
$$b^2 = 128$$
$$b = \sqrt{128} = \sqrt{64} \cdot \sqrt{2} = 8\sqrt{2}$$
$$b \approx 11.31$$

b.
$$5^2 + 12^2 = c^2$$
$$c^2 = 25 + 144$$
$$c = \sqrt{169} = 13$$

c. Let c be the length of the guy wire.
$$10^2 + 100^2 = c^2$$
$$c^2 = 10{,}100$$
$$c = \sqrt{10{,}100} = \sqrt{4} \cdot \sqrt{25} \cdot \sqrt{101}$$
$$= 10\sqrt{101} \approx 100.5$$

Unit 4 Checkpoint

1. $-3x^3 + 9x^2 + 6x$
2. $x^2 + 6x + 8$
3. $4x^2 - 22x + 10$
4. $x^2 - 14x + 49$
5. $4x^2 - 25$
6. $4x(x^2 - 3x + 6)$
   This polynomial cannot be factored since no products of 6 have a sum of -3.
7. $(x + 1)(x - 6)$
8. $2(x^2 - 25) = 2(x + 5)(x - 5)$
9. $(x - 5)(x - 10)$
10.
$$3x^2 - 6x + 2x - 4$$
$$= 3x(x - 2) + 2(x - 2)$$
$$= (3x + 2)(x - 2)$$
11. $\sqrt{64} = 8$
12. $\sqrt{150} \approx 12.5$ because $12^2 = 144$ and $13^2 = 169$.
13. $\dfrac{6}{\sqrt{3}} = \dfrac{6}{\sqrt{3}} \cdot \dfrac{\sqrt{3}}{\sqrt{3}} = \dfrac{6\sqrt{3}}{3} = 2\sqrt{3}$
14.
$$4^2 + 12^2 = c^2$$
$$c^2 = 16 + 144$$
$$c = \sqrt{160} = \sqrt{16} \cdot \sqrt{10}$$
$$= 4\sqrt{10} \approx 12.65$$

15.
$$a^2 + 15^2 = 12^2$$
$$a^2 = 144 - 225$$
$$a^2 = -81$$
Since $a^2 = -81$, the value of a is undefined, thus there is no solution.

Lesson 4

Try It 4.1

a.
$$x^2 + 7x + 12 = 0$$
$$x^2 + 3x + 4x + 12 = 0$$
$$x(x + 3) + 4(x + 3) = 0$$
$$(x + 3)(x + 4) = 0$$
$$x + 3 = 0 \quad \text{or} \quad x + 4 = 0$$
$$x = -3 \qquad\qquad x = -4$$

Check:
$$(-3)^2 + 7(-3) + 12 \overset{?}{=} 0$$
$$9 - 21 + 12 = 0$$
$$(-4)^2 + 7(-4) + 12 \overset{?}{=} 0$$
$$16 - 28 + 12 = 0$$

b.
$$4x^2 + 20x + 25 = 0$$
$$(2x + 5)^2 = 0$$
$$2x + 5 = 0$$
$$x = -\frac{5}{2}$$

Check:
$$4\left(\frac{-5}{2}\right)^2 + 20\left(\frac{-5}{2}\right) + 25 \overset{?}{=} 0$$
$$4\left(\frac{25}{4}\right) - 50 + 25 \overset{?}{=} 0$$
$$25 - 50 + 25 = 0$$

c.
$$4x^2 + 4x - 3 = 0$$
$$4x^2 - 2x + 6x - 3 = 0$$
$$2x(2x - 1) + 3(2x - 1) = 0$$
$$(2x - 1)(2x + 3) = 0$$
$$2x - 1 = 0 \qquad 2x + 3 = 0$$
$$x = \frac{1}{2} \qquad\quad x = -\frac{3}{2}$$

Check:
$$4\left(\frac{1}{2}\right)^2 + 4\left(\frac{1}{2}\right) - 3 \overset{?}{=} 0$$
$$4\left(\frac{1}{4}\right) + 2 - 3 \overset{?}{=} 0$$
$$1 + 2 - 3 = 0$$
$$4\left(\frac{-3}{2}\right)^2 + 4\left(\frac{-3}{2}\right) - 3 \overset{?}{=} 0$$
$$4\left(\frac{9}{4}\right) - 6 - 3 \overset{?}{=} 0$$
$$9 - 6 - 3 = 0$$

Try It 4.2

a.
$$x^2 + 10x - 3 = 0$$
$$x^2 + 10x = 3$$
$$x^2 + 10x + 25 = 3 + 25$$
$$(x + 5)^2 = 28$$
$$x + 5 = \pm\sqrt{28}$$
$$x = -5 \pm \sqrt{28}$$

b.
$$x^2 + 5x + 2 = 0$$
$$x^2 + 5x = -2$$
$$x^2 + 5x + \frac{25}{4} = -2 + \frac{25}{4}$$
$$\left(x + \frac{5}{2}\right)^2 = \frac{17}{4}$$
$$x + \frac{5}{2} = \pm\sqrt{\frac{17}{4}}$$
$$x = -\frac{5}{2} \pm \sqrt{\frac{17}{4}}$$
$$= -\frac{5}{2} \pm \frac{\sqrt{17}}{2}$$

c.
$$3x^2 + 18x - 4 = 0$$
$$3x^2 + 18x = 4$$
*Divide by 3.
$$x^2 + 6x = \frac{4}{3}$$
$$x^2 + 6x + 9 = \frac{4}{3} + 9$$
$$(x + 3)^2 = \frac{31}{3}$$
$$x + 3 = \pm\sqrt{\frac{31}{3}}$$
$$x = -3 \pm \sqrt{\frac{31}{3}}$$

Try It 4.3

a.
$$x = \frac{-(-7) \pm \sqrt{(-7)^2 - 4(1)(-1)}}{2(1)}$$
$$x = \frac{7 \pm \sqrt{49 + 4}}{2}$$
$$x = \frac{7 \pm \sqrt{53}}{2}$$
$$x \approx -0.14 \text{ or } x \approx 7.14$$

b.
$$x = \frac{-(-8) \pm \sqrt{(-8)^2 - 4(4)(-21)}}{2(4)}$$
$$x = \frac{8 \pm \sqrt{64 + 336}}{8}$$
$$x = \frac{8 \pm \sqrt{400}}{8}$$
$$x = \frac{8 \pm 20}{8} = 1 \pm \frac{5}{2}$$
$$x = -1.5 \text{ or } x = 3.5$$

Lesson 5

Explore It 5.1

1.

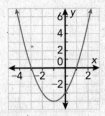

x	f(x)	(x, y)
−4	5	(−4, 5)
−3	0	(−3, 0)
−2	−3	(−2, −3)
−1	−4	(−1, −4)
0	−3	(0, −3)
1	0	(1, 0)
2	5	(2, 5)

2. vertex = $(-1, -4)$
axis of symmetry $x = -1$

3. $x = -3$ and $x = 1$

4. The solutions are the same.
$$x^2 + 2x - 3 = 0$$
$$(x + 3)(x - 1) = 0$$
$$x + 3 = 0 \text{ or } x - 1 = 0$$
$$x = -3 \text{ or } x = 1$$

5. $x = 0$

6.
$$x = -\frac{b}{2a}$$
$$x = -\frac{2}{2(1)} = -1$$
$$f(-1) = -4 = y$$

The equation finds the x-value of the vertex, which can be substituted into the equation to find the y-value.

Try It 5.1

a. $f(x) = 2x^2 + 3x + 1$
y-intercept:
$$f(0) = 2(0)^2 + 3(0) + 1$$
$$= 1$$
zeros:
$$2x^2 + 3x + 1 = 0$$
$$2x^2 + 2x + x + 1 = 0$$
$$2x(x + 1) + 1(x + 1) = 0$$
$$(x + 1)(2x + 1) = 0$$
$$x + 1 = 0 \qquad 2x + 1 = 0$$
$$x = -1 \qquad x = -\frac{1}{2}$$
vertex:
$$x = -\frac{b}{2a} = -\frac{3}{2(2)} = -\frac{3}{4} = -0.75$$
$$f\left(-\frac{3}{4}\right) = 2\left(-\frac{3}{4}\right)^2 + 3\left(-\frac{3}{4}\right) + 1$$
$$= -\frac{1}{8} = -0.125$$
$$(x, y) = \left(-\frac{3}{4}, -\frac{1}{8}\right)$$
axis of symmetry:
$$x = -\frac{3}{4}$$
graph:

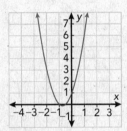

b. $f(x) = x^2 - 9$
y-intercept:
$$f(0) = (0)^2 - 9$$
$$= -9$$
zeros:
$$x^2 - 9 = 0$$
$$(x - 3)(x + 3) = 0$$
$$x - 3 = 0 \quad x + 3 = 0$$
$$x = 3 \qquad x = -3$$
vertex:
$$x = -\frac{b}{2a} = -\frac{0}{2(1)}$$
$$x = 0$$
$$f(0) = (0)^2 - 9$$
$$= -9$$
$$(x, y) = (0, -9)$$
axis of symmetry: $x = 0$
graph:

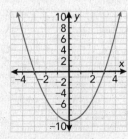

c. $f(x) = x^2 - 3x - 1$
y-intercept:
$$f(0) = (0)^2 - 3(0) - 1$$
$$= -1$$
zeros:
$$x = \frac{-(-3) \pm \sqrt{(-3)^2 - 4(1)(-1)}}{2(1)}$$
$$x = \frac{3 \pm \sqrt{9 + 4}}{2} = \frac{3 \pm \sqrt{13}}{2}$$
$$x \approx -0.3 \text{ or } x \approx 3.3$$
vertex:
$$x = -\frac{b}{2a} = -\frac{(-3)}{2(1)}$$
$$x = \frac{3}{2}$$
$$f\left(\frac{3}{2}\right) = \left(\frac{3}{2}\right)^2 - 3\left(\frac{3}{2}\right) - 1$$
$$= -\frac{13}{4} = -3.25$$
$$(x, y) = \left(\frac{3}{2}, -\frac{13}{4}\right)$$
axis of symmetry:
$$x = \frac{3}{2}$$
graph:

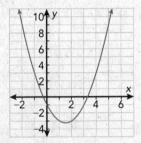

Try It 5.2

a. $f(x) = -(x - 3)^2 + 16$
y-intercept:
$$f(0) = -(0 - 3)^2 + 16$$
$$= -9 + 16 = 7$$
zeros:
$$-(x - 3)^2 + 16 = 0$$
$$-(x - 3)^2 = -16$$
$$(x - 3)^2 = 16$$
$$x - 3 = \pm 4$$
$$x = -1 \text{ or } x = 7$$
vertex: $(x, y) = (3, 16)$
axis of symmetry: $x = 3$
graph:

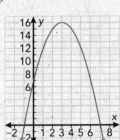

b. $f(x) = (x-3)^2 - 2$

 y-intercept:
$$f(0) = (0-3)^2 - 2$$
$$= 9 - 2 = 7$$

 zeros:
$$(x-3)^2 - 2 = 0$$
$$(x-3)^2 = 2$$
$$x - 3 = \pm\sqrt{2}$$
$$x = 3 \pm \sqrt{2}$$
$$x \approx 1.59 \text{ or } x = 4.41$$

 vertex: $(x, y) = (3, -2)$

 axis of symmetry: $x = 3$

 graph:

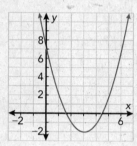

Try It 5.3

a.
$$(x-3)^2 + 4 = 0$$
$$(x-3)^2 = -4$$
$$x - 3 = \pm\sqrt{-4}$$
$$x = 3 \pm 2i$$

b.
$$x^2 + 3x + 5 = 0$$
$$x = \frac{-3 \pm \sqrt{(3)^2 - 4(1)(5)}}{2(1)}$$
$$= \frac{-3 \pm \sqrt{9 - 20}}{2}$$
$$= \frac{-3 \pm \sqrt{-11}}{2} = \frac{-3 \pm i\sqrt{11}}{2}$$

Lesson 6

Try It 6.1

a. The domain is the set of all real numbers. The range is $y \leq 16$ because the graph of the function is turned downwards.

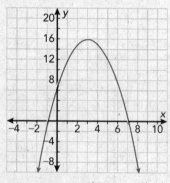

b. The domain is the set of all real numbers.
 Range:
$$x = -\frac{b}{2a} = -\frac{0}{2(1)} = 0$$
$$f(0) = (0)^2 - 9 = -9$$

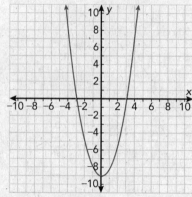

The range is all real values of y such that $y \geq 9$ because the graph of the function is turned upwards.

c. The domain is the set of all real numbers.
 Range:
$$x = -\frac{b}{2a} = -\frac{(-3)}{2(1)} = \frac{3}{2}$$
$$f\left(\frac{3}{2}\right) = \left(\frac{3}{2}\right)^2 - 3\left(\frac{3}{2}\right) - 1 = -\frac{13}{4}$$
$$= -\frac{13}{4} = -3.25$$

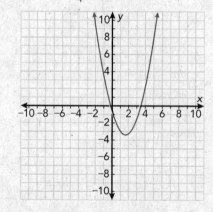

The range is all real values of y such that $y \geq -3.25$ because the graph of the function is turned upwards.

Try It 6.2

a. $h(t) = 96t - 16t^2$

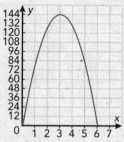

Maximum height:
$$t = -\frac{b}{2a} = -\frac{96}{2(-16)} = 3$$
$$h(3) = 96(3) - 16(3)^2$$
$$= 288 - 144 = 144$$

At $t = 3$ seconds, the rocket reaches its maximum height at $h = 144$ ft.

Height equals zero:
$$96t - 16t^2 = 0$$
$$t(96 - 16t) = 0$$
$$t = 0 \text{ or } 96 - 16t = 0$$
$$t = 0 \qquad t = 6$$

The rocket hits the ground at $t = 6$ seconds.

b. $h(t) = 100 - 16t^2$

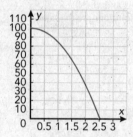

$$100 - 16t^2 = 0$$
$$16t^2 = 100$$
$$t^2 = \frac{100}{16}$$
$$t = \sqrt{\frac{100}{16}} = \frac{10}{4} = 2.5$$

The object hits the ground at $t = 2.5$ seconds.

Try It 6.3

a. Revenue = (# of units sold)(price)
$R(x) = x(50 - x) = 50x - x^2$
maximum revenue:

$$x = -\frac{b}{2a} = -\frac{50}{2(-1)} = 25$$

$R(25) = 50(25) - (25)^2 = 625$
price: $P(25) = 50 - 25 = 25$

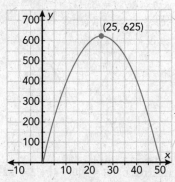

To achieve maximum revenue of $625, Rosa must sell 2,500 orders of roses at $25 each.

b. Revenue = (# of seats)(price)
$R(x) = (1,000 - 5x)(20 + 2x)$
$= 20,000 + 1,900x - 10x^2$
maximum revenue:

$$x = -\frac{b}{2a} = -\frac{1,900}{2(-10)} = 95$$

$R(95) = 20,000 + 1,900(95) - 10(95)^2$
$= 110,250$
number of seats:
#seats $= 1,000 - 5(95) = 525$

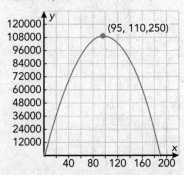

The theater will achieve maximum revenue of $110,250 when they sell 525 seats.

Unit 4 Self-Evaluation

1. $5x^3 + 15x^2 - 35x$
2. $x^2 + 2x - 8$
3. $3x^2 - 20x + 12$
4. $(4x - 1)(4x - 1) = 16x^2 - 8x + 1$
5. $9x^2 - 4$
6. $(x - 4)^2$
7. $(x - 5)(x + 3)$
8. $2(2x - 3)(2x + 3)$
9. $(2x + 1)(x + 6)$
10. $(2x + 1)(x - 7)$
11. $\frac{2}{\sqrt{2}} \cdot \frac{\sqrt{2}}{\sqrt{2}} = \frac{2\sqrt{2}}{2} = \sqrt{2}$
12. $\frac{5}{\sqrt{3}} \cdot \frac{\sqrt{3}}{\sqrt{3}} = \frac{5\sqrt{3}}{3}$

13.
$$6^2 + 8^2 = c^2$$
$$c^2 = 36 + 64$$
$$c^2 = 100$$
$$c = 10$$

14.
$$15^2 + b^2 = 20^2$$
$$b^2 = 400 - 225$$
$$b = \sqrt{175} = 5\sqrt{7}$$

15. Let b represent the height of the ladder.
$$3^2 + b^2 = 20^2$$
$$b^2 = 400 - 9$$
$$b = \sqrt{391} \approx 19.77 \text{ ft}$$

16. $x \approx -0.12$ or $x \approx 8.12$
17. $x = 3$ or $x = -3$
18. $x = 0.5$
19.
$$x = \frac{-(-2) \pm \sqrt{(-2)^2 - 4(5)(1)}}{2(5)}$$
$$= \frac{2 \pm \sqrt{4 - 20}}{10} = \frac{2 \pm \sqrt{-16}}{10}$$
$$= \frac{2 \pm 4i}{10} = \frac{1 \pm 2i}{5}$$

20. $x = -\frac{1}{2}$ or $x = \frac{1}{3} \approx 0.33$
21. $x = -5$ or $x = 1$
22. $x = -1$ or $x = \frac{1}{2}$
23. $x = \frac{-3 \pm i\sqrt{39}}{4}$
24. $x = -\frac{1}{4}$ or $x = \frac{1}{4}$
25. $f(x) = -(x + 1)^2 - 2$

y-intercept:
$$f(0) = -(0 + 1)^2 - 2$$
$$= -3$$
zeros:
$$-(x + 1)^2 - 2 = 0$$
$$-(x + 1)^2 = 2$$
$$(x + 1)^2 = -2$$
$$x + 1 = \sqrt{-2}$$
Since you have to take a negative root, there is no real-valued solution for the zeros of this equation. You would then have two complex zeros:
$$x = -1 \pm i\sqrt{2}$$
vertex: $(x, y) = (-1, -2)$
axis of symmetry: $x = -1$
graph:

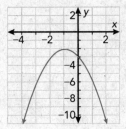

26. $f(x) = (x - 3)^2 - 1$
y-intercept:
$$f(0) = (0 - 3)^2 - 1$$
$$= 8$$
zeros:
$$(x - 3)^2 - 1 = 0$$
$$(x - 3)^2 = 1$$
$$x - 3 = \pm 1$$
$$x = 3 \pm 1$$
$$x = 2 \text{ or } x = 4$$
vertex: $x, y = (3, -1)$
axis of symmetry: $x = 3$
graph:

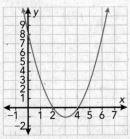

27. The domain is the set of all real numbers. The range is all *y*-values such that $y \leq -3$ because the graph of the function is turned downwards.

28. The domain is the set of all real numbers.
Range:
$$x = -\frac{b}{2a} = -\frac{3}{2(1)} = -\frac{3}{2}$$
$$f\left(-\frac{3}{2}\right) = \left(-\frac{3}{2}\right)^2 + 3\left(-\frac{3}{2}\right) - 1$$
$$= -\frac{13}{4} = -3.25$$
The range is all real values of y such that $y \geq -3.25$ because the graph of the function is turned upwards.

29. $h(t) = 144t - 16t^2$
Maximum height:
$$t = -\frac{b}{2a} = -\frac{144}{2(-16)} = \frac{9}{2} = 4.5$$
$h(4.5) = 144(4.5) - 16(4.5)^2 = 324$
At $t = 4.5$ seconds the rocket reaches its maximum height at $h = 324 \, ft$.
Height equals zero:
$$144t - 16t^2 = 0$$
$$t(144 - 16t) = 0$$
$$t = 0 \text{ or } 144 - 16t = 0$$
$$t = 0 \quad t = 9$$
The rocket hits the ground at $t = 9$ seconds.

30. Revenue = (# sold)(price)
$R(x) = x(75 - 3x) = 75x - 3x^2$
maximum revenue:
$$x = -\frac{b}{2a} = -\frac{75}{2(-3)} = 12.5$$
$R(12.5) = 75(12.5) - 3(12.5)^2 = 468.75$
price: $P(12.5) = 75 - 3(12.5) = 37.5$
To achieve maximum revenue of $468.75, Sam must sell 1,250 subscriptions at $37.50.

UNIT 5
Lesson 1

Try It 1.1
a. $|x-4| = 1$
$x - 4 = \pm 1$
$x - 4 = 1 \quad x - 4 = -1$
$x = 5 \qquad x = 3$

b. $|x + 2| = 4$
$x + 2 = \pm 4$
$x + 2 = 4 \quad x + 2 = -4$
$x = 2 \qquad x = -6$

c. $3|x + 2| = 5$

$|x + 2| = \dfrac{5}{3}$

$x + 2 = \pm \dfrac{5}{3}$

$x = -2 \pm \dfrac{5}{3}$

$x = -2 + \dfrac{5}{3} \quad x = -2 - \dfrac{5}{3}$

$x = -\dfrac{1}{3} \quad x = -3\dfrac{2}{3}$

Try It 1.2
a. $f(x) = |x - 3| + 5$
y-intercept: $f(0) = |0 - 3| + 5 = 8$
x-intercepts:
$|x - 3| + 5 = 0$
$|x - 3| = -5$
Since an absolute-value function cannot be negative, there is no real-valued solution. The graph does not pass through the x-axis.
vertex: $(x, y) = (3, 5)$
graph:

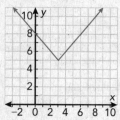

b. $f(x) = -|x + 1| + 3$
y-intercept: $f(0) = -|0 + 1| + 3 = 2$
x-intercepts:

$-|x + 1| + 3 = 0$

$-|x + 1| = -3$

$|x + 1| = 3$

$x + 1 = \pm 3$
$x = -1 + 3 \quad x = -1 - 3$
$x = 2 \qquad x = -4$
vertex: $(x, y) = (-1, 3)$
graph:

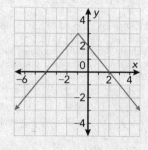

Lesson 2

Try It 2.1
a. $\dfrac{1}{4} + \dfrac{5}{x - 1} = \dfrac{1}{4} \cdot \dfrac{x - 1}{x - 1} + \dfrac{5}{x - 1} \cdot \dfrac{4}{4}$

$= \dfrac{x - 1}{4x - 4} + \dfrac{20}{4x - 4}$

$= \dfrac{x + 19}{4x - 4}$ when $x \neq 1$

b. $\dfrac{x - 1}{x - 3} - \dfrac{x}{x + 2} =$

$= \dfrac{x - 1}{x - 3} \cdot \dfrac{x + 2}{x + 2} - \dfrac{x}{x + 2} \cdot \dfrac{x - 3}{x - 3}$

$= \dfrac{x^2 + x - 2}{(x - 3)(x + 2)} - \dfrac{x^2 - 3x}{(x - 3)(x + 2)}$

$= \dfrac{x^2 + x - 2 - x^2 + 3x}{(x - 3)(x + 2)}$

$= \dfrac{4x - 2}{(x - 3)(x + 2)}$ when $x \neq -2, 3$

c. $\dfrac{x + 1}{3x - 6} + \dfrac{x + 3}{x^2 - 4x + 4} =$

$= \dfrac{x - 1}{3(x - 2)} + \dfrac{x + 3}{(x - 2)^2}$

$= \dfrac{x - 1}{3(x - 2)} \cdot \dfrac{(x - 2)}{(x - 2)} + \dfrac{x + 3}{(x - 2)^2} \cdot \dfrac{3}{3}$

$= \dfrac{x^2 - 3x + 2 + 3x + 9}{3(x - 2)^2}$

$= \dfrac{x^2 + 11}{3(x - 2)^2}$ when $x \neq 2$

Try It 2.2
a. $\dfrac{x^2 - 4x - 5}{6x} \cdot \dfrac{3x^2}{2x - 10} =$

$= \dfrac{(x - 5)(x + 1)}{\cancel{3} \cdot 2 \cdot \cancel{x}} \cdot \dfrac{\cancel{3} \cdot \cancel{x} \cdot x}{2(x - 5)}$

$= \dfrac{x + 1}{2} \cdot \dfrac{x}{2} = \dfrac{x^2 + x}{4}$

b. $\dfrac{x^2 + 5x + 6}{x - 2} \div \dfrac{x^2 - 9}{x^2 - 4}$

$= \dfrac{x^2 + 5x + 6}{x - 2} \cdot \dfrac{x^2 - 4}{x^2 - 9}$

$= \dfrac{(x + 2)(x + 3)}{(x - 2)} \cdot \dfrac{(x - 2)(x + 2)}{(x + 3)(x - 3)}$

$= \dfrac{(x + 2)^2}{(x - 3)}$

Lesson 3

Try It 3.1
a. $\left(\sqrt[3]{-27}\right)^2 =$
$(-27)^{\frac{2}{3}} = \left((-27)^{\frac{1}{3}}\right)^2 = (-3)^2 = 9$

b. $\left(\sqrt[4]{16}\right)^5 = (16)^{\frac{5}{4}} = \left(16^{\frac{1}{4}}\right)^5 = 2^5 = 32$

c. $\left(\sqrt{64}\right)^3 = (64)^{\frac{3}{2}} = \left(64^{\frac{1}{2}}\right)^3 = 8^3 = 512$

Try It 3.2
a. $\left(x^{\frac{2}{3}}\right)^4 = x^{\frac{8}{3}}$
b. $x^{\frac{4}{3}} \cdot x^{\frac{1}{3}} = x^{\frac{12}{15} + \frac{5}{15}} = x^{\frac{17}{15}}$
c. $\dfrac{\left(a^{\frac{3}{2}} \cdot b\right)^{\frac{1}{2}}}{ab} = \dfrac{a^{\frac{3}{4}} \cdot b^{\frac{1}{2}}}{ab} = \dfrac{1}{a^{\frac{1}{4}} \cdot b^{\frac{1}{2}}}$

Try It 3.3
a. $\sqrt[3]{81x^4} =$
$\sqrt[3]{27x^3 \cdot 3x} = \sqrt[3]{27x^3} \cdot \sqrt[3]{3x} = 3x \cdot \sqrt[3]{3x}$

b. $\sqrt{75x^7} =$
$\sqrt{25x^6 \cdot 3x} = \sqrt{25x^6} \cdot \sqrt{3x} = 5x^3 \cdot \sqrt{3x}$

c. $\sqrt[4]{81x^{13}} =$
$\sqrt[4]{81x^{12} \cdot x} = \sqrt[4]{81x^{12}} \cdot \sqrt[4]{x} = 3x^3 \cdot \sqrt[4]{x}$

Unit 5 Checkpoint
1. $x = 3$ or $x = -2$
2. $x = 0$ or $x = \dfrac{2}{3}$
3. There is no real-valued solution since an absolute-value function is never negative.
4. $f(x) = |x - 3| - 1$
   y-intercept: $f(0) = |0 - 3| - 1 = 2$
   x-intercept: $x = 2$ or $x = 4$
   vertex: $(x, y) = (3, -1)$
   graph:

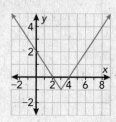

5. $f(x) = -|x - 4| + 2$
   y-intercept: $f(0) = -|0 - 4| + 2 = -2$
   x-intercept: $x = 2$ or $x = 6$
   vertex: $(x, y) = (4, 2)$
   graph:

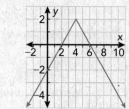

6. $\dfrac{1}{2} - \dfrac{3}{x - 4} = \dfrac{1}{2} \cdot \dfrac{x - 4}{x - 4} - \dfrac{3}{x - 4} \cdot \dfrac{2}{2}$

$= \dfrac{x - 4 - 6}{2x - 8} = \dfrac{x - 10}{2x - 8}$

7. $\dfrac{x}{x + 2} - \dfrac{x + 1}{x - 4}$

$= \dfrac{x}{x + 2} \cdot \dfrac{x - 4}{x - 4} - \dfrac{x + 1}{x - 4} \cdot \dfrac{x + 2}{x + 2}$

$= \dfrac{x^2 - 4x - x^2 - 3x - 2}{(x + 2)(x - 4)} = \dfrac{-7x - 2}{(x + 2)(x - 4)}$

8. $\dfrac{x - 1}{3x - 9} + \dfrac{x + 1}{x^2 - 9}$

$= \dfrac{x - 1}{3x - 9} + \dfrac{x + 1}{x^2 - 9}$

$= \dfrac{x - 1}{3(x - 3)} + \dfrac{x + 1}{(x + 3)(x - 3)}$

$= \dfrac{x - 1}{3(x - 3)} \cdot \dfrac{(x + 3)}{(x + 3)} + \dfrac{x + 1}{(x + 3)(x - 3)} \cdot \dfrac{3}{3}$

$= \dfrac{x^2 + 2x - 3 + 3x + 3}{3(x - 3)(x + 3)} = \dfrac{x^2 + 5x}{3(x - 3)(x + 3)}$

9. $\dfrac{x^2 - 2x - 3}{4x} \cdot \dfrac{3x}{2x - 6}$

$= \dfrac{(x - 3)(x + 1)}{4x} \cdot \dfrac{3x}{2(x - 3)}$

$= \dfrac{3x + 3}{8}$

10. $\dfrac{x^2 + 2x - 8}{x - 3} \div \dfrac{x - 2}{x^2 - 9}$

$= \dfrac{x^2 + 2x - 8}{x - 3} \cdot \dfrac{x^2 - 9}{x - 2}$

$= \dfrac{(x + 4)(x - 2)}{(x - 3)} \cdot \dfrac{(x - 3)(x + 3)}{(x - 2)}$

$= x^2 + 7x + 12$

11. $\left(64^{\frac{1}{3}}\right)^2 = 4^2 = 16$
12. $x^{\frac{27}{6} + \frac{4}{6}} = x^{\frac{31}{6}}$
13. $\dfrac{a^{\frac{3}{2}}}{a^2} = \dfrac{1}{a^{\frac{1}{2}}}$

14. $\sqrt{9x^2 \cdot 8x} = \sqrt{9x^2 \cdot 4 \cdot 2x}$
$= 3x \cdot 2\sqrt{2x} = 6x\sqrt{2x}$

15. $\sqrt[3]{8x^9 \cdot 6} = 2x^3 \cdot \sqrt[3]{6}$

Lesson 4

Try It 4.1

a. Since $2^5 = 32$, then $\log_2 32 = 5$.

b. Since $3^{-2} = \frac{1}{9}$, then $\log_3 \frac{1}{9} = -2$.

c. Since $10^5 = 100,000$,
then $\log_{10} 100,000 = 5$.

d. Since $4^{-3} = \frac{1}{64}$, then $\log_4 \frac{1}{64} = -3$.

Explore It 4.2

1. $\log_2 (4 \cdot 8) = \log_2 32 = 5$
$\log_2 4 + \log_2 8 = 2 + 3 = 5$

2. $\log_2 \left(\frac{64}{16}\right) = \log_2 4 = 2$
$\log_2 64 - \log_2 16 = 6 - 4 = 2$

3. $\log_2 (4^3) = \log_2 64 = 6$
$3\log_2 4 = 3(2) = 6$

Try It 4.2

a. $\log_4 8 + \log_4 8 = \log_4 (64) = \log_4 (4)^3$
$= 3 \log_4 4 = 3 \cdot 1 = 3$

b. $\log_4 a + 2 \log_4 b - \log_4 c$
$= \log_4 a + \log_4 b^2 - \log_4 c$
$= \log_4 ab^2 - \log_4 c$
$= \log_4 \frac{ab^2}{c}$

c. $2 \log_4 a + 3 \log_4 b$
$= \log_4 a^2 + \log_4 b^3$
$= \log_4 a^2b^3$

Try It 4.3

a. $\text{pH} = -\log[\text{H}^+]$
$= -\log[0.000042]$
≈ 4.38

b. $\text{pH} = -\log[\text{H}^+]$
$7.5 = -\log[\text{H}^+]$
$-7.5 = \log[\text{H}^+]$
$10^{-7.5} = \text{H}^+$

c. $k = 85 - 20\log(t + 1)$
$k = 85 - 20\log(24 + 1)$
$= 85 - 20\log(25)$
$\approx 57.04\%$

d. $k = 85 - 20\log(t + 1)$
$k = 85 - 20\log(99 + 1)$
$= 85 - 20\log(100)$
$= 85 - 20\log(10)^2$
$= 85 - 40\log(10)$
$= 85 - 401 = 45\%$

Lesson 5

Try It 5.1

a. $y = \frac{k}{x}, 3 = \frac{k}{7}, k = 21$

b. $V = \frac{k}{P}, 5 = \frac{k}{30}, k = 150$

c. $V = \frac{150}{12} = 12.5$

Try It 5.2

a. $y = \frac{x - 3}{x + 4}$

vertical asymptote:
$x + 4 = 0$
$x = -4$

horizontal asymptote: $y = \frac{1}{1} = 1$

y-intercept: $y = \frac{0 - 3}{0 + 4} = -\frac{3}{4}$

x-intercept:
$x - 3 = 0$
$x = -3$

graph:

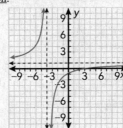

b. $y = \frac{2x - 6}{x - 2}$

vertical asymptote:
$x - 2 = 0$
$x = 2$

horizontal asymptote: $y = \frac{2}{1} = 2$

y-intercept: $y = \frac{3(0) - 6}{0 - 2} = 3$

x-intercept:
$2x - 6 = 0$
$x = 3$

graph:

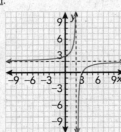

Try It 5.3

a. $\frac{x + 1}{2x - 1} = \frac{3x + 1}{4x - 1}$

$\frac{(2x - 1)(4x - 1)}{1} \cdot \frac{x + 1}{2x - 1}$

$= \frac{(2x - 1)(4x - 1)}{1} \cdot \frac{(3x + 1)}{4x - 1}$

$(4x - 1)(x + 1) = (2x - 1)(3x + 1)$
$4x^2 + 3x - 1 = 6x^2 - x - 1$
$2x^2 - 4x = 0$
$2x(x - 2) = 0$
$2x = 0 \quad \text{or} \quad x - 2 = 0$
$x = 0 \text{ or } x = 2$

b. $\frac{1,200}{500 - w} + \frac{1,200}{500 + w} = 10$

$\frac{(500 - w)(500 + w)}{1}$

$\cdot \left(\frac{1,200}{500 - w} + \frac{1,200}{500 + w}\right) =$
$\frac{(500 - w)(500 + w)}{1} \cdot \frac{10}{1}$

$\frac{(500 - w)(500 + w)}{1} \cdot \frac{1,200}{500 - w} +$
$\frac{(500 - w)(500 + w)}{1} \cdot \frac{1,200}{500 + w} =$

$\frac{(250,000 - w^2)}{1} \cdot \frac{10}{1}$

$1,200(500 + w) + 1,200(500 - w) =$
$10(250,000 - w^2)$

$600,000 + 1,200w + 600,000 - 1,200w =$
$2,500,000 - 10w^2$

$1,200,000 = 2,500,000 - 10w^2$
$10w^2 = 1,300,000$
$w^2 = 130,000$
$w \approx 360.55 \ mph$

Lesson 6

Try It 6.1

a. $y = -\sqrt{x - 2} + 1$

domain:
$x - 2 \geq 0$
$x \geq 2$

range: $y \leq 1$

x-intercept:
$-\sqrt{x - 2} + 1 = 0$
$-\sqrt{x - 2} = -1$
$\sqrt{x - 2} = 1$
$x - 2 = 1$
$x = 3$

y-intercept:
$y = -\sqrt{0 - 2} + 1$
$= -\sqrt{-2} + 1$

*Since to solve for the y-intercept you need to find a negative root, there is no real-valued solution.

graph:

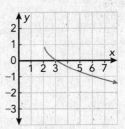

b. $y = \sqrt{-3 - x} + 2$

<u>domain:</u>
$$-3 - x \geq 0$$
$$-x \geq 3$$
$$x \leq -3$$

<u>range:</u> $y \geq 2$

<u>y-intercept:</u>
$$y = \sqrt{-3 - 0} + 2$$
$$= \sqrt{-3} + 2$$

*Since to solve for the y-intercept you need to find a negative root, there is no real-valued solution.

<u>x-intercept:</u>
$$0 = \sqrt{-3 - x} + 2$$
$$-2 = \sqrt{-3 - x}$$
$$(-2)^2 = (\sqrt{-3 - x})^2$$
$$4 = -3 - x$$
$$-x = 7$$
$$x = -7$$

graph:

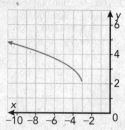

Try It 6.2

a.
$$\sqrt{3x + 5} = 2$$
$$3x + 5 = 4$$
$$3x = -1$$
$$x = -\frac{1}{3}$$

b.
$$\sqrt{x + 6} = x$$
$$x + 6 = x^2$$
$$x^2 - x - 6 = 0$$
$$(x - 3)(x + 2) = 0$$
$$x - 3 = 0 \quad x + 2 = 0$$
$$x = 3 \text{ or } x = -2$$

Try It 6.3

a. $P^2 = a^3$
$$P^2 = (0.39)^3$$
$$P^2 = 0.059319$$
$$P = \sqrt{0.059319} \approx 0.24 \text{ Earth years}$$

b. $30,000 = 15,000\sqrt{0.2x + 1}$
$$2 = \sqrt{0.2x + 1}$$
$$4 = 0.2x + 1$$
$$3 = 0.2x$$
$$x = 15$$

Unit 5 Self-Evaluation

1. $x = -6 \text{ or } x = -4$

2. $x = 0 \text{ or } x = 4$

3. There is no solution—an absolute-value function can never be negative.

4. $f(x) = |x - 1| + 3$

<u>y-intercept:</u> $f(0) = |0 - 1| + 3 = 4$

<u>zeros:</u>
$$|x - 1| + 3 = 0$$
$$|x - 1| = -3$$

*Since an absolute-value function cannot be negative, there is no real-valued solution. The graph does not pass through the x-axis.

<u>vertex:</u> $(x, y) = (1, 3)$

<u>graph:</u>

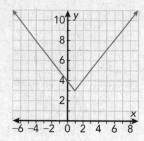

5. $f(x) = -|x - 1| + 4$

<u>y-intercept:</u> $f(0) = -|0 - 1| + 4 = 3$

<u>zeros:</u>
$$-|x - 1| + 4 = 0$$
$$-|x - 1| = -4$$
$$|x - 1| = 4$$
$$x - 1 = \pm 4$$
$$x = -3 \text{ or } x = 5$$

<u>vertex:</u> $(x, y) = (1, 4)$

<u>graph:</u>

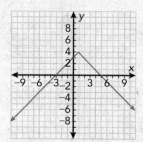

6. $\dfrac{1}{2} + \dfrac{4}{x + 3} = \dfrac{x + 3 + 8}{2(x + 3)} = \dfrac{x + 11}{2x + 6}$

7. $\dfrac{x + 1}{x - 3} - \dfrac{x}{x^2 - 9} =$

$$= \frac{(x + 1)}{(x - 3)} \cdot \frac{(x + 3)}{(x + 3)} - \frac{x}{(x - 3)(x + 3)}$$

$$= \frac{x^2 + 4x + 3 - x}{(x - 3)(x + 3)} = \frac{x^2 + 3x + 3}{x^2 - 9}$$

8. $\dfrac{x + 3}{x^2 - 1} - \dfrac{2x}{x^2 + x - 2} =$

$$= \frac{x + 3}{(x - 1)(x + 1)} \cdot \frac{(x + 2)}{(x + 2)}$$

$$- \frac{2x}{(x + 2)(x - 1)} \cdot \frac{(x + 1)}{(x + 1)}$$

$$= \frac{x^2 + 5x + 6 - 2x^2 - 2x}{(x + 1)(x - 1)(x + 2)}$$

$$= \frac{-x^2 + 3x + 6}{(x + 1)(x - 1)(x + 2)}$$

9. $\dfrac{x^2 - 4}{x} \cdot \dfrac{3x}{2x - 4} =$

$$= \frac{(x - 2)(x + 2)}{x} \cdot \frac{3x}{2(x - 2)}$$

$$= \frac{3x + 6}{2}$$

10. $\dfrac{x^2 + 2x + 1}{x - 3} \div \dfrac{x + 1}{x^2 - 9} =$

$$= \frac{(x + 1)(x + 1)}{(x - 3)} \cdot \frac{(x - 3)(x + 3)}{(x + 1)}$$

$$= x^2 + 4x + 3$$

11. $\left(\sqrt[3]{-64}\right)^2 = (-4)^2 = 16$

12. $x^{\frac{2}{3} \cdot \frac{1}{2}} = x^{\frac{4+3}{6}} = x^{\frac{7}{6}}$

13. $\dfrac{(a^2 \cdot b)^{\frac{1}{2}}}{a^3 b} = \dfrac{a \cdot b^{\frac{1}{2}}}{a^3 b} = \dfrac{1}{a^2 b^{\frac{1}{2}}}$

14. $\sqrt[3]{5^3 \cdot x^6} \cdot \sqrt[3]{5x} = 5x^2 \cdot \sqrt[3]{5x}$

15. $\sqrt[4]{2^4 \cdot x^8} \cdot \sqrt[4]{2x^3} = 2x^2 \cdot \sqrt[4]{2x^3}$

16. $\log_2 \dfrac{1}{8} = -3$ since $2^{-3} = \dfrac{1}{8}$

17. $\log 1{,}000 = 3$ since $10^3 = 1{,}000$

18. $\log a^3 + \log b^4 - \log c = \log \dfrac{a^3 b^4}{c}$

19. $\log_4 a^2 - \log_4 b = \log_4 \dfrac{a^2}{b}$

20. $k = 95 - 15\log(24 + 1) \approx 74.03$

21. $y = \dfrac{k}{x}, 2.5 = \dfrac{k}{10}, k = 25$

22. $y = \dfrac{x - 1}{x}$

<u>vertical asymptote:</u> $x = 0$

<u>horizontal asymptote:</u> $y = \dfrac{1}{1} = 1$

<u>y-intercept:</u> Since a vertical asymptote exists at $x = 0$, there is no y-intercept.

<u>x-intercept:</u>
$$x - 1 = 0$$
$$x = 1$$

<u>graph:</u>

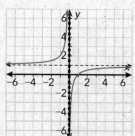

23. $y = \dfrac{2x - 4}{x + 1}$

vertical asymptote:
$$x + 1 = 0$$
$$x = -1$$

horizontal asymptote: $y = \dfrac{2}{1} = 2$

y-intercept: $y = \dfrac{2(0) - 4}{0 + 1} = -4$

x-intercept:
$$2x - 4 = 0$$
$$x = 2$$

graph:

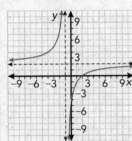

24.
$$\dfrac{x - 2}{2x - 1} = \dfrac{x + 4}{3x + 3}$$
$$(x - 2)(3x + 3) = (x + 4)(2x - 1)$$
$$3x^2 - 3x - 6 = 2x^2 + 7x - 4$$
$$x^2 - 10x - 2 = 0$$
$$x \approx -0.196 \text{ or } x \approx 10.196$$

25.
$$\dfrac{12}{5 + c} + \dfrac{12}{5 - c} = 5$$
$$\dfrac{12(5 - c) + 12(5 + c)}{(5 + c)(5 - c)} = 5$$
$$60 - 12c + 60 + 12c = 5(25 - c^2)$$
$$120 = 125 - 5c^2$$
$$5c^2 = 5$$
$$c = 1 \text{ mph}$$

26. $y = \sqrt{x - 2} - 1$

domain:
$$x - 2 > 0$$
$$x > 2$$

range: $y \geq -1$

x-intercept:
$$\sqrt{x - 2} - 1 = 0$$
$$\sqrt{x - 2} = 1$$
$$x - 2 = 1$$
$$x = 3$$

y-intercept:
$$y = \sqrt{0 - 2} - 1$$
$$= \sqrt{-2} - 1$$

*Since to solve for the y-intercept you need to find a negative root, there is no real-valued solution.

graph:

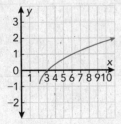

27. $y = -\sqrt{x - 2} + 4$

domain:
$$x - 2 \geq 0$$
$$x \geq 2$$

range: $y \leq 4$

x-intercept:
$$-\sqrt{x - 2} + 4 = 0$$
$$\sqrt{x - 2} = 4$$
$$x - 2 = 16$$
$$x = 18$$

y-intercept:
$$y = -\sqrt{0 - 2} + 4$$
$$= \sqrt{-2} + 4$$

*Since to solve for the y-intercept you need to find a negative root, there is no real-valued solution.

graph:

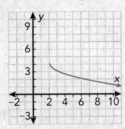

28. $\sqrt{x - 1} = 4$
$$x - 1 = 16$$
$$x = 17$$

29. $\sqrt{2x - 1} = x$
$$2x - 1 = x^2$$
$$x^2 - 2x + 1 = 0$$
$$(x - 1)^2 = 0$$
$$x - 1 = 0$$
$$x = 1$$

30. $500\sqrt{0.25x + 1} = 1{,}000$
$$\sqrt{0.25x + 1} = 2$$
$$0.25x + 1 = 4$$
$$0.25x = 3$$
$$x = 12 \text{ years}$$

Formulas

FORMULA	MEANING/EXPLANATION
SLOPE $$m = \frac{\Delta y}{\Delta x} = \frac{y_2 - y_1}{x_2 - x_1}$$	m = slope or rate of change
EQUATION OF THE LINE Slope-Intercept form: $y = mx + b$ Standard form: $ax + by = c$ Point-Slope form: $y = m(x - x_1) + y_1$	m = slope and b = y-intercept m = slope and (x_1, y_1) are the coordinates for the point
PERCENT EQUATION $R \cdot B = A$	*Rate $\cdot$ Base = Amount*
EXPONENTIAL FUNCTION $y = ab^x$	a is the initial value and b is the base.
PYTHAGOREAN THEOREM $a^2 + b^2 = c^2$	a and b are legs of a right triangle, and c is the hypotenuse.
SPECIAL PRODUCTS Trinomial Square: $(a + b)^2 = a^2 + 2ab + b^2$ Difference of Two Squares: $(a + b)(a - b) = a^2 - b^2$	• product of a binomial multiplied by itself • product = first term squared − second term squared
QUADRATIC EQUATION $ax^2 + bx + c = 0$	There may be 0, 1, or 2 real solutions.
QUADRATIC FORMULA $$x = \frac{-b \pm \sqrt{b^2 - 4ac}}{2a}$$	a, b, and c are from the quadratic equation $ax^2 + bx + c = 0$.
QUADRATIC FUNCTION General form: $y = f(x) = ax^2 + bx + c$ Vertex form: $y = f(x) = a(x - h)^2 + k$	The vertex is (h, k).
ABSOLUTE-VALUE FUNCTION $y = f(x) = a\lvert x - h \rvert + k$	The vertex is (h, k).
LOGARITHMIC EQUATION $b^x = a$ can be written as $\log_b a = x, b > 0, b \neq 1$	b is the base.
INVERSE-VARIATION EQUATION $y = \frac{k}{x}$	k is the constant of variation.
SQUARE-ROOT FUNCTION $f(x) = \sqrt{x}$	This is only defined for $x \geq 0$.

Glossary

─────────────────────────── A ───────────────────────────

absolute value   The absolute value of x is the distance from zero to x on a number line, denoted $|x|$.

$$|x| = \left.\begin{matrix} x \text{ if } x \geq 0 \\ -x \text{ if } x < 0 \end{matrix}\right\}$$

$|4| = 4$
$|-4| = 4$

absolute-value equation   An equation that contains absolute-value expressions.

$|x + 5| = 8$

absolute-value function   A function whose rule contains absolute-value expressions.

$|x + 5| = y$

algebraic expression   An expression that contains at least one variable.

$4x + 2y$
$5x$

asymptote   A line that a graph gets closer to as the value of a variable becomes extremely large or small.

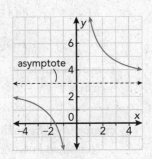

axis of symmetry   The line that divides a figure or graph into two mirror-image halves.

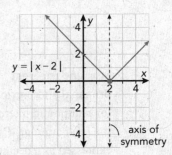

─────────────────────────── B ───────────────────────────

base   The number in a power that is used as a factor.

$2^4 = 2 \cdot 2 \cdot 2 \cdot 2 = 16$
2 is the base
3^4
↑
base

binomial   A polynomial with two terms.

$$x + y$$
$$2c^2 + 5$$
$$4x^2y^3 + 5xy^4$$

C

---

coefficient   A number multiplied by a variable.

In the expression $4x + 2y$, 4 is a coefficient of x and 2 is a coefficient of y.

common logarithm   A logarithm with base 10. For convenience, it is written without the base 10.

$$\log_{10} a = \log a$$

$$\log 100 = 2$$

completing the square   A process used to form a perfect-square trinomial. To complete the square of $x^2 + bx$, add $\left(\frac{b}{2}\right)^2$.

$$x^2 + 8x + \square$$
$$\left(\frac{8}{2}\right)^2 = 16$$
$$x^2 + 8x + 16$$

complex number   A number of the form $a \pm bi$ where $i = \sqrt{-1}$.

$$3 + 2gi$$

compound inequality   Two inequalities that are combined into one statement by the word *and* or *or*.

$x \geq 1$ and $x < 5$
(also written $1 \leq x < 5$)

compound interest   Interest earned or paid on both the principal and previously earned interest. The formula for compound interest is $A = P\left(1 + \frac{r}{n}\right)^{nt}$, where A is the final amount, P is the principal, r is the interest rate expressed as a decimal, n is the number of times interest is compounded, and t is the time.

consistent system   A system of equations that has a solution.

$$x + y = 8$$
$$x - y = 2$$
solution: (5, 3)

constant   A value that does not change.

$$4, 0, \pi$$

constant function   A function of the form $f(x) = c$. The graph of a constant function is a horizontal line.

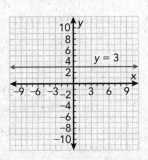

constant of variation   The constant k in a direct variation equation.

$$y = kx$$
$$y = 6x$$
6 is the constant of variation.

coordinate   A number used to identify the location of a point. On a number line, one coordinate is used. On a coordinate plane, two coordinates are used, called the x-coordinate and the y-coordinate.

$$x - 2y = 3$$
$$2x - 4y = 6$$

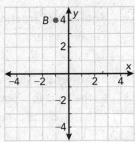

coordinate plane   A plane that is divided into four regions by a horizontal line called the x-axis, which is perpendicular to a vertical line called the y-axis.

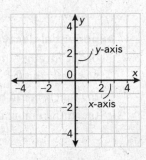

cube root   A number, written as $\sqrt[3]{x}$, whose cube is x.

$\sqrt[3]{8} = 2$, because $2^3 = 8$; 2 is the cube root of 8.

D

---

degree of a polynomial   The degree of the term of the polynomial with the greatest degree.

$$2xy^2 + 3x^2y^4 + 6x^2y^2$$
1st term degree 3; 2nd term degree 6; third term degree 4; polynomial degree: 6

dependent system A system of equations that has infinitely many solutions.

$$x - 2y = 3$$
$$2x - 4y = 6$$

difference of two squares The binomial $a^2 - b^2$. It is the special product of $(a + b)(a - b) = a^2 - b^2$.

$$(x + 2)(x - 2) = x^2 - 4$$

domain The set of input values of a function or relation.

The domain of $y = \sqrt{x}$ is $x \geq 0$.

E

---

equation A mathematical sentence that shows that two expressions are equivalent.

$$x + 5 = 7$$
$$4 + 3 = 8 - 1$$
$$(x - 2)^2 + (y - 3)^2 = 4$$

equivalent fractions Two or more fractions with the same value.

$$\frac{1}{2} = \frac{4}{8}$$

exponent The number that indicates how many times the base in a power is used as a factor. In general, with base, x, and exponent, n.

$$3^4 \longleftarrow \text{exponent}$$

$$x^n = \underbrace{x \cdot x \cdot x \cdots \cdot x}_{n \text{ factors of } x}$$

$$2^4 = 2 \cdot 2 \cdot 2 \cdot 2 = 16$$
4 is the exponent.

exponential-decay function An exponential function of the form $y = a \cdot b^x$, where a is the initial value at $x = 0$, and $0 < b < 1$. If r is the rate of decay, then the function can be written as $y = a(1 - r)^t$, where a is the initial amount and t is the time.

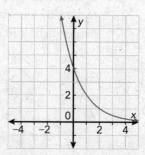

exponential function A function of the form $f(x) = ab^x$, where a and b are real numbers with $a \neq 0$, $b > 0$, and $b \neq 1$.

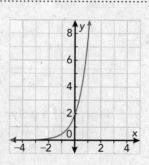

exponential-growth function An exponential function written as $y = a \cdot b^x$, where a is the initial value at $x = 0$, and $b > 1$. If r is the rate of growth, then the function can be written $y = a(1 + r)^t$, where a is the initial amount and t is the time.

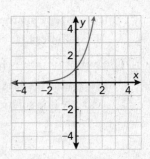

extraneous solution A solution of a derived equation that is not a solution of the original equation.

To solve $\sqrt{x} = -3$, square both sides:
$$x = 9$$
Check: $\sqrt{9} = 3$ is false, so 3 is an extraneous solution.

F

---

factor A number or expression that is multiplied by another number or expression to get a product.

$$10 = 2 \cdot 5$$
2 and 5 are factors of 10.
$$x^2 - 4 = (x + 2)(x - 2)$$
$(x + 2)$ and $(x - 2)$ are factors of $x^2 - 4$.

function A function is a rule that assigns to each input, x, one and only one output, y.

$$y = f(x) = 2x + 1$$

function notation If x is the independent variable and y is the dependent variable, then the function notation for y is $f(x)$, read "f of x," where f names the function.

equation: $y = 3x$
function notation: $f(x) = 3x$

G

---

greatest common factor (GCF) The largest natural number that divides two or more numbers evenly (no remainder).

The GCF of 4 and 29 is 1.
The GCF of 60 and 72 is 12.

I

---

imaginary number $\sqrt{-1}$ is written as i, and is called an imaginary number.

inconsistent system   A system of equations or inequalities that has no solution.

$$x + y = 2$$
$$x + y = 1$$

independent system   A system of equations that has exactly one solution.

$$x + y = 6$$
$$x - y = 2$$
solution: (4, 2)

inequality   A statement that compares two expressions by using one of the following signs: $<, >, \leq, \geq$, or $\neq$

$x \geq 3$

integer   A member of the set of whole numbers and their opposites.

$..., -3, -2, -1, 0, 1, 2, 3, ...$

inverse operations   Operations that undo each other.

Addition and subtraction are inverse operations:
$$4 + 3 = 7, 7 - 4 = 3$$
Multiplication and division are inverse operations:
$$2 \cdot 4 = 8, 8 \div 2 = 4$$

inverse variation   A relationship between two variables, x and y, that can be written in the form $y = \frac{k}{x}$, where k is a nonzero constant and $x \neq 0$.

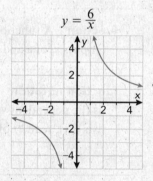

$y = \frac{6}{x}$

irrational number   A real number that cannot be written as a ratio of integers.

$\sqrt{3}, \pi$

L

leading coefficient   The coefficient of the first term of a polynomial in standard form.

$4x^2 + 2x + 5$
4 is the leading coefficient.

least common denominator (LCD)   The least common multiple of the denominators of two or more fractions.

The LCD of $\frac{5}{6}$ and $\frac{3}{8}$ is 24.

least common multiple (LCM) The smallest number that two or more natural numbers can divide into evenly.

The LCM of 6 and 8 is 24.

like terms Terms with the same variables raised to the same powers.

$2x^2y^3$ and $5x^2y^3$

linear function A function that can be written in the form $y = mx + b$, where x is the independent variable and m and b are real numbers. Its graph is a line.

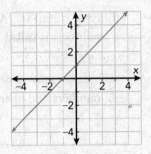

linear inequality in one variable An inequality that can be written in one of the following forms: $ax < b, ax > b, ax \le b, ax \ge b,$ or $ax \ne b$, where a and b are constants and $a \ne 0$.

$2x + 4 \le 3(x + 5)$

linear inequality in two variables An equation that can be written in one of the following forms: $y < mx + b, y > mx + b, y \le mx + b, y \ge mx + b,$ or $y \ne mx + b$, where m and b are real numbers.

$4x + 2y > 7$

logarithm An exponential equation with $b > 0, b \ne 1$ that can be written as a logarithmic equation. The log is the power to which the base is raised.

$b^x = a$ can be written as $\log_b a = x$.

Since $3^4 = 81$, then $\log_3 81 = 4$.

M

maximum of a function The y-value of the highest point on the graph of the function.

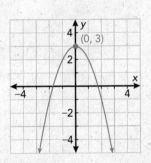

monomial   A number or a product of numbers and variables with whole-number exponents, or a polynomial with one term.

$5x^3y^2$

N

---

natural number   A counting number. The set of natural numbers is called N.

$N = \{ 1, 2, 3, 4, 5, 6, 7,... \}$

numeric expression   An expression that contains only numbers and operations.

$2 \cdot 5 + (6 - 8)$

O

---

opposite.   The opposite of a number a, denoted $-a$, is the number that is the same distance from zero as a, on the opposite side of the number line. The sum of opposites is 0.

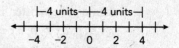

ordered pair   A pair of numbers that can be used to locate a point on a coordinate plane. The first number indicates the distance to the left or right of the origin, and the second number indicates the distance above or below the origin.

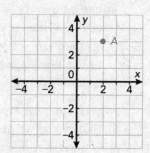

The coordinates of A are (2, 3).

origin   The intersection of the x- and y-axes in a coordinate plane. The coordinates of the origin are (0, 0). On a number line, the origin is at 0.

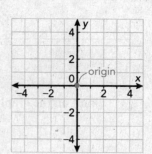

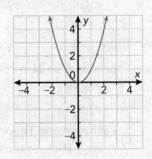

P

parabola The shape of the graph of a quadratic function.

parallel lines Lines in the same plane that do not intersect.

parent function The most basic function of a family of functions, or the original function before a transformation is applied.

$f(x) = x^2$ is the parent function for $h(x) = x^2 + 5$.

perfect square A number whose positive square root is a whole number.

49 is a perfect square because $\sqrt{49} = 7$.

perfect-square trinomial A trinomial whose factored form is the square of a binomial. A perfect-square trinomial has the form $a^2 - 2ab + b^2 = (a - b)^2$ or $a^2 + 2ab + b^2 = (a + b)^2$.

$x^2 + 10x + 25$ is a perfect-square trinomial because $x^2 + 10x + 25 = (x + 5)^2$.

perpendicular lines Lines that intersect at 90° angles.

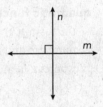

point-slope form $y - y_1 = m(x - x_1)$ where m is the slope and (x_1, y_1) is a point on the line.

$y - 4 = 2(x - 5)$

polynomial expression A monomial or a sum or difference of monomials.

$3x^2 + 4xy - 8y^2$

prime factored form A counting number that is written as a factor of only prime numbers.

The prime factorization of 36 is: $36 = 2 \cdot 2 \cdot 3 \cdot 3$

prime number   A number that has exactly two factors: the number itself and 1. The set of prime numbers is called P.

$P = \{2, 3, 5, 7, 11...\}$
Since only 3 and 1 can divide into 3 evenly, 3 is a prime number.

principal square root   The positive square root of a number, indicated by the radical sign.

$\sqrt{64} = 8$

Pythagorean Theorem   The theorem stating that in a right triangle, the sum of the squares of the legs, a and b, is equal to the square of the hypotenuse, c, which is the side opposite the right angle.

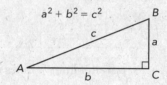

Pythagorean Triple   A set of three nonzero whole numbers a, b, and c such that $a^2 + b^2 = c^2$.

The numbers 3, 4, and 5 are a Pythagorean Triple because $3^2 + 4^2 = 5^2$.

Q

quadratic equation   An equation of the form, $ax^2 + bx + c = 0$ is called a quadratic equation.

$x^2 + 7x + 12 = 0$

quadratic formula   The formula used to find the solution(s) to a quadratic equation, $ax^2 + bx + c = 0$.

$x = \dfrac{-b \pm \sqrt{b^2 - 4ac}}{2a}$

quadratic function   A function that can be written in the form $f(x) = ax^2 + bx + c$, where a, b, and c are real numbers and $a \neq 0$, or in the form $f(x) = a(x - h)^2 + k$, where a, h, and k are real numbers and $a \neq 0$.

$f(x) = x^2 - 5x + 6$

R

radical equation   An equation that contains a variable within a radical.

$\sqrt{x + 2} + 5 = 9$

radical expression   An expression that contains at least one radical.

$\sqrt{x + 2} + 5$

radical function   A function that contains at least one radical.

$y = \sqrt{x - 1}$

radicand   The number or expression under a radical sign.

Expression: $\sqrt{x + 7}$
Radicand: $x + 7$

range   The set of output values of a function or relation.

range of a function   The set of all possible output values of a function.

The range of $y = 2x^2$ is $y \geq 0$.

rate of change   A ratio that compares the amount of change in the dependent variable to the amount of change in the independent variable.

rational equation   An equation that contains one or more rational expressions.

$$\frac{x + 3}{x^2 - 2x - 3} = 2$$

rational expression   An algebraic expression whose numerator and denominator are polynomials and whose denominator has a degree ≥ 1.

$$\frac{x + 3}{x^2 - 2x - 3}$$

rational function   A function whose rule can be written as a rational expression.

$$f(x) = \frac{x + 3}{x^2 - 2x - 3}$$

rational number   A number that can be written in the form $\frac{a}{b}$, where a and b are integers and $b \neq 0$.

$4, 2.75, 0.\overline{4}, -\frac{4}{5}, 0$

rationalizing the denominator   A method of rewriting a fraction by multiplying by another fraction that is equivalent to 1 in order to remove radical terms from the denominator.

$$\frac{1}{\sqrt{3}} \cdot \frac{\sqrt{3}}{\sqrt{3}} = \frac{\sqrt{3}}{3}$$

real number   The set of all rational and irrational numbers.

$1, -4, -\frac{3}{2}, \sqrt{14}, \pi$ are all real numbers.

reciprocal   For a real number $a \neq 0$, the reciprocal of a is $\frac{1}{a}$. The product of reciprocals is 1.

The reciprocal of 2 is $\frac{1}{2}$.

reflection   A transformation across a line, called the line of reflection. The line of reflection is the perpendicular bisector of each segment joining a point and its image.

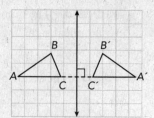

S

---

scatter plot   A graph with points plotted to show a possible relationship between two sets of data.

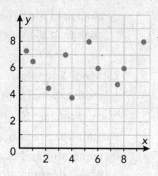

---

simplify   To perform all indicated operations.

$$12 - 10 + 8$$
$$2 + 8$$
$$10$$

---

slope   A measure of the steepness of a line. If (x_1, y_1) and (x_2, y_2) are any two points on the line, the slope of the line, known as m, is represented by the equation $m = \frac{y_2 - y_1}{x_2 - x_1}$.

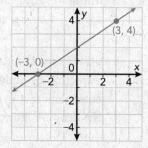

$$m = \frac{y_2 - y_1}{x_2 - x_1} = \frac{0 - 4}{-3 - 3} = \frac{-4}{-6} = \frac{2}{3}$$

---

slope-intercept form   A line with slope m and y-intercept b can be written in the form $y = mx + b$.

$$y = -3x + 5$$
The slope is -3.
The y-intercept is 5.

---

solution of a system of linear equations   An ordered pair or set of ordered pairs that satisfies all the equations in the system.

$(7, 1)$ is a solution of $\begin{array}{l} x - y = 6 \\ x + y = 8 \end{array}$

solution of an inequality in one variable   A value or set of values that satisfies the inequality.

4 is a solution of $x + 3 < 10$.

square root   A number that is multiplied by itself to form a product is called a square root of that product.

$\sqrt{25}$ is 5 because $5^2 = 5 \cdot 5 = 25$.

square-root function   A function whose rule contains a variable under a radical symbol.

$y = \sqrt{5x} - 6$

standard form of a linear equation $ax + by = c$, where a, b, and c are real numbers.

$3x + 5y = 6$

standard form of a quadratic equation $ax^2 + bx + c = 0$, where a, b, and c are real numbers and $a \neq 0$.

$3x^2 + 4x - 1 = 0$

standard form of a quadratic function $f(x) = ax^2 + bx + c$, where a does not equal 0.

$f(x) = 2x^2 - 3x + 5$

system of linear equations   A system of equations in which all of the equations are linear.

$2x + 4y = 2$
$x - 2y = 5$

T

term   A part of an expression or equation to be added or subtracted.

$4x^2 + 3x$
$4x^2$ and $3x$ are terms.

translation   A horizontal or vertical shift (or both) of the graph. A translation is sometimes called a slide.

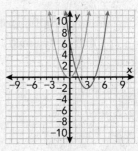

trinomial   A polynomial with three terms.

$4x^2 + 2xy - 7y^2$

U
---

unlike terms   Terms with different variables or the same
variables raised to different powers.

$3xy^2$ and $4x^2y$

V
---

variable   A symbol used to represent a quantity that
can change.

In the expression $x + 5$, x is
the variable.

....

vertex form of a quadratic function   The quadratic
function when $y = f(x) = a(x - h)^2 + k$, and the vertex
is (h, k).
For the quadratic $f(x) = (x + 4)^2 - 9$, the vertex
is $(-4, -9)$.

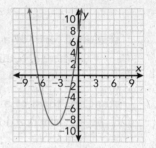

....

vertex of a parabola   The highest or lowest point on
a parabola.

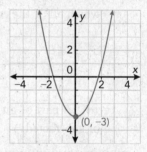

....

vertex of an absolute-value graph   The point on the
axis of symmetry of the graph.

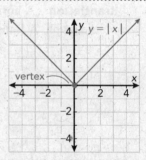

....

x-axis   The horizontal axis in a coordinate plane.

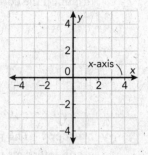

x-coordinate   The first number in an ordered pair, which indicates the horizontal distance of a point from the origin on the coordinate plane.

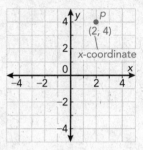

x-intercept   The x-coordinate(s) of the point(s) where a graph intersects the x-axis.

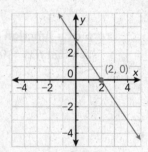

The x-intercept is 2.

y-axis   The vertical axis in a coordinate plane.

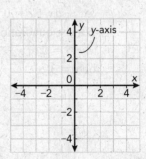

y-coordinate The second number in an ordered pair, which indicates the vertical distance of a point from the origin on the coordinate plane.

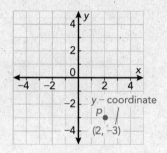

y-intercept The y-coordinate(s) of the point(s) where a graph intersects the y-axis.

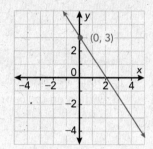

The y-intercept is 3.

Z

zero of a function For the function f, any number x such that $f(x) = 0$.

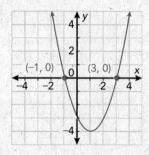

zeros of a quadratic equation The zeros of a quadratic equation are the x-values that satisfy $ax^2 + bx + c = 0$.
For the quadratic equation $(x + 5)(x - 3) = 0$
$x + 5 = 0$ or $x - 3 = 0$, and the zeros are $x = -5$ or $x = 3$.

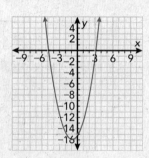

Index

equation, 231-232
expressions, 233-234
properties, 231, 233-234

M

maximum of a function, 202-204
Mental Math, 19, 23, 45, 49, 68, 69, 91, 92, 104, 105, 106,
    108, 110, 111, 112, 113, 114, 144, 161, 224
mixed number, 16
models
    add integers, 42
    area model, 155
    divide fractions, 6
    exponential models, 103-150
    linear models, 41-102
    multiply fractions, 24
    polynomial models, 152-210
    square numbers, 166
    subtract integers, 43
monomial, 152
    multiply, 152-153
multiplication
    binomial, 153-154
    equations, 34-35
    equivalent fractions, 10-15
    fractions, 23-25
    integers, 44-45
    monomial, 152-153
    polynomial, 152-157
    Property of Equality, 52
    Property of Inequality, 61
    rational expressions, 221-222
    rational numbers, 45-46

N

natural number, 6-9
negative number, 42
Note, 6, 7, 10, 23, 29, 30, 34, 36, 46, 52, 66, 67, 127, 161,
    169, 177, 180, 186, 190, 193, 199, 200, 212, 221, 223, 227,
    234, 237
number theory, 6-9
numerator, 10
numeric expression, 28

O

opposite, 43
ordered pair, 66-75
    graph, 66-70
    linear functions, 76-79
origin, 66
output variable, 66

P

parabola, 183-195
parallel lines, 84-86
parent function, 183
percent
    convert among fractions, decimals, and percents, 12-15
    equation, 104-118
    fraction and decimal equivalents, 23

percent-decrease problems, 113-115
percent-increase problems, 110-113
solve percent problems, 110-118
perfect-square, 166
perfect-square trinomial, 155-157, 176-179
perpendicular lines, 84-86
place value, 12
point of intersection, 67-75
point-slope form of a line, 84-86
polynomial, 152-210
    binomial, 153-154
    expression, 152-171
    factoring, 158-165
    models, 152-210
    monomial, 152-153
    multiply, 152-157
        special products, 155-157, 162
positive numbers, 42
Pretest, 1-3
prime factored form, 6-7, 158
prime number, 6-7
principal square root, 166
properties
    Distributive, 45-46, 110, 152-154
    of Equality, 52-54
    of exponents, 119-123, 225-226
    of Inequality, 61-63
    of logarithms, 231, 233-234
    to simplify radical expressions, 227-228
    rationalizing the denominator, 168-171
    Zero Product, 174-176
Pythagorean Theorem, 169-171
Pythagorean Triple, 169-171

Q

quadratic applications, 196-205
    business, 201-204
    physics, 199-201
quadratic equation, 174-182
    solve by completing the square, 176-179
    solve by factoring, 174-176
    solve using quadratic formula, 180-181
    solve with complex zeros, 192-195
quadratic formula, 180-181
quadratic function, 183-205
    domain, 197-198
    graph, 183-195
    parent function, 183
    range, 197-198
    transform, 188-191
    vertex form, 189-191
    zero of a function, 183

R

radical, 166-171
    equation, 245-250
        applications, 249-250
        solve, 248-250
    expression, 223-228
        compute values of, 223-225
        simplify, 227-228